SING A NEW SONG

Dedication

For my mother,
whose confidence in God
is still teaching me
the beginning of wisdom.

Timothy Radcliffe OP

SING A NEW SONG

THE CHRISTIAN VOCATION

TEMPLEGATE PUBLISHERS

This edition published 1999 by
Templegate Publishers
302 East Adams Street
P.O. Box 5152
Springfield, IL 62705
217-522-3353
www.templegate.com

ISBN 0-87243-247-5
Library of Congress Catalog Card Number:
99-75717

First published 1999 by
Dominican Publications
42 Parnell Square
Dublin 1
Ireland

Cover and book design by Bill Bolger
Cover painting by Kim En Joong OP

CONTENTS

PREFACE

Many of the pieces collected in this book were written, in the first place, for people who have made vows as members of religious orders, but I hope that they will be of some use to any one who is trying to live the Christian life. We struggle with much the same challenges as anyone else: trying to cope with our sexuality, dealing with money, saying our prayers, building community. In fact I would go further and say that religious life, a phrase I do not much like, only has meaning if it says something about the meaning of human life. Our vocation is to shed some light on the human vocation. If we do not, then we are wasting our time.

When I was elected Master of the Dominican Order in 1992, I was asked by many journalists whether I really thought that 'religious life' would survive into the next millennium. We are showing no signs of disappearing yet. It is true that our vows may seem crazy to our contemporaries, especially in the West. In a society which rightly sees freedom as fundamental to human dignity, how can we take a vow of obedience? When sexual realisation is seen as central to human fulfilment, then how can we vow to be chaste? In the world of consumerism, then it seems senseless to promise poverty. Yet it is precisely because our lives go against the grain of the times that religious life has more to say than ever before, and not just to Christians.

The title of this book, *Sing a New Song*, is intended to suggest the vitality of religious life today, as I have discovered travelling around the Order. It is true that in some Western countries religious orders are suffering a crisis of confidence. It is precisely then that we must dare to sing a new song. St Augustine said that we, like those who travel in the dark, must sing, especially when we are afraid of the wild beasts in the night. Song conquers fear and fear is the greatest enemy of Christian life.

The first chapter, on 'Jurassic Park and the Last Supper',

which was a talk for *The Tablet* Open Day, sets the scene by looking at some of the challenges that Christianity faces in the world of the global market. Then there are five letters to the Dominican Family. I find writing a letter to one person difficult enough, but writing to a whole religious family, young and old, men and women, in more than a hundred different countries, is quite a challenge. One would not choose quite the same words to talk about sexuality, for example, to a Bolivian brother, a Japanese nun, an American sister or a Lesotho lay Dominican. The remaining pieces owe their genesis to very different occasions, from a lecture to the Divinity Faculty of Yale University to a talk during the Dominican pilgrimage to Lourdes. Often they will touch on similar topics. Each of us only has a few coins to rattle around in his box, as someone said, like a beggar, which is what a Dominican is supposed to be.

I am aware that this title, *Sing a New Song*, might seem inappropriate, since nothing that I write is all that new. The last few years have been spent largely on the road, listening to my brothers and sisters, often living in difficult situations of violence, poverty and war. I simply share what I have received from them. Anyway, I have never believed in the absurd idea that one has to be original, and so I have not hesitated to grab every insight I have found during my travels and to share it. I am a mendicant friar after all. The newness of the song is the irrepressible novelty of God, not my own.

A final word about the cover of this book. When my brother Richard saw it, his immediate reaction was: 'What is it supposed to be?' Why do we have this painting for a cover? It is from a work by a Korean Dominican, Kim En Joong. First of all, I believe that one of the best ways of preaching the Gospel is through the arts: painting, sculpture and music. This gets behind the resistance to written words about God. Secondly, his paintings are explosions of colour, which are filled with the joy in God's creation. They are a much better way to 'Sing a New Song' than my tedious texts.

I am enormously indebted to my own Province of England, whose brethren are constantly cited. I especially acknowledge my debt to Herbert McCabe, Fergus Kerr, Simon Tugwell, and the late Cornelius Ernst. I thank my community of Santa Sabina in Rome, who restore me every time I come home, jet-lagged and travel-weary. I must say a special word of thanks to Paul Murray OP, for his poetry and gentle criticism, and to David Sanders OP, for his endless kindness and probing questions.

Above all I thank my parents, who gave me the gift not just of life but of faith.

Timothy Radcliffe OP

The Gospel in the World

Last Supper
painted by children in a barrio in Caracas

See page 226

JURASSIC PARK AND THE LAST SUPPER

Last year I had to give a ten-minute talk to the Union of Superiors General – the heads of religious orders – on the challenges to our mission as religious in the West. It seemed a pretty impossible task. What could one say in ten minutes? Then I went to see the film *Jurassic Park* – and it became clear that this is a story that shows us a wonderful picture of the world in which we have to live our faith today. It is one of the most successful films ever made. At one stage it was showing in one in three cinemas in Italy, and the French Minister of Culture has declared it a threat to the nation. In motorway cafes our children can buy dinosaur biscuits. Why has it been so successful? It is surely because every culture lives by stories, narratives that shape our perception of the world and of ourselves, which tell us what it means to be human. And this is a narrative in which millions of people, perhaps unconsciously, find themselves.

But we Christians claim to live by another tale, which we gather to remember and re-enact every Sunday, the story of the Last Supper, of the man who gathered his friends around him and shared with them a meal, who gave them himself, his body and his blood. This is the story that should, above all, shape our lives and self-awareness. So the challenge of being a Christian is for us not just that of trying to be good. There is no evidence to suggest that Christians are, on the whole any better than anyone else, and Jesus certainly did not call the saints but the sinners. The challenge is rather to live by and through a story that some of our contemporaries may find very odd, and which offers a different vision of the world and of being human. This evening I want to touch upon just a few of the differences between these two stories.

A talk given at *The Tablet* Open Day, London, June, 1994. An edited and shortened version of the talk was published in *The Tablet*, 18 June, 1994.

I assume that most of you have been to see *Jurassic Park*. You probably took your children, pretending that you were only going to make them happy but enjoyed it enormously. Just in case you have not seen it, here is the story. A millionaire (Richard Attenborough) uses experiments on DNA to bring the dinosaurs back to life. He creates a Mesozoic Longleat, where all the dinosaurs can run free. Unfortunately they break out, start killing the visitors, and so the human beings desert the island and fly away, leaving the jungle behind them. This may not seem to you to be much like life in the suburbs of London, unless things have changed a lot since I left for Rome, but I will suggest that it touches on important elements of our contemporary culture.

VIOLENCE
The first point I want to make is really pretty commonplace. *Jurassic Park* tells us of a violent world, of herds of dinosaurs roaming the plains, and devouring everything they meet. It is a violence to which the human beings can only reply with further violence. Our other story, that of the Last Supper, is also a story of violence, of the violence that is inflicted upon Jesus, and which he bears, 'like a sheep that is led to the slaughter, he did not open his mouth'. (Is 53:7)

When I asked recently a group of American Dominicans, brothers and sisters, what was the primary challenge for our preaching, they replied, without hesitation, that it was violence. In recent months I have visited Rwanda, Burundi, Haiti, Angola, Croatia and New York, and I have been confronted with the raw violence of much of our world. I suppose that most of human history has been violent and, except for the horrors of the two world wars, ours has not been much worse. Many societies in the past have glorified violence. I think that ours does so too, and in ways that are very subtle and hardly explicit.

Jurassic Park offers us a resurrected Darwinian jungle, in which animals compete to survive. The weak fail and die and become extinct, like the dinosaurs. The violent competition for food and territory is part of the creative process by which we come to be. That brutal struggle is what brings us into existence. It is our cradle. Ultimately, the film suggests, violence is fruitful. But Darwin's theory of evolution, which I cannot claim ever to have studied, is interesting as just one symptom of a deep shift in our understanding of what it means to be human which has occurred over the last two hundred or so years. It is the emergence of the conviction that all human society functions and flourishes through this fierce struggle between competing individuals, each pursuing their own good. The metaphor of the survival of the fittest, of life as a Darwinian jungle, haunts much of our language. Sumner, the Yale economist, even wrote that 'millionaires are a product of natural selection.... They may fairly be regarded as the naturally selected agents of society for certain work.'

One of the first indications of this deep shift in our understanding of human society was a little parody called the *Parable of the Bees*, written by a man called Mandeville in the eighteenth century. He argued that greed, envy, pride, all the traditional vices, may actually be very useful. They are what makes the world go round and human society flourish. They may be private vices but they are public virtues. The politics of greedy competition go back a long way. It is this understanding of what it means to be human that makes of our cities urban Jurassic Parks, violent inner city jungles, where the weak are destroyed. Our story, the tale of the Last Supper, offers a deep challenge, not just because here is the man who bears violence and refuses to pass it on. It offers a radically different image of what it means to be human. He offers us his body. This is the new covenant, our home and dwelling place. The meaning of our lives is given not in the pursuit of self-interest but by the reception of a gift of communion.

I think that most of us would agree, and it has often been argued, that the challenge of this moment is to break the fascination of what is ultimately a harmful and destructive image of what it is to be a human being, of us as solitary monads forever pursuing our own individual goods. We are flesh of each other's flesh, a communion that finds perfection in that flesh which Christ gives, his own body. That which we seek is most radically the common good. The problem is how we are to break the hold of this false myth of our humanity. What are we to do? As David Marquand put it *in The Unprincipled Society*:

> How can a fragmented society make itself whole? How can a culture permeated by possessive individualism restore the bonds of community? Granted that the common sense of nearly two hundred years is the chief obstacle to successful economic and political adjustment, how can common sense be redefined?[1]

The story of the Last Supper can liberate our imagination. It is the story of a community that is radically fractured, in which the man at the heart of the community is about to be betrayed and denied. All his friends will scatter in a moment. It is the story of the birth of a community which overthrows every form of alienation, betrayal, even death. It offers us hope.

WORDS

The central act of Jesus is to speak a powerful and transforming word: 'This is my Body and I give it to you.' He speaks a word. Words are not so very important in *Jurassic Park*. There is a lot of grunting and roaring, the sound of breaking bones, but you are

1. *The Unprincipled Society: New Demands and Old Politics*, Glasgow 1988, pp. 288.

not encouraged to chat to a Tyrannosaurus Rex. A Russian or Chinese could happily watch the film in English and not miss much. This difference is significant. I would say that one of the ways in which we build a human society, and transcend that trap of possessive individualism, is by recovering a reverence for words, and of their potency to form and sustain community.

We are human and we belong to each other because we can talk together. A society in disintegration is one in which there is contempt for words. When I was in San Salvador I went to visit the room where the Jesuits were gunned down in the University. The murderers also shot their books. You can see a copy of Kittel's *Theological Dictionary of the New Testament*, open at the page on the Holy Spirit, source of all wisdom, ripped across with bullet holes. I think of the library of a priest in Haiti, the books all destroyed and torn up. I think of a little village on the border of Croatia and Serbia, shelled out of existence, with the very bodies from the graves dug up and thrown around, and the missal in the Church ripped up, and desecrated with obscenities. What all these incidents speak of is both a hatred of words and a sense of their power.

When I land in England during my travels, to recover from jetlag and to wash my clothes, I do not read about MPs bursting into each other's rooms and ripping up their opponents' libraries. But I do get the impression of a culture in which we loose off words at each other with little thought as to their consequences, like children who play at cowboys and Indians without realizing that the guns they use are real. It is as if we had forgotten that speaking is a moral act, demanding the deepest responsibility. I could not help but be astonished at the difference between what was said about that fine man John Smith before and after his death. Was it all just words? Part of our deep social crisis is that we have lost confidence that words really show things as they are.

We have lost St Augustine's sense of awe when he says, 'Words, those precious cups of meaning.'

The Book of Genesis tells us that the vocation of Adam was to call things by their proper names. God made Adam to help with creation. He showed him a lion or a rabbit and Adam named it; he knew what things were and so assisted God in bringing a meaningful world out of chaos. His names were not just arbitrary labels stuck on things, so that he might just as well have called a rabbit a hare; they shared the power of God's words to bring to be, and to bring to light. To speak, to use words, is almost a divine vocation. Like God, it gives us the power of life and death. It is a religious matter.

The violence of our society impregnates the language that we use. The President of the Czech Republic, Vaclav Havel, contrasts the words of Salman Rushdie with the words of Ayatollah Khomeini. 'Words that electrify society with their freedom and truthfulness are matched by words that mesmerise, deceive, inflame, madden, beguile, words that are harmful – lethal even. The word as arrow.'[2] George Steiner has written:

> In words, as in particle physics, there is matter and antimatter. There is construction and annihilation. Parents and children, men and women, when facing each other in exchange of speech, are at ultimate risk. One word can cripple a human relationship, can do dirt on hope. The knives of saying cut deepest. Yet the identical instrument, lexical, syntactical, semantic, is that of revelation, of ecstasy, of the wonder of understanding that is communion.[3]

A Dominican sister from Taiwan told of a girl carrying the burden of a child on her back. Someone said to her: 'Little girl,

2. Quoted in *The Independent*, 9 December 1989, p. 29.
3. *Real Presences: Is There Anything in What We Say?*, London, 1989, p. 58.

you are carrying a heavy weight.' She replied 'I am not carrying a weight, I am carrying my brother.' A word that transforms.

The proponents of Political Correctness are on to the right thing in the wrong way. They have seen rightly that it matters desperately what words I use, because my words can be daggers that kill people. But the human community is not healed simply by us being forbidden to use certain words. As Robert Hughes wrote, in *The Culture of Complaint*, 'We want to create a sort of linguistic Lourdes, where evil and misfortune are dispelled by a dip in the waters of euphemism.' He points out that one does not overthrow the horror of death by ruling, as proposed in the *New England Journal of Medicine*, that a corpse should be referred to as a 'nonliving person'. A fat corpse, he points out, becomes a differently-sized nonliving person! The administrators of the University of San Francisco in Santa Cruz were wrong to believe that you could overcome racialism by banning expressions like there is 'a nip in the air' and a 'chink in one's armour' on the grounds that in some contexts they may seem to be racially disparaging!

We build communion and heal wounds not by banning nasty words but by using words that create communion, that welcome the stranger, that overthrow distance. At the heart of our typical story, the Last Supper, is a man who speaks words that bring a community into being: 'This is my Body and I give it to you.' And if the doctrine of the Real Presence, of these words as truly and deeply transforming, seems foolish and absurd to many of our contemporaries, then surely it is because we have forgotten just how powerful words are. Emily Dickinson wrote:

> Could mortal lip divine
> The undeveloped freight
> Of a delivered syllable,
> 'Twould crumble at the weight.

Christ's words of consecration disclose that to which all human language aspires, grace perfecting nature.

When the monks fled to the west coast of Ireland in the Dark Ages, they carried with them the texts of the gospels, which they copied and recopied and ornamented and revered. They founded communities which kept alive a reverence for these holy words. Perhaps what we are called to do is form communities in which there is a reverence for language, for truthful words, and words that build communion. If the Church is to be a place in which people can rediscover a deep sense of what it is to be human, to be those who in our deepest identity are one with each other, then we must be before all a community in which words are used with reverence and responsibility.

That means that we have to be a community of people which dares to debate, to argue, to dialogue in pursuit of the truth that we can never master. So often in our beloved Church there is a fear of debate. I do not mean of disagreement. There is plenty of vociferous disagreement. I mean that difficult struggle with one another, in which we both seek mutual enlightenment, that passionate argument in which one fights with the other precisely because one hopes to learn from them. In the *Summa*, St Thomas Aquinas always starts with the objections of his opponents, not just to prove them wrong but to discover in precisely what sense they are right. We wrestle with our opponent like Jacob struggling with an angel, so that we may demand a blessing.

Reverence for words implies a humility before the truth and the other person. Our words, both in the Church and in society, are so often heavy with arrogance. A last quote from Havel:

We should all fight together against arrogant words and keep a weather eye out for any insidious germs of arrogance in words that are seemingly humble. Obviously this is not just a linguistic task. Responsibility for words and towards words is a task which is intrinsically ethical. As such, however, it is situated beyond the horizon of the visible world, in that realm wherein dwells the Word that was in the beginning and is not the word of Man.[4]

FORGIVENESS

When we gather on a Sunday, to hear again our founding narrative, the powerful words that we hear are ones of forgiveness, of the blood which is shed for the forgiveness of sins. The word is a word that heals and absolves. Yet there is within our culture a deep resistance to the notion of forgiveness. Part of it comes, I would guess, from a suspicion that people who go on about forgiveness, especially Catholics, probably have an unhealthy obsession with guilt. Having been educated by the Benedictines, those humane men, this was not the sort of Catholicism in which I was raised. More fundamentally, I wonder whether in fact our culture is not suspicious of forgiveness because we suspect that it may not be a very good thing. Might it not be that within our contemporary culture there is a belief that, except in the most private and personal sense, forgiveness is harmful and even dangerous. If there was too much of it around society would fall apart. Like butter and chocolates and other good things, it should be strictly rationed! And yet it is central to our faith.

Certainly after Dachau and Auswitchz, after Dresden, and Hiroshima, one might be hesitant of too easy an idea of forgiveness. As if such horrors could be simply forgotten. Yet our hesitation is perhaps deeper still, and we can see clues in *Jurassic Park*. In the Darwinian jungle there can be no forgiveness. The necessary consequence of weakness and failure is extinction. And it is good that this happens; otherwise there would be no evolu-

4. ibid.

tion. We human beings are the result of a ruthless process which wipes out innumerable species because they could not adapt, but it leads to us. What is creative of our humanity is an unforgiving history. In *Jurassic Park* these dinosaurs are redeemed from death and we quickly discover that that is a great mistake. We should have left their DNA stuck in the drops of amber.

Now I cannot claim any expertise in economics. When the prioral accounts were explained in English, it did not take long for me to get lost. Now that I live in Santa Sabina, Rome, and the explanations are in Italian, the darkness is total. But I suspect that the image of the survival of the fittest operates in a similarly unforgiving way in much contemporary economics and politics and that one of the functions of government is precisely to remove whatever shields and protects the weak and ill-adapted industries. There should be no forgiveness. The weak should perish, and pity is a dangerous sentiment. I know that that is drastically over-simple, and that we believe in safety nets, and dream of the Social Market, and of benevolent capitalism, and yet it touches some deep instinct of our contemporary sensibility.

This mercilessness seems to deeply penetrate our culture. One of the joys of my wandering existence – sixty countries since July '92 – is, apart from reading *The Tablet*, coming across an English newspaper. It may be a few weeks old, but I fall upon it like a hungry man. And yet it is depressing how often it will tell of denunciation and accusation. The dominant model of arriving at the truth is that of exposure, of showing up someone's sins. No doubt this is all said to be done in the name of morality, of getting back to basics. Yet one must ask: What is really exposed? What is discovered and revealed? The truth of other human beings, with all their virtue and vice, goodness and badness, can only be attained through patient attentiveness. One must listen very carefully, and let the others disclose themselves. The truth is given not through exposure but in a moment of revelation. It needs tenderness and not denunciation. The truthful eye is always the compassionate eye, even the loving eye, for, as Thomas Aquinas taught us, the true and the beautiful are the same. The journalist with a scoop reminds me of Pompey storming up to the Temple in Jerusalem, demanding to see what was concealed behind the veil of the Holy of Holies. And when he rips it away he shouts out, 'But there is nothing, nothing at all.' There was nothing that he could see.

The forgiveness of the Last Supper is not primarily about forgetting. It does not reassure us that our God is willing to overlook our mistakes, to look the other way. It is a deeply creative act of healing. Forgiveness, within our tradition, is that utterly creative moment in which Jesus is raised from the dead. It is not what enables us to forget. It makes memory possible. It is the mystery of the ever fertile God who, in the mediaeval image, made the dead wood of the cross blossom with flowers, and can make our dead lives flourish. Our two stories, *Jurassic Park* and the Last Supper, differ most profoundly in their perception of creativity. In one, humans are created through a pitiless process which destroys the weak; in the other it is a creative word which heals and redeems and makes us whole.

The heroes of *Jurassic Park* are the dinosaurs. They are of course the victims, the ones who were condemned by the evolutionary process. And they are suitable heroes in our culture in which the victim so often has hero status. And the anger and bitterness of the victim, of abuse or molestation or injustice, surely derive from the feeling that nothing can ever be done to heal the damage, that they or we are condemned for ever to bear the wounds, to be casualties. To even mention the possibility of forgiveness would be to trivialise the hurt and to intensify the anger. All that can be done is to drive out the perpetrator. Surely it is only a belief in an utterly fecund God, who made everything out of nothing and raised Jesus from the dead, that can give us the courage to think on those whom we have wounded, or who have hurt us, and to hope for forgiveness.

In the Last Supper forgiveness is not just a private absolution, but the birth of a community. It is not just the offer of a personal interior peace, but the peace we live together. This was how it was seen in Europe, where the sacrament of reconciliation was the sacrament in which the community was healed, a public event until after the Council of Trent when we invented confessional boxes.

One of the most moving examples I saw of this shared forgiveness was in Burundi last year, during the massacres. The conflicts between Tutsi and Hutu that have decimated Rwanda this year had already begun in Burundi. Our brethren belonged to both ethnic groups, and everyone of them had lost members of their family. It was a time of deep pain for our brothers. How could we sustain and build a religious community in which traditional enemies lived together? That was our greatest priority. I toured the country with the Councillor of the General Council for Africa, who is Hutu, and the local superior who is Tutsi. We saw almost no one except the occasional band of armed men looking for their enemies. We visited the refugee camps and found the families of our brothers and sisters. It was enormously important that these accepted both these brothers, Tutsi and Hutu together. It was the first gesture of reconciliation and mutual forgiveness. And then before I left the capital, Bujumburu, we all sat down and tried to speak. Rather than the words of denunciation and accusation, each had to listen, to hear what the other had endured, so that he might remain a brother and not become a stranger. It was perhaps the most extraordinary moment of attentiveness that I have ever seen, of offering an hospitable ear to the one who seemed to speak from another world. It was a moment of deep silence, the sort of silence that accompanies words that are hard to find and hard to hear. Forgiveness here is not amnesia but the impossible gift of communion.

FATALISM

The last contrast that I would like to make between *Jurassic Park* and the Last Supper is deeply connected with the possibility of forgiveness. It is about the different understandings of freedom that they imply. *Jurassic Park* is a sort of parable, like the story of Frankenstein before it, about the failure of our scientific culture to live up to its dreams of absolute control. It is a story of a loss of control, a failure of freedom. In the book this is made quite explicit when the control room of the Park ceases to function and so all the dinosaurs can get out. Pausing for a moment of reflection as chaos is about to overwhelm them, the hero says, 'Ever since Newton and Descartes, science has explicitly offered us the vision of total control. Science has claimed the power to eventually control everything, through its understanding of natural laws. But in the twentieth century that claim has been shattered beyond repair.'[5] In the end, the only freedom that remains for our heroes is the freedom to run away, to escape the mess they have made. It also means that we can look forward to *Jurassic Park*, Part 2. It is the freedom not to belong, which is the final freedom of our modern human being, that isolated and solitary being for whom to belong is to be trapped.

Wonderful things have happened in these last years, unexpected freedoms have been achieved. We have seen the Berlin Wall fall, Nelson Mandela elected as President of South Africa. We may even be on the way to peace in the Middle East. Yet

5. Michael Crichton, *Jurassic Park*, p. 313.

despite all this, sometimes we are tempted by a sad fatalism, a feeling that nothing that we do can really face and overcome the growing poverty, the cruelty and the death. It is what Havel calls 'the general inability of modern humanity to be the master of its own situation.' Maybe that sense of fatalism is due not just to a failure of science to provide all the answers. In *The Culture of Contentment* the American economist, John Kenneth Galbraith, argues this fatalism is in fact implicit in our economic system, that our politics has been deeply influenced, for the past two hundred or so years, by the philosophy of *laissez faire*. This asserts that any interference in the market will have a harmful effect. We must let the market work under its principles and all will be all right in the end. 'Economic life has within itself the capacity to solve its own problems and for all to work out best in the end.'[6] It is a philosophy that encourages us all to think only in the short term, for, as Keynes said, 'In the long term we are all dead.'

The Last Supper offers freedom precisely in the face of death, that long or short term prospect. It offers us the memory of a man fated to death. It is necessary – one of the central words of Mark's Gospel – that the Son of Man will be handed over to suffer and to die. It is his fate. And yet in the face of destruction, the night before he was handed over, he performs an act of mad liberty. He takes his suffering and death, he grasps his fate, and makes of it a gift. 'This is my Body and I give it to you.' Fate is transfigured into freedom. And the form that this takes is the very opposite of that of *Jurassic Park*. It is precisely by refusing to escape from the disciples who will betray him and deny him. He places himself in their hands. He lets them do what they will with him. This is a very different freedom from the heroes of *Jurassic Park* escaping in their airplane from the chaos of rampaging dinosaurs. It is the

6. *The Culture of Contentment*, London, 1992, p. 79.

freedom to belong. It is the deepest freedom that we have because we are, whatever we may be tempted to think, flesh of each other's flesh and we cannot thrive alone. The freedom of escape is the flight from our own deepest nature.

If you were to ask me what I have most importantly learnt during these two years as Master of the Order, moving from airport to airport, I would say that I have learnt a tiny bit of what that freedom to belong might imply. What I have seen is so many people, women and men, so very often members of religious orders but also many lay people, who have dared to grasp that freedom to belong, to give their lives away, to make of their lives a gift. I have learnt just a little more about what it means to celebrate the Eucharist.

I have just come yesterday from Algeria, where the brethren have decided to stay on despite death threats from Islamic fundamentalists, as a sign of hope and future communion. Every Eucharist for them is celebrated in the face of death.

I think of a day in northern Rwanda, in the war zone, before these present troubles. I had visited the refugee camp with thirty thousand people and seen women trying to feed children who had just given up eating because they could not be bothered to live. I had visited the hospital run by the sisters, and seen ward after ward of children and young people with their limbs blown off. I remember one child, eight or nine, with both his legs blown off, and an arm and an eye, and his father sitting by the bed weeping. And we went back to the sisters' house and there was nothing to say. We could not find a single word. But we could celebrate the Eucharist, we could remember that Last Supper. It was the only thing to do, and which gave those sisters the courage to stay, and to belong.

To conclude, how are to break the hold, the entrancement, of the image of being human that holds our culture captive? How

are we to be liberated from this recent myth, that we are really just
solitary beings, each pursuing his or her own good in hot competition? How can we, as Marquand put it, redefine the common
sense of the last two hundred years and discover that we are
brothers and sisters, children of a single God, and siblings in
Christ, who share the same flesh and cannot find contentment
apart?

The deepest truth of our human nature is not that we are
greedy and selfish but that we hunger and thirst for God and in
God we will find each other. Alasdair McIntyre suggests we
should follow the example of our ancestors in the Dark Ages, and
form local communities 'within which the moral life could be
sustained so that both morality and civility might survive the
coming ages of barbarism and darkness.'[7] Certainly one of the
ways in which we will testify to what it is to be human is to gather
in small local communities and to re-enact this story of the Last
Supper, with its mystery of freedom and forgiveness. In England
we call some of these small communities parishes. They take
many different forms in the world. They should be communities
in which we are nourished in the knowledge that the good that
we seek is not our own private satisfaction but the common good.
But they should not be introverted little groups, celebrating their
own chumminess. I personally could not abide that. Here we
should nourish a wider sense of belonging, taste our communion
with all other humans, the saints and the sinners, and the living
and dead.

7. *After Virtue*, London, 1981, p. 244.

Letters to the Dominican Order

Blessed Jordan of Saxony (successor of Saint Dominic)
instituted the practice of Masters of the Order
writing letters to the Order.

Drawing by Sister Mary Grace Thul OP

VOWED TO MISSION

DARING TO VOW

In many parts of the world, especially those marked by Western culture, there has been a profound loss of confidence in the making of promises. This can be seen in the collapse of marriage, the high rate of divorce or the regular requests for dispensation from the vows. What sense can it make to give one's word *usque ad mortem*?

One reason why the giving of one's word may not seem to be a serious matter may be a weakening of our sense of the importance of our words. Do words matter that much in our society? Can they make a difference? Can one offer one's life to another, to God or in marriage, by speaking a few words? We preachers of the Word of God are witnesses that words matter. We are made in the image of God who spoke a word and the heavens and the earth came to be. He spoke a Word that became flesh for our redemption. The words that human beings speak to each other offer life or death, build community or destroy it. The terrible solitude of our vast cities is surely a sign of a culture that has sometimes ceased to believe in the importance of language, to believe that it can build community through language shared. When we give our word in the vows we witness to a fundamental human vocation, to speak words which have weight and authority.

Yet we cannot know what our vows will mean and where they will lead us. How do we dare to make them? Surely only because our God has done so, and we are his children. We dare to do as our Father did first. From the beginning, the history of salvation was of the God who made promises, who promised to Noah that

---

A letter to all the members of the Dominican Order, issued from Santa Sabina, Rome, in April 1994.

never again would the earth be overwhelmed by flood, who
promised to Abraham descendants more numerous than the
sand, and who promised Moses to lead his people out of bondage.
The culmination and astonishing fulfilment of all those promises
was Jesus Christ, God's eternal 'Yes'. As God's children we dare
to give our word, not knowing what it will mean. And this act is
a sign of hope, since for many people there is only the promise. If
one is locked in despair, destroyed by poverty or unemployment
or imprisoned by one's own personal failure, then maybe there is
nothing in which one can put one's hope and trust other than in
the God who has made vows to us, who again and again has
'offered a covenant to humanity and through the prophets taught
us to hope for salvation'.[1]

In this world so tempted by despair there may be no other
source of hope than trust in the God who has given us his Word.
And what sign is there of that vow given, other than men and
women who dare to take vows, whether of marriage or in
religious life. I have never understood so clearly the meaning of
our vows as when I went to visit a barrio on the edges of Lisbon,
inhabited by the very poorest of people, the forgotten and invisible of the city and found the quarter alive with rejoicing, because
a sister who shared their lives was to make her solemn profession.
It was their feast.

Ours has been called 'The Now Generation', the culture in
which there is only the present moment. This can be the source
of a wonderful spontaneity, a freshness and immediacy in which
we should rejoice. But if the present moment is one of poverty or
failure, of defeat or depression, then what hope can there be? The
vows of their nature reach out to an unknown future. For St
Thomas to make a vow was an act of radical generosity, because

1. Fourth Eucharistic Prayer.

one gave in a single moment a life which was to be lived successively through time.[2]

For many people in our culture this offer of a future which cannot be predicted may make no sense. How can I bind myself until death when I do not know who or what I shall become? Who will I be in ten or twenty years time? Whom will I have met and what will draw my heart? For us it is a sign of our dignity as the children of God and of trust in the God of providence, who offers unexpectedly the ram caught in the bushes. The taking of vows remains an act of the deepest significance, a sign of hope in the God who promises us a future, even when it is beyond our imagining, and who will keep his word.

It is true that sometimes a brother or sister may find themselves incapable of continuing in the vows they have taken. This may be because of a lack of discernment in the time of initial formation, or simply because this is a life that, in all honesty, they can no longer bear. Then there exists the wise provision of the possibility of dispensation from the vows. Let us at least give thanks for what they have given, and rejoice in what we have shared! Let us also ask whether, in our communities, we did all that we could to sustain them in their vows.

OBEDIENCE: THE FREEDOM OF THE CHILDREN OF GOD

The beginning of Jesus' preaching was his proclamation of the fulfilment of Isaiah's promise, freedom for prisoners and liberty for those who are oppressed.[3] The gospel which we are called to preach is of the irrepressible freedom of the children of God. 'For freedom Christ has set us free' (Gal 5:1). It is therefore paradoxical that we give our lives to the Order, to preach this gospel, by a

---

2. See *Summa Theologiae*, IIa IIae, q. 186, a 6, ad 2.
3. See Luke 4:18-21.

vow of obedience, the only vow we Dominicans pronounce. How can we speak of freedom who have given away our lives?

The vow of obedience is a scandal in a world which aspires to freedom as its highest value. But what is the freedom for which we hunger? This is a question that is being posed with particular intensity in the countries which have been liberated from Communism. They have entered the 'free world', but is this the freedom for which they have fought? There is certainly a certain important freedom gained, in the political process, but the freedom of the market place is often a disappointment. It does not bring the liberation that it promised, and tears apart the fabric of human society even more deeply. Above all, our supposedly free world is often characterised by a deep sense of fatalism, an impotence to take our destinies into our hands, to really shape our lives, that must make us question the freedom of the consumerist culture. The vow of obedience, then, is not for us merely an administrative convenience, a utilitarian means. It must confront us with a question: What is the freedom for which we long in Christ? How might this vow express that, and help us preachers of the Kingdom to live the exultant liberty of the children of God?

When the disciples find Jesus talking to the Samaritan woman by the well, he says to them: 'My food is to do the will of him who sent me' (Jn 4:34). The obedience of Jesus to the Father is not a limitation of his freedom, a restriction of his autonomy. It is the food that gives him strength and makes him robust. It is his relationship to the Father, the gift of all that he is, his very being.

This deep freedom of Jesus, to belong to the Father, is surely the context in which we reflect upon what it means for us to be free, and to give our lives to the Order. It is not the freedom of the consumer, with unrestricted choice between alternative purchases or courses of action; it is the freedom to be, the freedom of the one who loves. Within our own Dominican tradition this belonging together in mutual obedience is marked by a tension between two characteristics: an unqualified gift of our lives to the Order, and a search for consensus based on debate and mutual attentiveness and respect. Both are necessary if we are to be preachers of the freedom of Christ, the freedom for which the world thirsts. If we fail to really give ourselves to the Order, without condition, then we become merely a group of independent individuals who occasionally co-operate; if obedience is experienced as the imposition of the will of the superior, without the search for a common mind, then our vow becomes alienating and inhuman.

OBEDIENCE AND LISTENING

Obedience is not, in our tradition, fundamentally the submission of the will of a brother or sister to a superior. Because it is an expression of our fraternity with each other, the shared life within the Order, it is based on dialogue and discussion. As is so often remarked, the word *obedire* comes from *ob-audire*, to listen. The beginning of true obedience is when we dare to let our brother or sister speak and we listen to them. It is the 'principle of unity' (LCO, 17. 1). It is also when we are summoned to grow as human beings by being attentive to others. Married people have no option but to be drawn beyond themselves by the demands of their children and spouses. Our way of life, with its silence and solitude, can help us to grow in attentiveness and generosity, but we also run the risk of being locked within ourselves and our own concerns. Religious life can produce people who are deeply selfless or profoundly egoistic, depending upon whether we have listened. It requires all of our attention, complete receptivity. The fertile moment of our redemption was the obedience of Mary who dared to listen to an angel.

This is a listening that demands using our intelligence. In our tradition, we use our reason not so as to dominate the other, but so as to draw near to them. As P. Rousselot said, intelligence is 'the faculty of the other'. It opens our ears to hear. As Herbert McCabe wrote:

> it is first an openness of the mind such as is involved in all learning. Obedience only becomes perfect when the one who commands and the one who obeys come to share one mind. The notion of blind obedience makes no more sense in our tradition than would blind learning. A totally obedient community would be one in which no one was ever compelled to do anything.[4]

It follows that the primary place in which we practice obedience, in the Dominican tradition, is the community chapter, in which we argue with each other. The function of discussion within the Chapter is to seek unity of heart and mind as we seek the common good. We argue together, not so as to win but in the hope of learning from each other. What we seek is not the victory of the majority but, if at all possible, unanimity. This search for unanimity, even if it is sometimes unattainable, does not express just a desire to live in peace with each other. More radically it is a form of government born of a belief that those with whom we disagree have something to say, and we therefore cannot attain the truth alone. Truth and community are inseparable. As Malachy O'Dwyer wrote:

> Why did Dominic place so much trust and confidence in his companions? The answer is a simple one. He was profoundly a man of God, convinced that the hand of God lay upon everything and everyone ... If he was convinced that God was indeed speaking to him through voices other than his own

4. *God Matters*, London, 1987.

then he had to organise his family in such a way that all within the family could be heard.[5]

It follows that government within our tradition takes time. Most of us are busy and this time may seem wasted. Why should we spend time debating with each other when we could be out preaching and teaching? We do so because it is this shared life, this lived solidarity, that makes us to be preachers. We can speak of Christ only out of what we live, and the labour of seeking to be of one heart and mind trains us to speak with authority of the Christ in whom is all reconciliation.

Obedience for us is not the flight from responsibility. It structures the different ways in which we share it. Often the role of a prior is difficult because some brethren believe that, having elected him to office, he alone must bear the burden. This inculcates a puerile attitude to authority. Obedience demands that we grasp the responsibility that is ours, otherwise we shall never respond to the challenges that face the Order. As I said at the meeting of European Provincials at Prague in 1993:

Responsibility is the ability to respond. Will we? In my own experience as a Provincial I have seen 'the mystery of the disappearing responsibility'. It is as mysterious as a novel of Sherlock Holmes! A Provincial Chapter sees there is a problem and commissions the Provincial to face it and resolve it. A bold decision must be taken. He tells the Provincial Council to consider. The Council appoints a Commission to consider what is to be done. They take two or three years clarifying exactly what is the problem. And they then commit it to the next Provincial Chapter, and so the cycle of irresponsibility continues.

Sometimes what paralyses the Order and prevents us from

5. 'Pursuing Communion in Government: The Role of Community Chapter', *Dominican Monastic Search*, Vol. 2, Fall-Winter 1992, p. 41.

daring to do new things is the fear of accepting responsibility, of risking failure. We must each grasp the responsibility that is ours, even if it is painful to do so and we risk making the wrong decision, otherwise we shall die of irrelevancy.

It may be argued that our system of government is not the most efficient. A more centralised and authoritarian government would enable us to respond more rapidly to crises, to take wise decisions based on wide knowledge of the Order. There is often an impulse towards the centralisation of authority. But, as Bede Jarrett OP wrote seventy years ago,

> to those who live under its shadow, liberty in electing government is too blessed a thing to be put aside even at the risk of inefficiency. With all its inherent weakness, for them it mates better than autocracy, however beneficent, with the independence of human reason and the strengthening of human will. Democracy may mar results, but it makes men.[6]

It may sometimes lead to inefficiency but it makes preachers. Our form of government is profoundly linked to our vocation as preachers, for we can only speak with authority of our freedom in Christ if we live it with each other. But our tradition of democracy and of decentralisation can never be an acceptable excuse for immobility and irresponsibility. It should not be a way of hiding from the challenges of our mission.

OBEDIENCE AND SELF-GIFT

The democratic tradition of the Order, our stress on shared responsibility, and on debate and dialogue, might suggest that the demands upon us of obedience are less total than in a more autocratic and centralised system. Is not obedience, then, always a compromise between what I wish and what the Order asks? Might one not bargain for a certain limited autonomy? I do not

6. *The Life of St Dominic*, p. 128.

believe this to be so. Fraternity asks of us all that we are. Because, like all the vows, it is ordered towards *caritas*, an expression of love, then it must be whole-hearted. There will inevitably be a tension between the process of dialogue, the search for consensus, and the moment of handing oneself into the hands of the brethren, but it is a fruitful tension rather than a negotiated compromise. Although I speak most especially out of my experience of government by the brethren, I hope that much of what follows might be helpful to our sisters.

I started by pointing out the immensity of the challenges that we face as an Order. We can face these challenges only if we are able to form new common projects, and give up apostolates that may be dear to us as individuals or provinces. We must dare to try new experiments, risking failure. We must have the courage sometimes to give up institutions that have been important in the past and may still be significant. If we do not, we shall be prisoners of our past. We must have the courage to die if we are to live. This will demand mobility of mind and heart and body, as provinces and as individuals. If we are to build up proper centres of formation and study in Africa and Latin America, rebuild the Order in Eastern Europe, face the challenges of China, of preaching in the world of the young, dialogue with Islam and other religions, then inevitably there are apostolates that we will have to give up. Otherwise we shall never do anything new.

For me this wholehearted gift of one's life to the brethren is more than just the necessary flexibility which a complex organisation needs to respond to new challenges. It belongs to the freedom in Christ that we preach. It belongs to the *lex libertatis*, the law of freedom of the New Covenant. On the night he was betrayed, when his life was doomed to failure, Jesus took bread, broke it, gave it to his disciples and said: 'This is my body, and I give it to you'. Faced with his fate, for 'it was necessary that the

Son of man be handed over', he made this supreme gesture of liberty, giving his life away. Our profession, when we place our lives in the hands of the provincial, is a eucharistic gesture of mad liberty. This is my life and I give it to you. It is thus that we give ourselves to the mission of the Order, 'appointed entirely for the complete evangelisation of the Word of God'. (LCO 111)

When a brother gives his life into our hands this implies that we are under a corresponding obligation. We must dare to ask much of him. A Provincial must have the courage to believe that the brethren of his province are capable of doing wonderful things, more than they may ever imagine. Our system of government must express an astonishing confidence in each other, as when Dominic scandalised his contemporaries in sending out the novices to preach, saying 'Go confidently, because the Lord will be with you, and he will put into your mouth the word of preaching.' If a member of the Order has freely given his life then we honour that gift in freely asking of each other, even if it means leaving behind a project that he dearly loves and has flourished in. Otherwise the Order will be paralysed. We should invite each other to give our lives to new projects, to dare to grasp the challenges of the moment, rather than just to use them to keep alive institutions or communities that are no longer vital to our preaching.

There are challenges before us today where a response of the whole Order is necessary. The evangelisation of China may be one such. In such cases the Master will have to call upon the provinces to be generous and give brothers to new areas of mission, even if this has consequences that are hard to bear. I approached one Provincial to discuss the gift of a brother for our new General Vicariate in Russia and the Ukraine. It was with great hesitation since I knew that he was a brother whom this province could ill afford to lose. The Provincial said to me, 'If

God's providence has prepared this brother for this work, then we too must trust in God's providence for our needs.'

Nothing new can ever be born unless we dare to give up what has been proved to have value in favour of that which may turn out to be a failure. One cannot know in advance. The pressure of our society is that one should have a career, a life that goes somewhere. To give one's life to the preaching of the gospel is to renounce that reassurance. We are people who have no career, no prospects. That is our freedom. I think of the courage of our brethren who are establishing the Order in Korea, struggling with a new language and an unknown culture, with no guarantee in advance that this gift of their lives will bear fruit. That is only a gift of the Lord, as was the resurrection after the failure of the cross. A true gift is, of its nature, a surprise.

One of the ways in which we may have to live out this generosity is in accepting election as a prior, provincial or as a member of a conventual or provincial council. In many provinces it has become hard to find capable brethren who are prepared to accept office. The search for a superior becomes a matter of finding someone who is willing to let his name be proposed to chapter. We look for 'candidates'. Yet it seems to me that the only reason for accepting such a position is because one is obedient to the desires of one's brethren and not because one wishes to be a 'candidate'. There may be good objective reasons for refusing office, which must be taken seriously and possibly accepted, after confirmation by the higher authority. These should be grave reasons, rather than just the fact that one is not attracted by the idea of holding office.

On the Mountain of the Transfiguration, Peter is fascinated by the vision of glory that he has seen. He wishes to build tents and stay there. He resists the call of Jesus to walk on the way to Jerusalem, where he must suffer and die. He fails to see that it is in that death on the cross that the glory will be revealed. Sometimes we remain fascinated by the glory of our past, the glory of the institutions which our brethren before us built. Our gratitude to them should be expressed in searching for ways to meet today's challenges. Like Peter we may be hypnotised and paralysed, and resist the invitation to get up and walk, to share in death and resurrection. Every province must face death in every generation, but there is the sterile death of those who remain stuck on the Mountain of Transfiguration when the Lord has left, and there is the fertile death of those who have dared to take the road and travel with him to the mountain of Calvary, and which leads to resurrection.

POVERTY: THE GENEROSITY OF THE GRACIOUS GOD

Poverty is the vow for which it is hardest to find words that ring true, and this is for two reasons. Those brothers and sisters who have come closest to being really poor are often the most reticent to talk about it. They know how much of what we say about poverty, and about the 'option for the poor', is empty rhetoric. They know just how terrible are the lives of the poor, often without hope, with the daily, grinding violence, the boredom, the insecurity and the dependence. Those of us who have seen, even from afar, what poverty is like are usually suspicious of easy words. Can we ever really know ourselves what it means to live that degradation, insecurity and hopelessness?

A second reason that it is so hard to write about poverty is that what it means to be poor is so different from one society to another, depending upon the nature of family ties, the type of economy, the social provisions made by the State and so on. Poverty means one thing in India, where there is a long tradition of the holy beggar, another in Africa where in most cultures riches are seen as God's blessing, and yet another in the consumerist culture of the West. What it means for us to take a vow of poverty is more culturally determined than for obedience or chastity. The size and location of the community, the apostolates of the brethren impose different constraints that should make us wary of too easy judgments upon how well others are living this vow.

It is, like all the vows, in the first place, a means. It offers us the freedom to go anywhere and preach. You cannot be a wandering preacher if you must transport all your furniture every time you move. In the Bull *Cum Spiritus Fervore* of 1217 Honorius III wrote that Dominic and his brethren:

> in the fervour of the spirit that animated them, cast off the burden of the riches of this world and being shod with zeal to propagate the gospel had resolved to exercise the office of preaching in the humble state of voluntary poverty, exposing themselves to numberless sufferings and dangers for the salvation of others.

We are invited to give up not merely wealth to follow Christ, but 'brothers and sisters and mothers and fathers for my sake'. The renunciation that gives us freedom implies a radical break with our family ties as well, a disinheritance. The consequences of this need to be thought out with great delicacy, since the nature of the family has changed in many societies. Our families today are often marked by divorce and remarriage, and in some societies our religious brothers and sisters are increasingly likely to be only sons and daughters. We do have real obligations to our parents but how are these to be reconciled with the radical self-gift that we have made of our lives to the preaching of the gospel through our vows in the Order? It is paradoxical that it is often the members of the family who are in religious vows who are considered to be 'free' to help look after aged or ill parents. We will need to reflect on this with great sensitivity.

The vow of poverty offers us freedom to give ourselves without reservation to the preaching of the gospel but it is not just a
means in a narrow and utilitarian sense. Like the other vows it is,
as Saint Thomas wrote, ordered towards *caritas*, the love that is
the very life of God. How can we live it so that we can talk about
God with authority?

One way to answer this would be to explore how poverty
touches fundamental aspects of that sacrament of love which is
the Eucharist. For the Eucharist is the sacrament of unity which
poverty destroys; it is the sacrament of vulnerability, which the
poor endure; it is the moment of gift, which our culture of
consumption resists. To ask how we may and should be poor is
to ask how we should live eucharistically.

INVISIBILITY

On the night before he died Jesus gathered the disciples
around the table to celebrate the new covenant. It was the birth
of a home in which all might belong, since he embraced all that
might destroy human community: betrayal, denial, even death.
The scandal of poverty is that it rips apart what Christ has made
one. Poverty is not just an economic condition, the lack of food
and clothing or employment. It tears apart the human family. It
alienates us from our sisters and brothers. Lazarus at the door of
the rich man's house is not merely excluded from sharing his food
but from sitting at his table. The unbridgeable abyss that sepa-
rates them after death merely reveals what had been the case
during their lifetimes. In our world today the rift between rich
and poor countries, and within these countries themselves, is
becoming ever more acute. Even within the rich countries of the
European Community there are almost twenty million unemployed. The body of Christ is dismembered.

The voluntary poverty that we vow has value not because it is in any sense good to be poor. Poverty is terrible. It matters only if it is a reaching out across the boundaries that separate human beings from each other, a presence with our separated brothers and sisters. What possible authority could our words about our unity in Christ have if we do not dare to make this journey? During the last year I have seen how much our sisters have to teach the brethren, by their quiet presence among the poor in so many parts of the world. They know the importance of just being there as a sign of the Kingdom.

The Eucharist is the foundation of the universal human home. Would a poor person feel at home and welcomed in our communities? Would they feel that their dignity was respected? Or might they feel intimidated and small? Do our buildings attract or repel? One of the ways that the poor are removed from the human community is by becoming invisible and inaudible. They disappear, the *desaparecidos*, like Lazarus at the door of the rich man. When one arrives at Calcutta Railway Station, the beggars rush up and thrust their deformities at one. They demand to be seen, to be visible. Do we dare to look for fear of what we might see, a brother or a sister?

VULNERABILITY

In the Last Supper Christ embraced his suffering and his death. He accepted the ultimate vulnerability of being human, the liability to be wounded and killed. Our vow of poverty surely invites us to embrace our human vulnerability. In the Bull of Honorius III that I quoted above, Dominic and the brethren are praised not merely for being poor but for 'exposing themselves to numberless sufferings and dangers for the salvation of others'. In what sense do we ever share even a glimpse of the vulnerability of the poor?

However little we eat, for us there is always an escape route if we can endure it no more. The Order will not let us die of hunger. Yet I have met brothers and sisters who have dared to go as far as they can, for example in one of the most violent barrios of Caracas. They endure the danger and exhaustion of living every day in a world where violence is all pervasive. That is a real vulnerability which could cost them their lives. I think of our brothers and sisters in Haiti, whose brave stand for justice put their lives at risk. In Algeria and Cairo our brothers choose to remain, despite all the dangers, as a sign of their hope for reconciliation between Christians and Muslims. In Guatemala our indigenous sisters wear clothes of their own people, so that they may share their daily humiliation. If they wore a traditional habit they would be insulated from that. Not all of us are called to this degree of exposure. There are different tasks within the Order. But we can support them, listen to them and learn from them. The seedbed of our theology is their experience.

This call of Christ to vulnerability must put questions as to how we live the vow of poverty together. Do we dare even live the vulnerability which is presupposed by the common life? Do we really live out of the common purse? Do we live the insecurity of giving to the community all that we receive, exposed to the risk that they might not give us all that we think we need? How can we speak of the Christ who put himself into our hands, if we do not? Are our communities divided into financial classes? Are there some who have access to more money than others? Is there a real sharing of wealth between the communities of a Provinces, or between Provinces?

GIFT

At the heart of our lives is the celebration of that moment of utter vulnerability and generosity, when Jesus took bread and broke it and gave it to his disciples saying 'Take and eat, this is my body, given to you.' At the centre of the gospel is a moment of pure gift. This is where the *caritas* which is the life of God becomes most tangible. It is a generosity that our society finds hard to grasp, for our society is a market in which everything is bought and sold. What sense can it make of the God who shouts out 'Come to me all you who are thirsty and I will give you food without price.' All human societies have markets, the buying and selling and exchange of goods. Western society differs in *being* a market. It is the fundamental model that dominates and forms our conception of society, of politics and even of each other. Everything is for sale. The infinite fertility of nature, the land, water have become commodities. Even we human beings are on the 'labour market'. This culture of consumerism threatens to engulf the whole world, and it claims to do so in the name of freedom, but it locks us in a world where nothing is free. Even when we become aware of the distress of the poor and seek to respond, so often *caritas* has been monetarised into 'charity', in which the gift of money is substituted for the sharing of life.

How can we be preachers of the gracious and generous God, who gives us his life, if we are caught up in this all-pervasive culture? One of the most radical demands of the vow of poverty is surely that we so live in simplicity as to see the world differently and gain some glimpse of the utterly gracious God. The lives of our communities should be marked by a simplicity which helps to liberate us from the illusory promises of our culture of consummation, and from 'the domination of wealth' (LCO, 31.I). The world looks different from the back of a Mercedes than it does from the seat of a bicycle. Jordan of Saxony said that Dominic was 'a true lover of poverty', perhaps not because poverty is in itself lovable but because it can disclose to us our deepest desires. I have often been struck by the joyfulness and spontaneity of our brothers and sisters who live in simplicity and poverty.

In some parts of the Order the very language that we use when describing our common life suggests that we should be attentive to the dangers of absorbing the values of the world of business. The brothers or sisters become 'personnel'; we have 'personnel boards'; the role of a superior becomes that of 'management' or 'administration', and we study 'management techniques'. Can one imagine Dominic as the first President of the Order of Preachers Incorporated? How often does a Provincial prevent a brother from seeking new and creative ways of preaching and teaching because the Province would suffer financially?

The buildings in which we live are gifts. Do we live in them and treat them with gratitude? Do we have a responsible attitude to what we are given, for the fabric of our buildings, for what we receive? Do we need the buildings that we have? Could our buildings be better used? Bursars often have a thankless task, even though they have a vital role in helping us to live with the responsibility that we owe to those who are generous to us.

CHASTITY: THE FRIENDSHIP OF GOD

We have an urgent need to think together about the meaning of the vow of chastity. It touches issues central to our humanity: our sexuality, our bodiliness, our need to express and receive affection, and yet frequently we fear to talk. So often it is an area in which we struggle alone, afraid of judgement or incomprehension.

It is of course true that this vow is, like the others, a means. It gives us the freedom to preach, the mobility to respond to needs. But with this vow it is perhaps especially important that it is not merely endured as a grim necessity. Unless we can learn, perhaps through much time and suffering, to embrace it positively, then it can poison our lives. And we can do so because it is, like all the vows, ordered towards *caritas*, towards that love which is the very life of God. It is a particular way of loving. If it is not that, then it will lead us to frustration and sterility.

The first sin against chastity is a failure to love. It was said of Dominic that 'since he loved all, he was loved by all.' What is at issue, yet again, is the authority of our preaching. How can we speak of the God of love if that is not a mystery that we live? If we do so, then it will ask of us death and resurrection. The temptation is to take flight. One common escape route is activism, to lose ourselves in hectic work, even good and important work, so as to flee the solitude. We may even be tempted to flee from the fact of our sexuality, our bodiliness. Yet the Dominican Order was born precisely in the struggle against such dualism. Dominic was the one who preached against the division of body and soul, spirit and matter. It remains a modern temptation. Much of modern culture is deeply dualistic. Pornography, which appears to delight in sexuality, is in reality a flight from it, a refusal of that vulnerability that human relationship demands. The voyeur keeps his distance, invulnerable and in control, afraid.

It is our corporeality that is blessed and made holy in the Incarnation. If we are to be preachers of the Word become flesh, then we cannot deny or forget what we are. Do we care for the bodies of our brethren, making sure that they have enough food, tend them when they are sick, be tender to them when they are old? Bede Jarrett OP wrote to encourage a young Benedictine who was enduring the first sufferings of friendship:

> I am glad because I think your temptation has been towards Puritanism, a narrowness, a certain inhumanity. Your tendency was almost towards the denial of the hallowing of matter. You were in love with the Lord, but not properly with the Incarnation. You were really afraid.[7]

7. *The Letters of Bede Jarrett OP*, ed. Bede Bailey, Aidan Bellenger and Simon Tugwell, Bath, 1989, p. 180.

The basis of our chastity can never be fear, fear of our sexuality, fear of our bodiliness, fear of people of the other sex. Fear is never a good foundation for religious life, for the God who drew near to us dared to become flesh and blood even though it led to crucifixion. Ultimately this vow demands of us that we follow where God has gone before. Our God has become human, and invites us to do so as well.

St. Thomas Aquinas makes the startling claim that our relationship with God is one of friendship, *amicitia*. The good news that we preach is that we share in the infinite mystery of the friendship of Father and Son which is the Spirit. And indeed Thomas argues that the 'evangelical counsels' are the counsels offered by Christ in friendship. One way that we live that friendship is the vow of chastity. To help us reflect upon what it demands of us, let us briefly reflect upon two aspect of that Trinitarian love. It is utterly generous and unpossessive, and it is the love between equals.

AN UNPOSSESSIVE LOVE

It is that utterly generous and unpossessive love by which the Father gives all that he is to the Son, including his divinity. It is not a sentiment or a feeling, but the love that grants the Son being. All human love, of married people or religious, should seek to live and share in this mystery, in its unpossessive generosity.

We must be completely unambiguous as to what this loving demands of us who are vowed to chastity. It means not just that we do not marry but that we abstain from sexual activity. It asks of us a real and clear renunciation, an asceticism. If we pretend otherwise and willingly accept compromises, then we enter upon a path that may be ultimately impossible to sustain and cause us and others terrible unhappiness.

The first thing that we are asked to do is to believe that the vow of chastity really can be a way of loving, that though we may pass through moments of frustration and desolation, it is a path that can lead to our flourishing as affectionate, whole human beings. The older members of our community are often signs of hope for us. We meet men and women who have passed through the trials of chastity, and emerged into the liberty of those who can love freely. They can be for us signs that with God nothing is impossible.

The entry into this free and unpossessive love will take time. We may endure failures and discouragement on the way. Now that many people enter the Order when they are older, having had sexual experience, then we must not think of it so much as an innocence that we may lose but an integrity of heart into which we may grow. Even moments of failure may, in the grace of God, belong to the path by which we mature, for 'we know that in everything God works for good with those who love him' (Rom 8:28).

Our communities should be places in which brothers or sisters must give each other courage when one person's heart hesitates, forgiveness when another fails and truthfulness when anyone is tempted by self-deceit. We must believe in the goodness of our brothers or sisters when they cease to believe it of themselves. Nothing is more poisonous than self-despising. As Damian Byrne [8] wrote in his letter on 'The Common Life':

> While the deepest sanctuary of our hearts is given to God, we have other needs. He has made us so that a large area of our life is accessible to others and is needed by others. Each one of us needs to experience the genuine interest of the other members of the community, their affection, esteem and fellowship ... Life together means breaking the bread of our minds and

8. Master of the Order 1983-1992; died February 1996.

hearts with each other. If religious do not find this in their communities then they will seek it elsewhere.[9]

Sometimes the passage to real freedom and integrity of heart will demand that we pass through the valley of death, that we find ourselves faced only, it may seem, with sterility and frustration. Is it really possible to make this journey without prayer? There is first of all the prayer that we share with the community, the daily prayer that is fundamental to our lives. But there is also the silent and private prayer, that brings us face to face with God, in moments of unavoidable truth and astonishing mercy. Here one can learn to hope. Dominic himself would sometimes, when he walked, invite the brethren to go ahead so that he could be alone to pray and in an early version of the Constitutions Dominic said that the novice master should teach his novices to pray in silence. Our nuns have much to teach the brethren about the value of prayer in silence.

THE LOVE THAT GIVES EQUALITY

Finally, the love that is at the heart of God is utterly fertile. It is generative, creative of all that is. What we struggle with in chastity is not just the need for affection but the desire to beget, to bring to birth. Our care for each other must surely include an attentiveness to the creativity that each one of us has, and which our lives as Dominicans should liberate for the gospel. This may be the creativity of a brother or sister bringing a community into being in a parish, or the intellectual labour of a theologian, or the pre-novices in El Salvador performing spontaneous theatre. Our chastity must never be sterile.

The love that is God is so fertile as to create equality. The Trinity is without domination or manipulation. It is not patronising or condescending. This is the love that our vow of chastity

9. *A Pilgrimage of Faith*, Dublin, 1991, pp. 44-45.

invites us to live and preach. As Thomas wrote, friendship finds or creates equality. The fraternity of our Dominican tradition, the democratic form of government in which we delight, expresses not just a way of organising our lives and taking decisions, but expresses something of the mystery of the life of God. That the brethren are known as the *Ordo Fratrum Praedicatorum* embodies what it is that we preach, the mystery of that love of perfect equality that is the Trinity.

This should characterize all our relationships. The Dominican Family, with its recognition of each other's dignity, and the equality of all members of the family belongs to our living this vow well. The relationship between sisters and brothers, religious and laity, should also be a 'holy preaching'. Even our search for a more just world, in which the dignity of every human being will be respected, is not merely a moral imperative, but an expression of the mystery of the love that is the life of the Trinity which we are called to embody.

CONCLUSION

When Dominic used to walk through villages where his life was threatened by the Albigensians, he used to sing loudly so that everyone knew that he was there. The vows have any value only if they liberate us for the mission of the Order with some of Dominic's courage and joy. They should not be a heavy burden to weigh us down, but grant us a freedom to walk lightly as we go to new places to do new things. What I have written in this letter gives only a very inadequate expression of how this may be so. I hope that together we may build a shared vision of our life as Dominicans, vowed to mission, that may strengthen us on the journey and free us to sing.

THE WELLSPRING OF HOPE:
STUDY AND THE ANNUNCIATION
OF THE GOOD NEWS

When St Dominic wandered through the south of France, his life in danger, he used to sing cheerfully. 'He always appeared cheerful and happy, except when he was moved by compassion for any trouble which afflicted his neighbour.'[1] And this joy of Dominic is inseparable from our vocation to be preachers of the good news. We are called to 'give an account of the hope that is within us' (1 Pet 3:15). Today, in a world crucified by suffering, violence and poverty, our vocation is both harder and more necessary than ever. There is a crisis of hope in every part of the world. How are we to live Dominic's joy when we are people of our time, and we share the crises of our peoples and the strengths and weaknesses of our culture? How can we nurture a deep hope, grounded in God's unshakeable promise of life and happiness for his children? The conviction which I explore in this letter to the Order is that a life of study is one of the ways in which we may grow in that love which 'bears all things, believes all things, hopes all things, endures all things'. (1 Cor 13:7)

The time has come to renew the love affair between the Order and study. This is beginning to happen. All over the world I see new centres of study and theological reflection opening, in Kiev, Ibadan, Sao Paolo, Santo Domingo, Warsaw, to name a few. These should offer not just an intellectual formation. Study is a way to holiness, which opens our hearts and minds to each other, builds community and forms us as those who confidently proclaim the coming of the Kingdom.

1. Cecilia *Miracula B Dominici* 15 *Archivum Fratrum Praedicatorum* XXXVII, Rome, 1967 p. 5 ff.

A Letter to all members of the Dominican Order, issued from Santa Sabina, Rome, on 21 November, 1995.

THE ANNUNCIATION

To study is itself an act of hope, since it expresses our confi- //
dence that there is a meaning to our lives and the sufferings of our
people. And this meaning comes to us as a gift, a Word of Hope
promising life. There is one moment in the story of our redemption which sums up powerfully what it means to receive that gift
of the good news, the Annunciation to Mary. That meeting, that
conversation, is a powerful symbol of what is meant by being a
student. I will use this to guide our reflection upon how study
grounds our hope.

First of all it is a moment of attentiveness. Mary listens to the
good news that is announced to her. This is the beginning of all
our study, attentiveness to the Word of Hope proclaimed in the
Scriptures. 'Orally and by letter brother Dominic exhorted the
brothers to study incessantly the New and the Old Testament'.[2]
We learn to listen to the One who says 'Sing, O barren one, who
did not bear; break forth into singing and cry aloud, you who
have not been in travail'. (Is 54:1) Do our studies offer us the hard
discipline of learning to hear the good news?

Secondly, it is a moment of fertility. There she is, as Fra
Angelico portrays her, with the book on her knees, attentive,
waiting, listening. And the fruit of her attentiveness is that she
bears a child, the Word made flesh. Her listening releases all her
creativity, her female fertility. And our study, the attentiveness to
the Word of God, should release the springs of our fertility, make
us bear Christ in our world. In the midst of a world which often
seems doomed and sterile, we bring Christ to birth in a miracle
of creativity. Whenever the Word of God is heard, it does not just
tell of hope, but of a hope that takes flesh and blood in our lives
and words. Congar loved to quote the famous words of Peguy

2. Process of Canonisation, No. 29.

'Not the Truth, but the Real ... That is to say, the Truth histori-
cally, with its concrete state in the future, in time.' This is the test
of our studies: Does it bring Christ to birth again? Are our studies
moments of real creativity, of Incarnation? Houses of study
should be like maternity wards!

Thirdly, in a moment when God's people seem deserted and
without hope, God gives his people a future, a way to the
Kingdom. The Annunciation transforms the way in which
God's people could understand its history. Instead of leading to
servitude and despair, it opens a way to the Kingdom. Do our
studies prepare the way for the coming of Christ? Do they
transform our perception of human history so that we may come
to understand it, not from the point of view of the victor but of the
small and crushed whom God has not forgotten and whom he
will vindicate?

LEARNING TO LISTEN

And he came to her and said, 'Hail, O favoured one, the Lord
is with you.' But she was greatly troubled at the saying and
considered in her mind what sort of greeting this might be. (Lk
1:29-30)

Mary listens to the words of the angel, the good news of our
salvation. That is the beginning of all study. Study is not learning
how to be clever but how to listen. Simone Weil wrote to a French
Dominican, fr Perrin, that 'the development of the faculty of
attentiveness forms the real object and almost the sole interest of
studies'.[3] This receptivity, this opening of the ear which marks all
study, ultimately is deeply linked to prayer. They both require of
us that we be silent and wait for God's Word to come to us. They
both demand of us an emptiness, so that we wait upon the Lord

3. Simone Weil, *Attente de Dieu,* Paris, 1950, p. 71.

for what He may give us. Think of Fra Angelico's picture of Dominic, sitting at the foot of the cross and reading. Is he studying or praying? Is this even a relevant question? True study makes mendicants of us. We are led to the thrilling discovery that we do not know what this text means, that we have become ignorant and needy, and so we wait, in intelligent receptivity for what will be given.

For the great Dominican Scripture scholar, M.J. Lagrange, the *Ecole Biblique*, which he founded, was a centre of scriptural studies precisely because it was a house of prayer The rhythm of the life of the community was a movement between the cell and the choir. He wrote: 'I love to hear the gospel sung by the deacon at the ambo, in the middle of the clouds of incense: the words penetrate my soul more deeply when I meet them again in an article'.[4] Our monasteries should play an important role in the life of study of the Order, as oases of peace and places of attentive reflection. Study in our monastries belongs to the asceticism of Dominican monastic life. It cannot just be left to the brethren. Every nun deserves a good intellectual forrnation as part of her religious life. As the Constitutions of the Nuns say, 'The blessed Dominic recommended some form of study to the first nuns as an authentic observance of the Order. It not only nourishes contemplation but also removes the impediments which arise through ignorance and forms a practical judgement.' (LMO 100 II)

Mary listened to the promise spoken to her by the angel, and she bore the Word of Life. This seems so simple. What more do we need to do than to open ourselves to the Word of God spoken in scripture? Why are so many years of study necessary to form preachers of the good news? Why do we have to study philosophy, read fat and difficult books of theology when we have God's

---

4. Bernard Montagnes, *Le Pére Lagrange,* Paris, 1995, p. 57.

own Word? Is it not simply enough to give an 'account of the hope that is within us'? God is love and love has conquered death. What more is there to say? Do we not betray this simplicity in our complex discussions? But it was not so simple for Mary. This story begins with her puzzlement. 'But she was greatly troubled at the saying and considered in her mind what sort of greeting this might be.' Listening begins when we dare to let ourselves be puzzled, disturbed. And then the story continues with her question to the messenger: 'How can this be, since I am a virgin?'

THE CONFIDENCE TO STUDY

The story is told that St Albert the Great was once sitting in his cell studying. And the Devil appeared to him disguised as one of the brethren, and tried to persuade him that he was wasting his time and energy studying the secular sciences. It was bad for his health. Albert just made the sign of the cross and the apparition disappeared.[5] Alas, the brethren are not always so easy to convince! All the disciplines – literature, poetry, history, philosophy, psychology, sociology, physics, etc – that try to make sense of our world, are our allies in our search for God. 'It must be possible to find God in the complexity of human experience.'[6] This world of ours, for all its pain and suffering, is ultimately the fruit of 'that divine love which first moved all beautiful things.'[7] The hope that makes us preachers of good news is not a vague optimism, a hearty cheerfulness, whistling in the dark. It is the belief that in the end we can discover some meaning in our lives, a meaning that is not imposed, which is there, waiting to be discovered. It follows that study should be above all a pleasure, the pure delight of discovering that things do, despite all the evidence to

5. Thomas of Chantrimpé.
6. Cornelius Ernst OP, *Multiple Echo*, ed. Fergus Kerr OP and Timothy Radcliffe OP, London, 1979, p. 1.
7. Dante, *Inferno*, Canto 1, 40.

the contrary, make sense, whether our own lives, human history or the particular bit of scripture with which we have been struggling all morning. Our centres of study are schools of joy because they are founded upon the belief that it is possible to arrive at some understanding of our world and our lives. Human history is not the senseless and endless conflict of *Jurassic Park*, the survival of the fittest. This creation in which we live and of which we are part is not the result of chance, but it is the work of Christ: 'all things were created through him and for him, He is before all things, and in him all things hold together' (Col 1:16f). Wisdom dances before the throne of God to express her joy in creating this world, and the aim of all study is to share her pleasure. Simone Weil wrote in April 1942 to fr Perrin, 'The intelligence can only be led by desire. For there to be desire there must be pleasure and joy in the work. The joy of learning is as indispensable to study as breathing is to running.'[8] The Constitutions talk of our *propensio* (LCO 77) to the truth, a natural inclination of the human heart. To study should be simply part of the joy of being fully alive. The truth is the air that we are made to breathe.

This is a beautiful idea, but let us admit straightaway that it is very far from the experience of many of us! For some Dominicans, brothers and sisters, the years of study have not been a time of learning to hope but of despair. So often I have seen students struggling with books that seem arid and remote from their experience, longing for it all to be over so that they can get on with preaching, swearing never to open another book of theology after they have escaped from their studies. And even worse than the aridity is, for some, the humiliation, struggling with Hebrew verbs without success, never managing to understand the difference between the Arians and the Apollinarians, and finally

8. Simone Weil, op. cit., p. 71.

defeated by German philosophy!

Why is study so hard for many of us? In part it is because we are marked by a culture which has lost confidence that study is a worthwhile activity and which doubts that debate can bring us to the truth for which we long. If our century has been so marked by violence it is surely partly because it has lost confidence in our ability to attain the truth together. Violence is the only resort in a culture which has no trust in the shared search for truth. Dachau, Hiroshima, Rwanda, Bosnia – these are all symbols of the collapse of a belief in the possibility of building a common human home through dialogue. This lack of confidence may take two forms: a relativism which despairs of ever attaining to the truth, and a fundamentalism which asserts that the truth is already completely possessed.

In the face of that despair which is relativism, we celebrate that the truth may be known and in fact has come to us as a gift. With St Paul we can say: 'What I received from the Lord, I also delivered to you.' (1 Cor 11:23) Studying is a eucharistic act. We open our hands to receive the gifts of tradition rich with knowledge. Western culture is marked by a profound suspicion of all teaching, since it is equated with indoctrination and bigotry. The only valid truth is that which one has discovered for oneself or which is grounded in one's feelings: 'If it feels right for me, then it is OK'. But teaching should liberate us from the narrow confines of our experience and our prejudices and open up the wide open spaces of a truth which no one can master. I remember, as a student, the dizzy excitement of discovering that the Council of Chalcedon was not the end of our search to understand the mystery of Christ but another beginning, exploding all the tiny coherent little solutions in which we had tried to box him. Doctrine should not indoctrinate but liberate us to continue on the journey.

But there is also the rising tide of fundamentalism which derives from a profound fear of thinking, and which offers 'the false hope of a faith without ambiguity'. (Oakland Chapter No 109) Within the Church this fundamentalism sometimes takes the form of an unthinking repetition of received words, a refusal to take part in the never-ending search for understanding, an intolerance of all for whom tradition is not just a revelation but also an invitation to draw nearer to the mystery. This fundamentalism may appear to be a rocklike fidelity to orthodoxy, but it contradicts a fundamental principle of our faith, which is that when we argue and reason we honour our Creator and Redeemer who gave us minds with which to think and to draw near to him. We can never do theology well unless we have the humility and the courage to listen to the arguments of those with whom we disagree and take them seriously. St Thomas wrote: 'As nobody can judge a case unless he hears the reasons on both sides, so he who has to listen to philosophy will be in a better position to pass judgement if he listens to all the arguments on both sides.'[9] We have to lose those certainties that banish uncomfortable truths, see both sides of the argument, ask the questions that may frighten us. St Thomas was the man of questions, who learnt to take every question seriously, however foolish it might appear.

Our centres of study are schools of hope. When we gather together to study, our community is a 'holy preaching'. In a world which has lost confidence in the value of reason, it witnesses to the possibility of a common search for the truth. This may be a university seminar arguing over a case of bio-medical ethics, or a group of pastoral agents studying the Bible together in Latin America. Here we should learn confidence in each other as

9. Metaph III lec 3.

partners in the dialogue, companions in the adventure. Humiliation can have no part in study, if we are to give each other the courage for the journey. No one can teach unless they understand from within another's panic upon opening a new book, or struggling with a new idea. So the teacher is not there to fill the pupils' heads with facts, but to strengthen them in their deep human inclination towards the truth, and to accompany them in the search. We must learn to see with our own eyes and stand on our feet. When Lagrange taught at the *Ecole Biblique* he used to say to his pupils, 'Look! You will not say Father Lagrange said this or that, because you will have seen for yourself'.[10] Above all, the teacher should give the student the courage to make mistakes, to risk being wrong. Meister Eckhart said that 'one seldom finds that people attain to anything good unless they have first gone somewhat astray.' Children can ever learn to walk unless they have fallen flat on their faces several times. The child who is frightened remains for ever on its bottom!

THE BREAKING OF IDOLS

In the earliest days, the study of the brethren was essentially biblical, in preparation for pastoral work, above all the sacrament of penance. The first theological works of the Order were confessional manuals. But when St Thomas was teaching those beginners in theology at Santa Sabina he realised that our preaching would only be useful for the salvation of souls if the brethren received a profound theological and philosophical formation. This was for two reasons. Firstly, the simplest questions often require the most profound thought: Are we free? How can we ask God for things? Secondly because, according to the biblical tradition, what stands between us and a true worship of God is

10. Bernard Montagnes, op. cit., p. 54.

not so much atheism as idolatry. Humanity has a tendency to build false gods, and then to worship them. The exodus from this idolatry requires of us a hard journey, in how we live and think. It is not enough just to sit and listen to the Word of God. We need to break the hold of those false images of God which hold us captive and block our ears.

All his life St Thomas was fascinated by the question: What is God? As Herbert McCabe OP says, his sanctity lay in the fact that he let himself be defeated by this question. Central to the teaching of Aquinas is this radical ignorance, for we are joined to God 'as to one, as it were, unknown.'[11] We have to be liberated from the image of God as a very powerful and invisible person, manipulating the events of our lives. Such a God would ultimately be a tyrant and a rival to humanity against whom we would be forced to rebel. Instead we have to discover God as the ineffable source of my being, the heart of my freedom. We have to lose God if we are to discover him, as St Augustine said, 'closer to me than I am to myself.'[12]

Teaching theology, then, is not just a matter of communicating information, but of accompanying students as they face the loss of God, the disappearance of a well-known and loved person, so as to discover God as the source of all who has given himself to us in his Son. Then we can indeed say, 'Blessed are those who mourn; they shall be comforted'. McCabe writes, 'It is one of the special pleasures of teaching in our *studium* to watch the moment which comes to every student sooner or later, the moment of conversion you might say, when he realises that ... God is not less than the source of all my free acts, and the reason why they are my

11. *Summa Theologiae*, 1a, Q. 12, a. 8, ad 1. See Acts of the Caleruega Chapter, 32. This text provoked one of the most passionate debates of the Chapter. It was good to see the brothers arguing over theology!
12. Confessions, 111, 6.

own. [13] The intellectual discipline of our study has this ultimate purpose, to bring us to this moment of conversion when our false images of God are destroyed so that we may draw near to the mystery. But thinking is not enough. Dominican theology began when Dominic got off his horse and became a poor preacher. The intellectual poverty of Thomas before the mystery of God is inseparable from his choice of an Order of poor preachers. The theologian must be a beggar who knows how to receive the free gifts of the Lord.

For us, listening to the Word will demand of us that we free ourselves from the false ideologies of our time. Who are our false gods? Surely they include the idolatry of the State, upon whose altars millions of innocent lives have been shed this century; the worship of the market, and the pursuit of wealth. I have written often enough about the dangers of the myth of consumerism. Our whole world has been seduced by a mythology, that everything can be bought and sold. Everything has been transformed into commodities, everything has a price. The world of nature, the fertility of the earth, the fragile ecology of forests, all this is put on sale. Even we ourselves, the sons and daughters of the Most High, are to be bought and sold on the labour market. The Industrial Revolution saw the uprooting of whole communities, expelled from their land and enslaved in the new cities. This massive migration continues today. The most acute and scandalous example was the enslaving of millions of our brothers and sisters from Africa, transformed into marketable goods for profit and export. As it was written at the Chapter of Caleruega: 'Men and women may not be treated as commodities, nor may their lives and work, their culture and potential for flourishing in society be counted among negotiable tokens in the game of profit

13. *God Matters,* London, 1987, p. 241.

and loss.' (20.5)

Our centres of study should be places in which we are liberated from this reductive view of the world, and where we learn again to wonder in gratitude at the good gifts of God. It is through study, by seeking to understand things and each other, that we recover a sense of astonishment at the miracle of creation. Simon Tugwell OP writes, 'When we get to the bottom of things, reaching their very essence with our minds, what we find is the inscrutable mystery of God's creative act ... Really to know something is to find ourselves tipped headlong into a wonder far surpassing mere curiosity.' [14] The truth does indeed set us free. This intellectual liberation goes hand in hand with the real freedom of poverty. Like Dominic and Thomas we have to become beggars who receive God's good gifts. The vow of poverty and a closeness to the poor is the proper Dominican context in which to study.

In our struggle to liberate ourselves from this perception of the world, we are helped by being an Order which is truly world-wide. Many cultures do not have a vision of reality which is based upon domination and mastery. Our brothers and sisters from Africa can help us towards a theology which is based more upon mutuality and harmony. The Asian religious traditions can also help us towards a more contemplative theology. We have to be present in these other cultures, not just so that we may inculturate the gospel there, but so that they may help us to understand the mystery of creation, and of God the giver of all good things.

THE BIRTH OF COMMUNITY

The Angel said to her, 'Do not be afraid, Mary, for you have found favour with God. And behold you will conceive in your

14. *Reflections on the Beatitudes*, London, 1979, p. 100.

womb and bear a son, and you shall call his name Jesus.' (Lk
1:30)

The purpose of our studies is not merely to impart information
but to bring Christ to birth in our world. The test of our studies
is not so much whether they make us well informed, but whether
they make us fertile. Every new-born child is a surprise, even to
its parents. They cannot know beforehand whom they are bringing into the world. So too our study should prepare us to be
surprised. Christ comes among us in every generation in ways
that we could never have anticipated and may only slowly
recognise as authentic, as it took time for the Church to accept the
new shocking theology of St Thomas. In the mountains of
Guatemala, in our centre of reflection on inculturation AK'KUTAN
in Coban, the brothers and sisters seek to help the Order to be
born with the richness of the indigenous culture. In Takamori,
behind Mount Fuji, our brother Oshida seeks to bring Christ to
birth in the world of Japan, or there is our brother Michael
Shirres in New Zealand, who has for twenty years been struggling to meld the fertile seeds of Maori spirituality with Christian
faith. This may happen in all sorts of ways that are not academic.
In Croatia one of our brothers heads a rock band called the
Messengers of Hope. In Japan I have seen the wonderful paintings
of our brothers Petit and Carpentier. Or it may be in the miraculous birth of community in a village in Haiti. How can our
preaching bring Christ to birth among the drug addicts of New
York or the slums of London? How can the Word become flesh
in the words of today, take body in the languages of philosophy
and psychology, through our prayer and study? It is for this
incarnation of the Word of God in every culture, that the establishment of houses of study, of theological excellence, in every
continent, must be a priority of the Order.

I wish to argue that a life of study builds community, and so prepares a home for Christ to dwell among us. There is no more cruel experience of despair than that of utter solitude, the human person introverted upon his or her self. If our society is tempted so often by despair, then maybe it is because this is the dominant image of the human being in our world, the solitary individual in pursuit of his or her own desires and private good. The radical individualism of our time seems like a liberation, but it can plunge us into a lonely hopelessness. The community offers us an 'ecology of hope'.[15] It is only together that we may dare to hope for a renewed world.

The scholar may seem to be the perfect example of the solitary figure, alone with his or her books or computer screen, and with a sign saying 'Do not disturb' on the door. It is true that study will demand of us often that we be alone and struggle with abstract questions. But this is a service that we offer our brothers and sisters. The fruit of this solitary labour is to build community by opening up the mysteries of the Word of God. We learn through study to belong to each other and so to hope.

THE TRANSFORMATION OF MIND AND HEART

Even the very image of the self as utterly alone, an isolated individual, is challenged. For the doctrine of creation shows us that our Creator is more intimately close to us than any being could be, since he is the ever-present source of our being. We cannot be alone, because alone we could not even be!

In Western culture there is an obsession with self-knowledge. But how can I know myself apart from the one who sustains me in being? St Catherine was deeply modern in inviting her brethren to enter into the 'cell of self-knowledge', but that self-knowledge was inseparable from a knowledge of God. We can

15. Jonathan Sachs, *Faith in the Future,* London, 1995, p. 5.

see neither our own dignity nor the defects which spoil the beauty of our soul, unless we look at ourselves in the peaceful sea of God's being in which we are imaged.'[16] Even the moments of utter desolation, of the dark night of the soul, when we seem to be utterly deserted, can be transfigured into moments of meeting: 'The night that joins the beloved with her loved one, the night transfiguring the beloved in her loved one's life.'[17]

Study can never be just the training of the mind; it is the transformation of the human heart. 'A new heart I will give you, and a new spirit I will put within you; and I will take out of your flesh the heart of stone and give you a heart of flesh.' (Ezek 36:26) The first General Chapter of the Order at Bologna said that novices are to be taught 'how they should be intent on study, so that by day and by night, at home or on a journey, they should be reading or reflecting on something; whatever they can, they should try to commit to memory.'[18] All the time we are letting our hearts be formed, reading newspapers and novels, watching films and the television. All that we read and see is forming our heart. Do we give it good things to nourish it? Are we moulding it with violence and triviality, giving ourselves hearts of stone?

St Catherine of Siena says of Thomas that 'With his mind's eye he contemplated my Truth ever so tenderly and there gained light beyond the natural.'[19] Study then teaches us tenderness, and even Thomas was a great theologian because he was soft-hearted. Fr Yves Congar once wrote that his growing illness and paralysis meant that he became increasingly dependent on his brothers. He could do nothing at all without their help. He said, 'I have

16. Letter 226, *Catherine of Siena, Passion for Truth, Compassion for Humanity,* ed
    Mary O'Driscoll OP, New York, 1993, p. 26.
17. St John of the Cross, *Canciones de Alma,* 5.
18. Primitive Constitutions, 1, 13.
19. Mary O'Driscoll OP, ibid, p. 127.

understood above all, since I became ill and in constant need of my brothers' services ... that whatever we can preach and say, however sublime it may be, is worthless if not accompanied by *praxis*, by real, concrete action, of service, and of love. I think that I have been lacking a little of that in my life, I have been a bit too intellectual.'[20]

When Savanarola talks about St Dominic's understanding of the Scriptures, he says that it was founded on *carità*, charity. Since it was the love of God which inspired the Scriptures, it is only the loving person who can understand them: 'And you, brothers, who wish to understand the Scriptures, and who wish to preach: learn charity and she will teach you. Having charity you will understand her.'[21]

Study transforms the human heart through its discipline. It is 'a form of asceticism by its own perseverance and difficulty' (LCO 83) that belongs to our growth in holiness. It offers us the hard discipline of remaining in our rooms in silence, struggling to understand, when we long to escape. One of the innovations of the Order was in offering those especially given to study the solitude of an individual cell, but it is a solitude that can be an asceticism. When we are alone, struggling with a text, then we will think of a thousand valid reasons why we should stop and go and see someone to talk. We will quickly convince ourselves that we have a duty to do so, and that to continue studying would be a betrayal of our vocation and of Christian duty! Yet unless we endure this solitude and silence, we will have nothing of value to give. In the *Letter to Brother John*, we are told: 'love your cell by making constant use of it, if you want to be admitted into the wine

20. *Allocution de fr Congar, en remerciement a la Remise du prix de I 'Unité chrétienne*, 24 November 1984.
21. 'Dalle Prediche di fra' Gerólamo Savanarola', ed L. Ferretti, in *Memorie Dominicane*, XXVII, 1910.

cellar'.[22] Evidently the thirteenth century novice's idea of paradise! Much study is indeed and inevitably boring. Learning to read Hebrew or Greek is hard and tedious work. Often we will wonder whether it is worthwhile. It is precisely an act of hope, that this labour will bear fruit in ways that we cannot now imagine.

STUDY AND THE BUILDING OF COMMUNITY IN THE ORDER

Study not only should open our hearts to the other but introduce us into a community. To study is to enter into a conversation, with one's brothers and sisters and with other human beings in our search for the truth that will set us free. Albert the Great wrote of the pleasure of seeking the truth together: *'in dulcedine societatis quaerere veritatem.'* [23]

Scholars often reflect the values of our society. Much of academic life is based upon production and competition, as if we were making cars and not seeking wisdom. Universities can be like factories. Articles must pour off the production line, and rivals and enemies must be wiped out. Yet we can never say an illuminating word about God unless we do theology differently, uncompetitively and with reverence. One cannot do theology alone. Not only because no one today would be able to master all the disciplines but because understanding the Word of God is inseparable from building community. Much of the preparation for the Second Vatican Council was done by a community of brothers in Le Saulchoir, especially of Congar, Chenu and Ferret, working together and sharing their insights

There is a story that while eating with the King of France, Thomas is supposed to have thumped the table and shouted, 'That's settled the Manichees!' This may suggest that he was not

22. *De Modo Studendi.*
23. In Libr viii *Politicorum.*

paying much attention to the other guests, but it also shows that theology can be a struggle. We can never build community unless we dare to argue with each other. I must stress, as so often, the importance of debate, argument, the struggle to understand. But one struggles with one's opponent, like Jacob wrestling with the angel, so as to demand a blessing. One argues with an opponent, because you wish to receive what he or she can give you. One wrestles so that the truth can win. We have to argue out of a sort of humility. The other person always has something to teach us and we fight with them so as to receive the gift.

One of my most powerful memories of my year in Paris was of fr Marie-Dominique Chenu, the master who was always eager to learn from every one he met, even an ignorant young English Dominican! Often, late in the evening, he would return from some meeting with bishops, students, trades unionists, artists, happy to tell you of what he had learnt and to ask what you had learnt that day. The true teacher is always humble. Jordan of Saxony said that Dominic understood everything, 'humili cordis intelligentia',[24] through the humble intelligence of his heart. The heart of flesh is humble, but the heart of stone is impenetrable.

Theology is not just what is done in centres of study. It is the moment of illumination, of new insight, when the Word of God meets our ordinary daily experience of trying to be human, of sin and failure, of trying to build human community and make a just world. All the world of scholarship, of biblical experts, patristic scholars, philosophers and psychologists, are there to help that conversation be fertile and truthful. Good theology happens when, for example, the scripture scholar helps the brother working in pastoral work to understand his experience, and when the brother with pastoral experience helps the scholar to understand

24. *Libellus* 7.

the Word of God. The recovery of our theological tradition demands not only that we train more brothers in the various disciplines but that we do theology together. Unless we can build our provinces as theological communities then our studies may become sterile and our pastoral work superficial. Much of Thomas' work was answering the questions of the brethren, and his teacher Albert had to cope with some rather foolish questions from the Master of the Order![25]

Where do we do theology? We need the great theological faculties and the libraries. But we also need centres where theology is done in other contexts – with those who struggle for justice, in dialogue with other religions, in poor slums and hospitals. Especially at this moment in the life of the Church, true study involves the building of community between women and men. A theology which grows solely out of male experience would limp on one leg, breathe with one lung. That is why today we need to do theology with the Dominican Family, listening to each other's insights, making a theology which is truly human. As God says to St Catherine of Siena: 'I could well have made human beings in such a way that they all had everything, but I preferred to give different gifts to different people, so that they would all need each other.'[26]

All human communities are vulnerable, liable to dissolve, needing constant reinforcement and repair. One of the ways in which we make and remake community together is through the words that we speak to each other. As servants of the Word of God, we should be deeply aware of the power of our words, a power to heal or to hurt, to build or to destroy. God spoke a word, and the world came to be, and now God speaks the Word that is

25. See James A. Weisheipl, *Albertus Magnus and the Sciences: Commemorative Essays 1980*, pp. 41-42.
26. Dialogue 7.

his Son, and we are redeemed. Our words share in that power. At the heart of all our education and study must be a deep reverence for language, a sensitivity to the words that we offer to our brothers and sisters. With our words we can offer resurrection or crucifixion, and the words that we speak are often remembered, kept in our brothers' hearts, to be reflected upon, returned to, for good or ill, for years. A word may kill.

Our study should educate us in responsibility, responsibility for the words that we use. Responsibility in the sense that what we say responds to the truth, corresponds to reality. But also we have the responsibility of saying words that build community, that nurture others, that heal wounds, and offer life. St Paul, in prison, wrote to the Philippians, 'Finally brethren, whatever is true, whatever is honourable, whatever is just, whatever is pure, whatever is lovely, whatever is gracious, if there is any excellence, if there is anything worthy of praise, think about these things' (4:8).

STUDY AND THE BUILDING OF A JUST WORLD

Our world has seen the triumph of a single economic system. It has become hard to imagine an alternative. The temptation of our generation may be to resign ourselves to the sufferings and injustices of this time and to cease to hunger for a world made new. But we preachers must be the guardians of hope. We have been promised the freedom of the children of God, and God will be true to that Word. In San Sisto there is a picture of St Dominic studying, with a dog at his feet holding a candle. In the background another Dominican chases a dog with a stick. The inscription tells us that Dominic did not oppose the devil with violence but with study! Our study prepares us to speak a liberating word. It does this through teaching us compassion, showing us that God is present even in the midst of suffering and it is there that we must forge our theology. It offers us an intellectual discipline that opens our ears to hear God summoning us into freedom.

Felicissimo Martinez OP once described Dominican spirituality as 'open-eyed'. And in the General Chapter of Caleruega, Chrys McVey commented, 'Dominic was moved to tears – and to action – by the starving in Palencia, by the innkeeper in Toulouse, by the plight of some women in Fanjeaux. But that is not enough to explain his tears. They flowed from the discipline of an open-eyed spirituality that did not miss a thing. Truth is the motto of the Order – not its defence (as often understood), rather its perception. And keeping one's eyes open so as not to miss a thing, that can make the eyes smart.' Our study should be a discipline of truthfulness that opens the eyes. As St Paul says, 'Look at the evidence of your eyes' (2 Cor 10:7).

It is painful to see what lies before us. It is easier to have a heart of stone. Often enough I have been to places which I have longed to forget, hospital wards of young people in Rwanda with their limbs amputated, the beggars on the streets of Calcutta. How can one bear to see so much misery? Yet we must obey Paul's command to look at the evidence of our eyes and to see a tortured world. The books which we read must prise open our hearts. Franz Kafka wrote: 'I think that we ought to read only the kind of books that wound and stab us ... we need the books that affect us like a disaster, that grieve us deeply, like the death of someone whom we love more than ourselves, like being banished into forests far from everyone, like a suicide. A book must be the axe for the frozen sea within us.' [27]

Yet it is not enough just to see these places of human suffering, and to be the tourists of the world's crucifixion. These are places

27. Letter to Oskar Pollak, 27 January 1904.

in which theology is to be done. It is in these places of Calvary that
God may be met and a new word of hope discovered. Think of
how much of the greatest theology has been written in prison,
from the letter of St Paul to the Philippians, the poems of St John
of the Cross, to the letters of Dietrich Bonhoeffer in a Nazi
concentration camp. We are, said St John of the Cross, like
dolphins who plunge into the dark blackness of the sea to emerge
into the brilliance of the light. A refugee camp in Goma or a bed
in a cancer ward; these are places where a theology that brings
hope may be discovered.

It is not only in situations of extreme anguish that God may be
encountered. Vincent de Couesnongle [28] wrote: 'There can be no
hope without fresh air, or oxygen or a new vision. There can be
no hope in a stuffy atmosphere.' [29] Ours has been from the
beginning a theology of the city and the market place. St Dominic
sent his brothers to the cities, the places of new ideas, of new
experiments with economic organisation and democracy, but
also where the new poor gathered. Do we dare to let ourselves be
disturbed by the questions of the modern city? What is the word
of hope that may be shared with young people who face unemployment for the rest of their lives? How may God be discovered
in the suffering of an unmarried mother or a frightened immi-
grant? These too are places of theological reflection. What have
we to say to a world becoming sterile with pollution? Will we let
ourselves be interrogated by the questions of the young and enter
the minefields of moral issues such as sexual ethics, or do we
prefer to be safe?

So then, we must dare to see what is before our eyes; we must
believe that it is where God seems most distant and where human

28. Master of the Order 1974-1983; died July 1992.
29. *Le Courage du Futur,* chapter 8.

beings are tempted by despair that theology may be done. Yet surely, as Dominicans, we must assert a third requirement. Our words of hope will only have authority if they are rooted in a serious study of the Word of God and an analysis of our contemporary society. In 1511 the Spanish Dominican Anthony Montesino preached his famous sermon in what is now Haiti against the oppression of the Indians in Latin America and asked: 'Are they not human beings? Have they not rational souls? Are you not obliged to love them as you love yourselves? Do you not understand this? Do you not grasp this?' Montesino was inviting his contemporaries to open their eyes, and see the world differently. For clarity, compassion is not enough. Hard study was needed to see through the false mythologies of the *conquistadores* and it was the source of Las Casas' prophetic stand.

Chenu commented, 'It is extremely interesting to draw attention to the encounter between the speculative doctrine of [Francisco de Vittoria OP, the] first great master of international law (at this moment when nations were being born outside the pale of the Holy Roman Empire) and the evangelism of Las Casas. The theologian, in Vittoria, envelopes the prophet'.[30] It is not enough to be indignant at the injustices of this world. Our words will only have authority if they are rooted in serious economic and political analysis of the causes of injustice. St Antoninus grappled with the problems of a new economic order in Renaissance Florence, as in this century L. J. Lebret OP analysed the problems of the new economics. If we are to resist the temptation of easy clichés, then we need some brothers and sisters who are trained in scientific, social, political and economic analysis.

The building of a just society does not demand only the

30. M.-D. Chenu, *Prophétes et Théologiens dans l'Eglise*, Parole de Dieu' in *La Parole de Dieu II*, Paris 1964, p. 211.

equitable distribution of wealth. We need to build a society in which we may all flourish as human beings. Our world is being reduced to a cultural desert through the triumph of consumerism. The cultural poverty of this dominant perception of the human person is ravaging the whole world, and 'the people perish for the lack of a vision.' (Prov 29:18)[31] There is a hunger not just for food but for meaning. As the General Chapter of Oakland said, 'To speak truthfully is an act of justice' (109). St Basil the Great says that if we have extra clothes they belong to the poor. One of the treasures that we possess and which our centres of study should preserve and share are the poetry, the stories of our people, the music, and traditional wisdom. All this is a wealth for the building of a human world.

Being a prophet is no excuse for not studying the scriptures. We ponder the Word of God, seeking to know his will rather than to discover evidence that God is on our side. It is easy to use the scriptures as a source book for easy slogans, but the study of God's Word is the pursuit of a deeper liberation than we could ever imagine. Through the discipline of study we seek to catch the echo of a voice that summons us to an ineffable freedom, God's own liberty. When Lagrange faced the problems raised by modern historical criticism he quoted the words of St Jerome, 'Sciens et prudens, manum misi in ignem'[32] ('Knowingly and prudently, I put my hand in the fire'). Knowing that it might cost him pain and suffering, he plunged his hand into the fire. Lagrange's commitment to the new intellectual disciplines of his time was a real token of trust that the Word of God would surely show itself to be a truly liberating word, and that we need not fear to pass by the way of doubt and questioning. He submitted the

31. See the Jamaican National Anthem.
32. Bernard Montagnes op. cit., p. 84.

Word of God to rigorous analysis because he trusted that it would show itself to be a word that could never be mastered. Do we dare to share his courage? Do we dare plunge our hands in the fire, or do we prefer not to be disturbed?

THE GIFT OF A FUTURE

He will be great, and will be called the Son of the Most High; and the Lord God will give to him the throne of his father David, and he will reign over the house of Jacob for ever; and of his Kingdom there will be no end. And Mary said to the angel, 'How can this be, since I have no husband?' (Lk 1:32-34)

How can this be? How can a virgin give birth to a child? How can a woman of this small and unimportant colony of the Roman Empire give birth to the Saviour of the world? Who could have guessed that the history of this people had the seed of such a future? Two thousand years ago it seemed that David's line had failed, but unexpectedly he was given a son to sit upon his throne.

Much of our studies are studies of the past. We study the story of the people of Israel, the evolution of the Bible, the history of the Church, of the Order, and even of philosophy. We learn about the past. Central to study is the acquisition of a memory. Yet this is not so that we may know many facts. We study the past so as to discover the seeds of an unimaginable future. Just as a virgin or a barren woman becomes pregnant with a child, so our apparently barren world is discovered to be pregnant with possibilities that we had never dreamt of, the Kingdom of God.

'History does more than any other discipline to free the mind from the tyranny of present opinion.'[33] History shows us that things need not be as they are, and that history may open us out to an unexpected future. We discover, in the words of Congar,

33. Owen Chadwick, *Origins*, 1985, p. 85.

that there is not only the Tradition, but a multitude of traditions which open up riches of which we had never dreamt. The Second Vatican Council was a moment of new beginning because it was a retelling of the past. We were brought back before the divisions of the Reformation, back before the Middle Ages, to rediscover a sense of the Church prior to the divisions of east and west. It was a memory that set us free for new things.

History introduces us to a wider community than those who just happen to be alive today. We find that we are members of the community of saints and the community of our ancestors. They too have a right to a voice in our deliberations. We test our insights against their witness, and they invite us to a larger vision than we could find in the small confines of our own time.

The retelling of history liberates us not just from present opinion but from the 'the rulers of this age' (1 Cor 2:8). History is normally told from the point of view of the victor, of the strong, of those who build empires, and the history that they tell confirms them in their power. We must learn to tell history from another point of view, from the side of the small and forgotten, and that is a story that sets us free. This is why to remember is a religious act, the primordial religious act of the Jewish and Christian traditions. When we gather to pray to God, we 'remember the wonderful works that he has done.' (Ps 105:5)

Ultimately we are brought back to the memory of a small and apparently insignificant people, the people of Israel. We tell the story from the point of view not of the great empires, of the Egyptians or the Assyrians, the Persians, the Greeks or the Romans, but of a tiny people whose history was barely registered in the books of the great and the powerful, yet whose history was pregnant with the birth of the Son of the Most High. And the history in which we discover ourselves is finally that of a virgin who hears the message of the angel and of a man who was nailed on a cross in a sea of crosses, a man whose story was that of failure. This is the story that we remember in every Eucharist. In this story we learn how to tell the history of humanity and it is a history that does not end on the cross.

Do we dare to tell the history of the Church and even of the Order with such courage? Do we dare to tell a history of the Church which is freed from all triumphalism and arrogance, and which recognises the moments of division and sin? Surely the good news, the ground of our hope, is that God has accepted precisely such fallible, quarrelling people as his people. So often when we learn about Dominican history we are told of the glories of the past. Do we dare to tell of the failures, of the conflicts? The previous archivist of the Order, Emilio Panella OP, wrote a study[34] of what the chronicles do not say, what they omitted. Such a story finally gives us more hope and confidence since it shows that God always works with 'earthen vessels to show that the transcendent power belongs to God and not to us' (2 Cor 4:7). He may even achieve something through us. At the General Chapter of Mexico, we dared to remember the fifth centenary of our arrival in the Americas. We remembered not only the great deeds of our brothers, of Las Casas and Montesino, but also the silences and failures of others. But they are all our brothers. Above all we remembered those who were reduced to silence or extinction. We remembered so as to hope for a more just world.

There are memories which are hard to bear, of Dachau and Auschwitz, of Hiroshima and the bombing of Dresden. There are acts so terrible that we would rather forget. What history could be told that could bear all that suffering? And yet at Auschwitz the monument to the dead says, 'O earth, cover not

34. 'Quelle che la Cronica Conventuale non dice', *Memorie Domenicane,* 18, 1987, 227-235.

their blood.' Maybe we can only dare to remember and to tell of the past truthfully, if we remember the one who embraced his death, who gave himself to his betrayers, who made of his passion a gift and communion. In that memory we dare to hope. We can know that 'history does not ultimately lie in the hands of the slaughterer. The dead can be named; the past must be known. In that naming and knowing, God is to be met, and in God lies the possibility for us of a different world, a different apprehension of power, a voice for the dumb.'[35] 'For the poor shall not always be forgotten: the patient abiding of the meek shall not perish for ever.' (Ps 9:18)

St Dominic walked through the countryside singing, not just because he was courageous, and not just because he had a cheerful temperament. Years of study had given him a heart formed to hope. Let us study so as to share his joy.

> History says, *Don't hope*
> *on this side of the grave.*
> But then, once in a lifetime
> The longed-for tidal wave
> Of justice can rise up,
> And hope and history rhyme.
>
> So hope for a great sea-change
> On the far side of revenge.
> Believe that a further shore
> Is reachable from here.[36]

35. Rowan Williams, *Open to Judgement*, London 1994, p. 242
36. Seamus Heaney, *The Cure at Troy: version of Sophocleses' 'Philocpetes'*, London, 1990.

FREEDOM AND RESPONSIBILITY:
TOWARDS A SPIRITUALITY
OF GOVERNMENT

DOMINIC A MAN OF FREEDOM AND GOVERNMENT

Dominic fascinates us by his freedom. It was the freedom of the poor itinerant preacher, the freedom to found an Order unlike any that had existed before. He was free to scatter the fragile little community which he gathered around him and send them to the Universities, and free to accept the decisions of brothers in Chapter, even when he disagreed with them. It was the freedom of the compassionate person, who dared to see and to respond.

The Order has always flourished when we have lived with Dominic's freedom of heart and mind. How can we renew today the freedom that is properly and deeply Dominican? It has many dimensions: a simplicity of life, itinerancy, prayer. In this letter I wish to focus on just one pillar of our freedom, which is good government. I am convinced, after visitating so many Provinces of the Order, that typical Dominican freedom finds expression in our way of government. Dominic did not leave us a spirituality embodied in a collection of sermons or theological texts. Instead we have inherited from him and those earliest friars, a form of government that frees us to respond with compassion to those who hunger for the Word of God. When we offer our lives for the preaching of the gospel, we take in our hands the book of the Rule and Constitutions. Most of those Constitutions are concerned with government.

This may appear surprising. In contemporary culture, it is usually assumed that government is about control, about limiting

---

A letter to all the members of the Dominican Order, issued on the feast of Saint Antoninus, 10 May 1997.

the freedom of the individual. Indeed many Dominicans may be tempted to think that freedom lies in evading the control of meddlesome superiors! But our Order is not divided into 'the governors' and 'the governed'. Rather government enables us to share a common responsibility for our life and mission. Government is at the basis of our fraternity. It forms us as brothers, free to be 'useful for the salvation of souls'.[1] When we accept a brother into the Order we express our confidence that he will be capable of taking his place in the government of his community and province, and that he will contribute to our debates and help us to arrive at and implement fruitful decisions.

The temptation of our age is towards fatalism, the belief that faced with the problems of our world we can do nothing. This passivity can infect religious life too. We share Dominic's freedom when we are so moved by the urgency to preach the gospel that we dare to take difficult decisions, whether to undertake a new initiative, close a community or endure in an apostolate that is hard. For this freedom, good government is necessary. The opposite of government is not freedom but paralysis.

In this letter I will not try to make detailed observations about the application of the Constitutions. That is the responsibility of the General Chapters. Rather I wish to suggest how our Constitutions touch some of the deepest aspects of our religious life: our fraternity and our mission. It is not enough simply to apply the Constitutions as if they were a set of rules. We need to develop what might be called a spirituality of government, so that through it we grow together as brothers and preachers.

These comments will be based upon my experience of government by the brethren. So what I have to say will not always be applicable to the other branches of the Dominican Family. I

---

1. Prologue of the Primitive Constitutions.

hope, however, that it will be helpful for our nuns, sisters and laity as you face analagous challenges.

'The Word became flesh and dwelt among us full of grace and truth; we have beheld his glory, glory as of the only Son of the Father' (Jn 1:14). These words of John will help to structure these very simple reflections on government. It may seem absurd to take such a rich theological text as the basis of an exploration of government. I wish to show how the challenge of good government is to make flesh among us that grace and truth.

1. The Word that comes among us is 'full of grace and truth'. The first section of the letter reflects upon the purpose of all government, which is that we be liberated for the preaching of the gospel. All government in the Order has the common mission as its goal.

2. This Word 'dwells among us'.
In the second section of the letter, we consider the fundamental principles of Dominican government. Central to our practice of government is that we meet in chapter, engage in debate, vote and take decisions. But these meetings will be nothing more than mere administration at the best, and party politics at the worst, unless they belong to our welcoming of the Word of God who would make his home among us. Government needs to be nourished by lived fraternity.

3. This Word of God became flesh.
Finally, this beautiful theory of government must become flesh in the complex reality of our lives, in our priories, provinces and the whole Order. In the last section I will share a few observations on the relationship between the different levels of responsibility in the Order.

1. THE WORD WAS MADE FLESH, 'FULL OF GRACE AND TRUTH': THE PURPOSE OF DOMINICAN GOVERNMENT

FREEDOM FOR THE MISSION

In St Catherine's vision the Father says of Dominic, 'He took the task of the Word, my only begotten Son. Clearly he appeared as an apostle in the world, with such truth and light did he sow my word, dispelling the darkness and giving light.'[2] All government within the Order has as its goal the bringing forth of the Word of God, the prolongation of the Incarnation.

The test of good government is whether it is at the service of this mission. That is why, from the beginning of the Order a superior has had the power of dispensation from our laws, 'especially when it seems to him to be expedient in those matters which seem to impede study, preaching or the good of souls'.[3]

Fundamental to the life of the brethren is that we gather in Chapter, whether conventual, provincial or general, to take decisions about our lives and mission. From the beginning of the Order we have arrived at these decisions democratically, by debate leading to voting. But what makes this democratic process properly Dominican is that we are not merely seeking to discover what is the will of the majority, but what are the needs of the mission. To what mission are we sent? The Fundamental Constitution of the Order makes quite explicit this link between our democratic government and the response to needs of the mission: 'This communitarian form of government is particularly suitable for the Order's development and frequent renewal ... This continual revision of the Order is necessary, not only on account of a spirit of perennial Christian conversion, but also on account of the special vocation of the Order which impels it to accommo-

2. Dialogue 158.
3. *LCO*, I.VI.

date its presence in the world for each generation' (VII).

Our democratic institutions enable us to grasp responsibility or to evade it. We are free to take decisions that may turn our lives upside down, or we may settle for inertia. We can elect superiors who may dare to ask more of us than we feel we can give, or we choose a brother who will leave us in peace. But let us be clear about this: our democracy is only Dominican if our debating and voting is an attempt to hear the Word of God summoning us to walk in the way of discipleship.

Every institution can be tempted to make its perpetuation its ultimate aim. A company that makes cars does not exist out of a compassionate desire to respond to humanity's need for cars, but so that the organisation may itself expand and grow. We too may fall into this trap, and especially if we talk about our own institutions in terms which derive from the world of business: the provincial and council may become 'The Administration', and the syndic the 'Business Manager'! The brethren may even be referred to as 'personnel'. What mother, announcing the birth of a new child, says that the personnel of the family has increased? But our institutions exist for another purpose, outside ourselves, which is to mobilise the brethren for the mission.

There is a story told in *The Lives of the Brethren* of how a great lawyer in Vercelli came running to Jordan of Saxony, threw himself down before him, and all he could say was 'I belong to God'. Jordan replied 'Since you belong to God, in his name we make you over to him'.[4] Each brother is a gift from God, but he is given to us so that we may give him away, in forming him for the mission and freeing him to preach.

The beginning of all good government is attentiveness, listening together for the Word of God, opening our ears to the needs

4. IV 10 iv.

of the people. In a thirteenth century Dominican blessing, the brethren prayed for the Holy Spirit, 'to enlighten us and give us eyes to see with, ears to hear with, and hands to do the work of God with, and a mouth to preach the word of salvation with, and the angel of peace to watch over us and lead us at last, by our Lord's gift, to the Kingdom.'[5] Whenever we gather in Council or Chapter, we pray for the Holy Spirit, that we may have eyes to see and ears to hear, but what we see and hear may well summon us where we would rather not go. Compassion may turn our lives upside down.

And if mission is the end of all government, then what is its beginning? Surely it is that 'we have beheld his glory, glory as of the only Son of the Father'. If government is the exercise of responsibility, then this ultimately expresses our response to the one who has revealed his glory to us. Contemplation of the only begotten Son is the root of all mission, and so the mainspring of all government. Without this stillness there is no movement. All government brings us from contemplation to mission. Without it, then we practise mere administration.

THE TASK OF GOVERNMENT IS THE COMMON MISSION

The Word was made flesh and dwelt among us. The Word of salvation gathers us together into communion, in the Trinity and with each other. In that Word we find our true freedom, which is the freedom to belong to each other in grace and truth. The good news that we preach is that we may find our home in the life of the Triune God.

If the preaching of the gospel is the summons to communion, then the preacher can never be a solitary person, engaged just in his or her mission. All of our preaching is a sharing in a common

5. 'A Dominican Blessing', *Early Dominicans Selected Writings,* edited by Simon Tugwell OP, New York 1982, p. 153.

task, the invitation to belong in the common home. If the end of government in the Order is the mission of preaching, then its principal challenge is in gathering the brethren into the common mission, the mission of the Order and of the Church. The disciples are not sent out alone.

Nothing so cripples good government as an individualism, by which a brother may become so wedded to 'my project', 'my apostolate', that he ceases to be available for the common mission of the Order. This privatisation of the preaching not only makes it hard for us to evolve and sustain common projects. More radically, it may offer a false image of the salvation to which we are called – unity in grace and truth. Ultimately it is a surrender to a false image of what it means to be truly human: the solitary individual whose freedom is that of self-determination, liberated from the interference of others.

One of the principal challenges of government is to refuse to let the common mission of the Order be paralysed by such an individualism. That freedom of Dominic, which we think of as so characteristic of the Order, is not the freedom to plough our own furrow, free from the intervention of superiors. It is the freedom to give ourselves, without reserve, with the mad generosity of the Word made flesh.

Some forms of preaching the gospel cannot be easily shared. For example, a brother or sister who preaches through writing poetry, through painting, or even through research, may often have to labour alone. Even then we must show that they are not just 'doing their own thing', that they too are contributing to common mission. The Order is most often alive when it harnesses the dynamism of the brethren. Sometimes the most liberating thing that a superior can do is to command a brother to do what he most deeply wishes and is able to do. Sometimes the common mission may demand of us that we accept tasks we would not have chosen, that we give up a cherished apostolate for the common good. We need not only preachers and pastors, but bursars and secretaries, superiors and administrators. But this too is part of the preaching of that Word who gathers us into community.

2. THE WORD WAS MADE FLESH AND DWELT AMONG US. THE BASIC PRINCIPLES OF DOMINICAN GOVERNMENT

The Constitutions tell us that 'the primary reason why we are gathered together is that we may dwell in unity, and that there may be in us one mind and one heart in God' (LCO 2.i). This may appear to contradict the fundamental purpose of the Order, which is that we are sent out to preach the Word of God. In fact it is a healthy and necessary tension which has always marked Dominican life. For the grace and truth that we are sent to preach we must live together, otherwise we will have nothing to say. The common mission which we share is grounded in the common life we live.

This tension is found in our government. For if the end of all government is that the brethren be freed for preaching, yet it is founded on our fraternity. Unless we seek to live together in unity of heart and mind, then our democracy will fail. In her vision, the Father says to St Catherine that the ship of St Dominic is one in which 'both the perfect and the not-so-perfect fare well.'[6] The Order is a home for sinners. And this means that to build good government, it is never enough just to apply the Constitutions, to hold Chapters, to vote and take decisions. T. S. Eliot tells us of people who are 'dreaming of systems so perfect that no one will need to be good'.[7] Our system of government ultimately is grounded upon a search for virtue. The flesh must become word

6. Dialogue 158.
7. Chorus from 'The Rock', 1934, VI.

and communion, and the mixed group of individuals that we are a community.

POWER, AUTHORITY AND RESPONSIBILITY

Good government depends upon a right living of our relationships of power, authority and responsibility. It may seem strange that I do not include a section on obedience. This is because I have already written about obedience at length in my Letter to the Order 'Vowed to Mission'.[8] Also, virtually all that I write in this letter about government comments upon the implications of our vow of obedience, through which we give ourselves unconditionally to the common mission of the Order.

Power. Our common life confronts us inevitably with the question of power. We do not usually like to speak of power, unless we feel that it is being misused. The word seems almost inappropriate for the relationship of brotherhood which unites us. Yet every human community is marked by relationships of power, and Dominican communities are not exempt. When we make profession we place ourselves into the hands of the brethren. Our brethren will take decisions about our lives that we may not welcome, and which we may even feel are unjust. We may be assigned to places to which we do not wish to go, or elected to positions of responsibility which we do not wish to hold.

Every brother has power, by what he says or does not say, and by what he does or does not do. All the issues we shall address in this letter – the democracy of the chapter, voting, the relationship of the different levels of government in the Order – all explore aspects of the power that we all have in our relationships with one another. And if our preaching is to have power then we must live these relationships of power openly, healthily and in accordance with the gospel.

8. Pages 31-53, *supra.*

The life of Jesus shows a paradoxical relationship to power. He was the man of powerful words, who summoned the disciples to follow him, who healed the sick, cast out demons, raised the dead and dared to confront the religious authorities of his time. And yet he was the powerless one who refused the protection of the sword of Peter, and who was hung upon a cross.

With this strong and vulnerable man, power was always healing, and life-giving. It never cast down, diminished, made little, destroyed. It was not a power over people, so much as a power that he gave to them. Indeed he was most powerful precisely in refusing to be a channel of violence, in bearing it in his body, in letting it stop with him. He took his passion and death into his own hands, and made it fruitful, a gift, Eucharist.

Good government in our communities demands that we live relationships of power in this way, granting power to our brothers rather than undermining them. This demands of us the courage to be vulnerable. Josef Pieper wrote,

> Fortitude presumes vulnerability; without vulnerability there is no possibility of fortitude. An angel cannot be courageous because it is not vulnerable. To be brave means to be ready to sustain a wound. Since human beings are substantially vulnerable, then we can be courageous.[9]

Our government invites to live such a courageous vulnerability.

Authority. All government is dependent upon the exercise of authority. The fact that the supreme authority of the Order is the General Chapter is a recognition of the fact that for us authority is granted to all the brethren. The sequence of our General Chapters, of diffinitors and provincials, suggests that for us authority is multifaceted. Superiors enjoy authority in virtue of

---

9. Josef Pieper, *A Brief Reader on the Virtues of the Human Heart,* translated Paul C. Duggan, San Francisco, 1991, p. 24.

their office; theologians and thinkers by virtue of their knowledge; brothers engaged in pastoral apostolates enjoy authority because of their contact with people in their struggle to live the faith; the older brothers enjoy authority because of their experience; younger brethren have an authority which comes from their knowledge of the contemporary world with its questions.

Good government works well when we acknowledge and respect the authority that each brother has, and refuse to absolutise any single form of authority. If we were to make absolute the authority of superiors, the Order would cease to be a fraternity; if we were to absolutise the authority of the thinkers, then we would become just a strange academic institution; if we were to absolutise the authority of the pastors, then we would betray our mission in the Church; if we were to make indisputable the authority of the old, then we would have no future; if we were to give authority only to the young, then we would have no roots. The health of our government depends on allowing the interplay of all the voices that make up our community.

Furthermore, we are part of the Dominican Family. This means that we also are called to be attentive to the voice of our nuns, sisters and laity. They too must have authority in our deliberations. The nuns have an authority which derives from lives dedicated to contemplation; our sisters have an authority which comes from their lives as women with a vast variety of pastoral experience. Often they can teach us much through their closeness to the People of God, especially the poor. Increasingly too, there are sisters who have a theological training who have much to teach us. The laity have an authority because of their different experiences, knowledge, and sometimes marriage and parenthood. Part of what we offer to the Church lies in being a community in which each of those authorities should be recognised.

Responsibility. All government is the exercise of our shared responsibility for the life and mission of the Order. Its foundation is the confidence that we should have in each other. When St Dominic sent out the young friars to preach, the Cistercians were scandalised at his confidence in them, and he told them: 'I know, I know for certain, that my young men will go out and come back, will be sent out and will return; but your young men will be kept locked up and will still go out'.[10]

The aim of all our formation is to form brethren who are free and responsible, and that is why the Constitutions say that the person who has primary responsibility for his formation is the candidate himself (LCO 156). Our government is founded upon a trust in the brethren. We show our trust in accepting a brother for profession; that same trust is present in the election of superiors. Superiors too must trust the brethren whom they appoint to posts of responsibility. Sometimes we will be disappointed, but that is no reason to renounce that fundamental mutual confidence. As Simon Tugwell OP wrote, 'In the last analysis, if Dominicans are to do their job properly, they have got to be exposed to certain hazards, and they have got to be trusted to cope with them – and the Order as a whole has got to accept that some, perhaps many, individuals will abuse this trust'.[11]

Such a trust demands that we overcome fear, fear of what may happen if the brethren are not controlled! We must form the brethren to live with that freedom of Dominic. As Felicísimo Martínez OP says, 'There is no greater service to a person than to educate him or her to freedom ... The fear of freedom may be rooted in the good-will of those who feel responsible for others, and it can be legitimated by an appeal to realism, but this makes

---

10. Tugwell, ibid, p. 91.
11. *Dominican Ashram*, December 1983, 'Dominican Risks' p. 187.

it no less a lack of faith in the vigour and force of the Christian experience. Fear and the lack of faith always go hand in hand'.[12]

Fear destroys all good government. St Catherine wrote to Pope Gregory XI, 'I desire to see you free of any servile fear, for I am aware that the fearful person does not persevere in the strength of holy resolution and good desire.... Father, get up courageously, because I tell you, there is nothing to fear!'[13] Fear is servile, and therefore is incompatible with our status as the children of God, and brothers and sisters of each other. It is above all wrong in a superior, who is called to help his brothers grow in confidence and fearlessness.

But this confidence that we have in each other is not an excuse for mutual neglect. Because I have confidence in my brother, it does not mean that I can forget about him and let him just go his own way. If good government gives us shared responsibility, then it is rooted in the mutual responsibility that we are called to have for each other. When we make profession we place our hands in those of a brother. It is a gesture of extraordinary vulnerability and tenderness. We hand our life over to our brothers, and we do not know what they will do with it. We are in each other's hands.

The *Lives of the Brethren* tell us about a certain Tedalto[14] whose vocation passed through a hard time. 'Everything that he saw and felt seemed like the second death to him.' He had joined the Order as a pleasant and calm man, but now he had become so bad-tempered that he even hit the subprior with the Psalter. This is an experience that we have all had! Even though we may consider that Tedalto should never have been accepted into the

---

12. *Caminos de Liberación y de Vida* Bilbao, 1989, p. 24.
13. Letter 233, quoted from Mary O'Driscoll OP, *Catherine of Siena, Selected Spiritual Writings*. New York, 1993, p. 37.
14. III 6.

Order, Jordan of Saxony refused to give up on him, and prayed with him until his heart was healed. In accepting a brother for profession we accept a responsibility for him, for his happiness and flourishing. His vocation is our common concern.

Do we always fight for our brother's vocation? If a brother passes through a time of crisis, do I look the other way? Do I pretend that respect for his privacy can justify my negligence? Am I afraid to hear the doubts that he may share with me? I hope that if ever I am driven to hitting the subprior with the breviary, then my brothers will have care for me! Also I must have the confidence, in times of crisis, to share with my brethren, confident of their understanding and mercy.

As preachers of the Word made flesh, we have a special responsibility for the words that we speak. The Word must become flesh above all in the words of 'grace and truth'. The Primitive Constitutions ordain that the novice-master must teach the novices 'never to speak about people who are absent except to speak well of them' (I.13). This is not a pious squeamishness, which flies from facing the reality of what our brethren are actually like. It is an invitation to speak words of 'grace', a recognition of the power of our words to hurt, to destroy, to subvert and undermine our brothers.

It is just as much a challenge to learn to speak words of truth. Fundamental to our democracy is that we dare to speak truthfully to each other, that we dare to bring to word the tensions and conflicts that hurt the common life and impede the common mission. If we do so, then often it may be with anyone except the brother concerned. If we are disturbed by the behaviour of our brother, then we must dare to talk truthfully with him, gently and fraternally. Chapter is not always the first place in which to do this. We must dare to knock on his door and speak alone with him (Mt 18:15). We must take the time to speak to each other, especially those from whom we are estranged. Communication in the Chapter will depend upon a vast labour of communication outside. If we make that effort, then we will have strengthened the fraternity between us so that hard questions can be addressed together. Then we will be able to have those open debates about our common life, about how we fail and can grow, which were the aim of the old Chapter of faults. The General Chapter of Caleruega (43, 2) makes some excellent recommendations as to how this may happen today.

One of the signs that there is confidence in the brethren is when we are prepared to elect them to positions of responsibility even when they are young or inexperienced. Jordan was chosen to be Provincial of Lombardy when he was just over a year in the Order, and Master after two years. What an extraordinary sign of trust in a man who today would not even have made solemn profession. Sometimes in the Order we may find older men hanging on to responsibility, perhaps out of fear for what the young may do and where they may take us. And often these 'young' are not so very young anyway, certainly old enough to be fathers of families and hold important positions in the secular world. Sometimes they are even not much younger than I am! But our formation and mode of government should make us dare to entrust our lives to brothers who will take us we know not where. At profession a brother may place his hands in ours. But accepting him, as a brother with a voice and vote, means that we too have placed ours in his.

DEMOCRACY

When I was asked during a television interview in France what was central to our spirituality, I was almost as surprised as the interviewer when I replied 'democracy'. Yet it is central to our lives. To be a brother is to have a voice and a vote. Yet we do not have votes merely as groups of private individuals, seeking compromise decisions that will leave each person with as much private freedom as possible. Our democracy should express our brotherhood. It is one expression of our unity in Christ, a single body.

Democracy for us is more than voting to discover what is the will of the majority. It also involves discovering what is the will of God. Our attentiveness to our brother is an expression of that obedience to the Father. This attentiveness demands intelligence. Alas, God does not always speak clearly through my brother. Indeed sometimes what he says is evidently wrong! Yet, at the heart of our democracy is the conviction that even when what he says is foolish and mistaken, yet there is some grain of truth waiting to be rescued. However much I may disagree with him, he is able to teach me something. Learning to hear: that is an exercise in imagination and intelligence. We must take the time to speak to each other, especially those from whom we are estranged. I must dare to doubt my own position, to open myself to another's questions, to become vulnerable to his doubts. It is an act of charity, born of a passion for truth. It indeed is the best preparation to be a preacher of 'grace and truth'.

Fergus Kerr OP, in his sermon for the opening of the Chapter of the English Province in 1996, said:

> If there is one thing we should surely manage to do at a chapter it is to demonstrate this commitment to look for the truth, to listen to what we can agree with in what we disagree with, to save what is true in what other people think ... What I prize more and more the longer I am in the Order ... is a way of thinking – of expecting other people to have views we may disagree with; expecting also to be able to understand why they believe what they do – if only we have the imagination, the courage, the faith in the ultimate power of truth, the charity,

to listen to what others say, to listen especially for what they are
afraid of when they seem reluctant to accept what we want
them to see: there are many ways of finding the truth, but that
is one way that I hope the Order of Preachers will always try
to practise.[15]

This beloved democracy of ours takes time. It is time that we owe
each other. It can be boring. Few people find long meetings as
boring as I do. It is not efficient. I do not believe that we will ever
be one of the most efficient Orders in the Church, and it would
be wrong for us to seek to be so! Thanks be to God there are more
efficient Orders than ours. Thanks be to God that we do not seek
to emulate them. A certain efficiency is necessary if we are not to
lose our freedom through paralysis. But if we make efficiency our
goal, then we may undermine that freedom which is our gift to
the Church. Our tradition of giving each brother a voice and a
vote is not always the most efficient at arriving at the best
decisions, but it is a witness to evangelical values that we offer to
the Church, and which the Church needs now more than ever.

VOTING

The aim of this dialogue in our Chapters is that the community
should attain unanimity. This is not always possible. Then we
must arrive at a decision through a vote. One of the most delicate
responsibilities of a superior is to judge the time when there must
be a vote. He must bring the brethren as near to an unanimity as
possible, without waiting so long that a community is left paralysed by indecision.

When we come to a vote, the aim is not to win. Voting in a
chapter is utterly different from in a parliament or a senate.
Voting, like debate, belongs to the process whereby we seek to
discern what is required by 'the common good'. The purpose of

15. Acts of the Provincial Chapter of the English Province, 25 April 1996, p. 13.

voting is not to determine whether my will, or that of the other brethren, will triumph, but to discover what the building of the community and the mission of the Order requires.

Voting, in our tradition, is not a contest between groups, but the fruit of an attentiveness to what *all* the brethren have said. As far as possible, without betraying any fundamental convictions, I should seek to vote for proposals that reflect the concerns, fears and hopes of all the brethren, not just the majority. Otherwise I may indeed 'win', but the community will lose. In politics one's vote expresses one's allegiance to a party. For us, voting expresses who we are, brethren given to the common mission of the Order.

It follows that the result of a vote is the decision of the community, and not just of those who voted in its favour. It is the community that has arrived at a decision. I am free to disagree with the result, and even eventually to campaign for its reversal, but I express my identity as a member of the community by implementing the decision. To trust in the simple majority vote was a profound innovation of the Dominican tradition.[16] Previously the choice of the superior had either been through consensus, or the decision of the 'wiser' brethren. It was considered too risky to trust the majority. For us it is an expression of our confidence in the brethren.

Never is this more so than in the election of superiors. It is natural that with like-minded brethren one will discuss who might be a good superior, but it would be contrary to the nature of our democracy for a brother to be presented as the 'candidate' of a party. Therefore I am doubtful as to whether it is appropriate to approach a brother beforehand to ask whether he is prepared to 'stand' as a candidate. It is of course helpful to know whether a brother would accept or refuse an election, but there is the

16. Tugwell, ibid, p. 182.

danger of him being seen as the candidate of a group, and of
accepting election as its representative. Also, few brethren who
would be good superiors would ever wish to be candidates,
though they may be more likely to accept election as an act of
obedience to their brothers. To look for candidates who express
their willingness to be superiors may well lead us not to choose the
brethren most suited to office.

A superior is elected to serve all the brethren, for the common
good of the Order. His election is the result of a vote that 'we' have
made, regardless of for whom we voted. And once he is elected
he needs the support of the whole community, for we have
elected him regardless of how I individually voted. We have
prayed for the guidance of the Holy Spirit before we voted, and
we must trust that guidance has indeed been given.

One of the most solemn responsibilities that our democracy
may require of us is to vote for the admittance to the Order of
candidates, and for the profession of our brothers. It is a beautiful
expression of our common responsibility. Here we vote as a
search for the truth, as part of a process of discerning whether the
brother is called by God to share our life. It can never be an
expression of party politics, or our personal like or dislike of a
brother. Voting has to be an expression of truthful charity,
seeking to discern what is best for that brother. If we do so, then
a brother who is refused profession will not feel that he is rejected,
but that we have helped him to discern what is indeed the will of
God for him. If our vote expresses power struggles within the
community, ideological tussles, friendships or enmities, then we
will have betrayed a profound responsibility. We will encourage
those in formation to conceal their true selves, and we will form
brothers who will be unfit to govern in their turn.

3. THE WORD WAS MADE FLESH:
THE LEVELS OF DOMINICAN GOVERNMENT

GRASPING RESPONSIBILITY

The Word which we proclaim is not an abstract word, for it became flesh and blood. What we preach is not a theory of salvation but the grace that was embodied in the life, death and resurrection of a man some two thousand years ago. So too for us, it is not enough that we have a fine theory of responsibility. We have to live it. We have wonderful democratic structures, which offer us freedom, but it is a freedom that we must grasp.

I have become convinced during my visitations of the Provinces that one of the greatest issues that we face is to respond effectively and responsibly to the challenges of today. Sometimes we suffer from what I have often called 'the mystery of disappearing responsibility'.[17] How is it that we, for whom responsibility is central, so often let it slip through our fingers? Our Chapters, General and Provincial, are usually moments of truth, when we look honestly at what is to be done and how we are to do it. Great decisions are made. Wonderful texts are written. But sometimes, having seen and analysed all so clearly, we are like a man 'who observes his natural face in a mirror; for he observes himself and goes away and at once forgets what he was like' (Jam 1:23).

One reason why we escape responsibility is that although we are called to freedom, freedom is frightening and responsibility is burdensome and so it is tempting to escape. We have many levels of responsibility in the Order, and often it is attractive to imagine it is at some other level that it must be exercised. 'Something must be done', and yet it is usually by someone else, the superior or the Chapter or even the Master of the Order! 'The Province must act', but what is the Province if not ourselves? If

17. See, for example, 'Vowed to Mission, A Letter to the Order', *supra*, pp. 31-53.

we are to be truly the heirs of Dominic's freedom, then we must identify the responsibility that is properly ours and grasp it. We must articulate the relationship between the different levels of government in the Order.

The Constitutions say that our government 'is noted for an organic and balanced participation of all its members', and that the universal authority of its head is shared 'proportionately and with corresponding autonomy by the provinces and convents'. (LCO 1 VII). If our government is indeed to be 'organic and balanced' and recognise the proper autonomy of each brother, convent and province, then we must clarify the relationship between the different levels of government in the Order. I dislike the word 'levels' but I have been unable to think of a better word.

The relationship between the different levels of responsibility in the Order is articulated by at least three fundamental principles.

Itinerancy

No brother is, or should be, superior for too long. There is a limit to the number of terms that a brother can serve as Prior or Provincial without postulation. We do not have abbots for life. There should be no caste of superiors, for government is the shared responsibility of all the brothers. If we are elected to be a superior, then it is a service that we must offer. But there is no career, no promotion, in the Order of Friars Preachers.

We must strengthen each other

There can be no competition for power of responsibility, either to grab it or to flee from it. We must strengthen each other. One of the primary responsibilities of a prior is to strengthen his brethren,[18] to have confidence in their ability to do more than they ever imagined, and to support them when they take a brave

18. St Thomas, *Summa Theologiae*, II.IIae, q. 88, a. 12, ad 2.

stand on any issue. When Montesinos preached his famous
sermon on the rights of the Indians, it was his prior, Pedro de
Córdoba, who stood by him, saying that it was the whole community which had preached that sermon. Each brother is a gift to the
community and it is an obligation of the superior to welcome and
value the talents of the brethren whom God has given us.

But this relationship is reciprocal. Every brother, in turn, has
an especial responsibility for the brother whom we have elected.
One of the ways in which we affirm the value of a brother is in
electing him to be a superior. Having placed a burden on his
shoulders, we have a duty to support him, care for him, and
encourage him. If he fails, then he needs our forgiveness. If we
have a superior who is inefficient, or who lacks vision, then it is
because we have chosen that brother. Let us not blame him for
faults which we knew when the community chose him. Rather
than burden him with his failure, we must help him to do all of
which he is capable.

What the Lord said to Peter he says to us all: 'Strengthen your
brothers' (Lk 22:32). If our system of government, with all its
complexity, works for mutual disempowerment, then we are all
paralysed and we have lost the freedom of Dominic. But if it
works for the strengthening of all, then we can do great things.

The discernment of the common good

The discernment and pursuit of the common good is the
principal task of government, and it is here that relationships
between different levels of government may become most tense
and painful (cf 1.2, *supra*). A brother may find himself assigned
to a community in which he does not wish to live or to a task for
which he feels himself unfit. Or a Province may find itself asked
to release a brother whom it can ill afford to lose for some mission
of the Order. This may be hard, and yet it is the clearest expres-

sion of our unity in a common mission, and often the wider common good must receive priority over the more local if the Order is not to fragment into a loose association of individuals.

It can be painful to ask, for both. Rather than face that pain, it may be tempting for a superior to ask for volunteers, or to declare that nothing can be done. Yet this would be a flight from the responsibility for which one has been elected, and would lead to paralysis.

At times we must dare to govern, precisely because we value the freedom which is at the heart of Dominican life. We cherish that freedom of the brethren to gather in Chapter and take decisions about our common mission and life which can be realised and not remain mere declarations on paper. We also cherish the freedom with which a brother has given his life to the Order, and to its common mission. Not to dare to ask a brother to give himself to some mission would be to fail to respect that free self-gift which he made at profession. I admit that often I have hesitated to ask of a brother what I suspect he does not wish to give. Who am I to ask this of my brother? Yet I am not asking for submission to my will, but acceptance of that common good which the brethren have defined together. Sometimes one may even have to insist 'under obedience'. Yet, if it comes to this, it would be a mistake to think that this is the best image of what obedience is all about, since for us it is above all grounded in mutual attentiveness, in which we both seek together to understand what is right and best.[19]

I will now share with you a few brief observations about some of the challenges that we face in grasping responsibility at the different levels of government in the Order. This is by no means a complete picture. That would need a book.

19. See 'Vowed to Mission, A Letter to the Order: Obedience' Rome 1994, *supra*, at pp. 33-42; also Herbert McCabe OP, *God Matters*, 'Obedience' London, 1987.

CONVENTUAL GOVERNMENT

Fundamental to the life of the Order is that we share responsibility in the communities in which we live. We do not elect a brother as superior of the community, to relieve us of responsibility for our common life and mission, but to help us to share it. In some Provinces it is hard to find brothers who are willing to accept election as Prior. One reason may be that we expect him to bear all responsibility alone. The Prior, having been a majestic figure, has sometimes become the domestic manager, the one who must be perpetually solving the problems of the community. If my light bulb does not work or the central heating does not function, then it is the Prior who must solve the problem. It was only when I became Prior of Oxford that I was confronted with the question of how the milk gets from the cow to the jug, so that I may have milk with my coffee! The Prior is indeed called to 'serve with charity' (LCO 299) but this does not mean that we can pile all responsibility upon his shoulders, leaving him alone and helpless. The right that we have to elect a superior implies the duty to support him in building our common life and mission.

Superiors also need support from the Provincial and his Council. Many Provinces hold annual meetings of superiors at which they can discuss the challenges that they face and offer each other support and encouragement. The Province of St Albert the Great in the United States even produced an excellent booklet, to help new superiors understand their role, and how to survive it.

As the servant of the common good, one of the Prior's principal tasks is to preside over the Chapter and to help the brethren seek consensus. Above all he has to ensure that all the brethren have a voice, especially those who are most timid or who hold minority views. He is there to protect the weak against the strong. 'There are fragile brothers who may suffer much from being crushed, perhaps involuntarily, by the brethren with strong personalities. The role of the Prior is to protect them, on the one hand by valuing their gifts, and on the other by making the strong aware of their duty not to overwhelm the others.'[20] St Catherine of Siena wrote to the rulers of Bologna, that they often let the strong get away with anything, yet with the weak, 'who seem insignificant and whom they do not fear, they display tremendous enthusiasm for "justice" and, showing neither mercy nor compassion, they exact hard punishments for small faults.'[21] Even a superior in a Dominican community may be tempted to show more zeal in pointing out the failures of the weak than the strong.

The superior must take time with every brother. It is not enough to preside at the community meeting. He must be attentive to every brother, and regularly meet him alone, so that the brother may share his hopes and fears with freedom, certain of an open ear. Above all a superior must have care for the dignity of every brother. If there is one piece of advice that I would give it is this: Never ever let any brother be humiliated.

One of the most important tasks of the superior is to help the community define its 'community project'. The centrality of this to our common life and mission has been underlined by the last three General Chapters of the Order, but in some Provinces it is neglected. Sometimes this is because it has been misunderstood to mean that every community must identify a single task to which all the brethren must be committed, such as a school or a parish. The first step is for each brother to tell the community about his life and ministries, to share the joys and disappoint-

---

20. Joseph Kopf OP, 'Etre Prieur aujourdhui' in *Prieurs et Supérieurs dans le gouvernment des couvents*, published by Province Dominicaine de France, Réunion des Prieurs/Supérieurs, mars 1995.
21. Letter 268, translation *Catherine of Siena, Passion for the Truth and Compassion for Humanity*, ed Mary O'Driscoll OP, New York, 1993, p. 39.

ments that he faces. But it must lead us further, to a deep collaboration in each other's tasks, and the emergence of a common mission. It is a moment for a community to assess together the apostolic presence of the Order in a region, and how far it conforms to the priorities of the Order. I strongly support the recommendation of the General Chapter of Caleruega (44), that every community hold an annual day, to assess the ministries of the brethren, and to plan for the year ahead.

Democracy does not mean that the Prior must bring everything to the Chapter. We elect brethren to hold particular responsibilities so that we may be free for the mission. Having elected a brother to govern, we must leave him free to do so. The Constitutions lay down when the Prior must consult the community, or when the Chapter or Council has the power of decision. But the superior should not use this as an excuse to deny the Community responsibility for anything that it is of importance for the brethren. 'What touches all must be approved by all'.[22] The fundamental principle was laid down by Humbert of Romans in the thirteenth century, which is that the Prior ought to consult the community in all matters of importance, but not bother to do so if the question is insignificant, and that in intermediate matters prudence would demand that he consult some of his councillors.[23]

Democratic rule of the Chapter is so central to our life that sometimes we may be tempted to assume that the Prior is merely the chair of the Chapter, that his sole role is to guide the debate so that the brethren may arrive, if possible, at a consensus. But the Constitutions (LCO 299, 300) also make clear that the Prior has a role as the guardian of the religious and apostolic life of the

22. Codex Iuris Canonici 119 3.
23. Opera de vita regulari II pp. 284-285.

community. For example he is to preach to the brethren regularly. This does not in any way undermine the democratic principle. It demonstrates that the local community is a part of the Province, just as the Province is part of the Order, and so the local community cannot make decisions which contradict what the brethren at a Provincial or General Chapter have ruled. It is precisely in the name of our wider democracy that a local Prior might find that he cannot accept the will of the majority. If the brethren were to vote that a sauna bath be installed in every cell, he would have to refuse his consent!

PROVINCIAL GOVERNMENT

At the General Chapter of Mexico, the Province is described as being the normal centre of animation of the Order's apostolic dynamism (No 208). It is at the Provincial level that much of the practical planning for the mission of the Order must take place. Having now visitated some thirty-five entities of the Order, I will have to struggle to limit what I write. Be grateful that I did not wait another year before writing this letter! I regret that there has not been space to write about the relationships of the Vicariates to the Provinces.

Creating new projects

Each Province needs to establish projects and institutions, which give body and form to our common mission. Most of us are drawn to the Order because we wish to be preachers. But what form does that preaching take? What projects give flesh and blood to our Dominican charism today?

We may succumb to the profound suspicion of institutions which is part of contemporary culture, and yet the foundation of the Order was an act of supreme institutional creativity. Dominic and his brothers responded to the need to preach the gospel with extraordinary imagination, the invention of a new institution, our Order. We need such creativity. Institutions need not be complex or expensive: a radio station or an Internet home page, a university or a musical band, a priory or an art gallery, a book shop or a team of itinerant preachers. All these are 'institutions' which can sustain new ways of preaching. The incarnation of the Word of God at new frontiers demands new conceptions.

When we gather in Chapters to plan the missions of our Provinces, then we must always ask whether the institutions that we maintain serve the mission of the Order. Do they give us a voice in the debates of today? St Dominic sent the friars to the new universities, because it was there that the important issues of the time where being argued over. Where would he send us today?

The planning of the mission requires of us that institutional creativity, the ability to imagine new projects, new pulpits, that give the Order a voice and a visibility. At one stage the young French Dominicans invented a new form of mission, 'the mission to the beach', which was very popular! An American brother, charged with a mission to the Protestant south of the country, transformed a caravan into a mobile chapel with a pulpit. If we really urgently wish to share the good news of Jesus Christ, then we will use our imagination fully.

If we do not have that courage and inventiveness, then either we will be stuck, waiting in our churches for the people to come to us, while they are elsewhere, hungry for a word. Or else we will find ourselves working for other institutions, founded by other groups, even religious orders, who have had more daring and imagination than we have.

We need young brethren and new vocations to preach in ways that we cannot now imagine. When the Province of Chicago was accepting novices a few years ago, who could then have guessed that today these same young men would be preaching on the

World Wide Web, and even considering the foundation of a Virtual Centre of Studies?

Planning

'In dreams begin responsibility',[24] said W. B. Yeats. Provincial Chapters should be moments when we dare to respond to the challenges by dreaming of new projects. Often Chapters take brave and bold decisions, to be more committed to justice and peace, to develop our presence in the mass media, to send brethren on the missions. Thanks be to God! And yet often four years later nothing much has happened. There is a prayer for Chapters from the old Dominican missal, in which the brethren pray for the gift of the Holy Spirit 'that they may seek to discern those things that you will, and use their strength to accomplish them'. Presumably this prayer was necessary because the brethren then as now found that it was easier to make decisions than to execute them. Yet unless we learn both to make decisions and to implement them, then we will become disillusioned with all government, and our freedom and responsibility will be destroyed.

Bringing the Word to flesh in our time, finding new forms of preaching now, must begin in dreams, but end in hard practical planning. Good government relies on the virtue of prudence, a practical wisdom. We must come to an agreement as to what we can achieve. We cannot do everything at once, and so we must determine the order in which projects will be realised. We must face the consequences of our choices, even if this means a profound re-orientation of the mission and life of the Province. We must decide the process by which a project may be planned, proposed, evaluated and implemented. If the process does not work, then we must seek to understand why and how this may be remedied.

24. W. B. Yeats, *Collected Poems*, London, 1st ed., 1933, p. 111.

Challenges of growth and shrinkage

There are specific moments in the life of an entity of the Order when careful planning is especially important.

The transition to a full Dominican identity. There are successive moments in the birth of the Order in a new country. Sometimes, at the beginning, to gain acceptance and to enter a new culture we may have to accept apostolates that do not fully express our charism as preachers and teachers.

All over the Order, in Africa, Latin America, Eastern Europe and Asia, I have seen the excitement and the difficulty of making the transition to the next stage of Dominican life. It is a moment of profound transformation, as the brethren try to form communities, give up some parishes, adopt new apostolates, establish centres of formation and study, build up a body of professors. The flourishing of the Order depends upon the brethren being able to live through this time of transition with mutual understanding and support.

For the older brethren, perhaps 'the founding fathers', it can be a painful time, because the aspirations of the young may feel like a rejection of all that they have done. They have welcomed young men into the Order who appear to wish to destroy the work of their lives, and in the name of being 'fully Dominican'. For the young it can also be a time of anxiety, when they may wonder whether they will be able to fulfil their dreams of a more developed Dominican life.

Such moments of transition need careful planning and consultation. But this is not a question solely of administration. We have to both show that we value what the older brethren have done, and live through this moment as a time of death and rebirth, walking in the steps of Christ. When Bishop Paul Andreotti was giving a retreat to the brethren in Pakistan, at the time of the birth of the new Vice-Province, he said to the brothers who had come from abroad, 'Some of you may now decide to return to your own provinces, but those who choose to stay must be very sure of their motivations. I believe that Jesus is offering us a way of dying.' If the older brethren can walk this way with joy then they will give the most profound formation to the young. For formation, especially for a mendicant itinerant friar, is always an introduction to dispossession. Gilbert Markus OP said at the General Chapter of Caleruega:

> If these young men are coming to the Order to follow Christ, they themselves must also be given guidance in the art of dying. They have entrusted themselves to the Order, and part of the responsibility which we accept when we receive their profession is the responsibility of teaching them the art. There is no hope for a young Dominican who cannot realise during his formation something of how he must lose himself, die to himself. This is not an excuse for the older men to cling defensively to their own position or to resist change. They need instead to lead the young on that sacrificial path, and that means to travel it with them, to give an example of generosity.[25]

Shrinkage Very few Provinces in the Order are dying, though some, especially in Western Europe, are shrinking. How can such Provinces remain capable of undertaking new projects and fresh initiatives?

A Province must ask itself what it really wishes to do. What is its mission today? What new challenges must it face? What new forms of preaching can it evolve? To have such a freedom it may well have to take drastic action. It may be necessary to close two houses so as to have the freedom to open one that will offer

25. *Ars Moriendi*, Gilbert Markus OP, The First Three Days, Papers for the General Chapter of Caleruega, Santa Sabina, 1995, pp. 10 f.

new possibilities. But it is better to take firm action so that we may be free, rather than simply to beat a slow retreat in which we are the passive victims of circumstances beyond our control. How can we preach the freedom of the children of God if we have renounced all freedom ourselves? How can we be messengers of hope if we have given up all hope of doing something new for God? Unless we are seen to grasp that freedom, then we will never attract or retain any vocations.

The Provincial and Council

The Provincial Council is elected to assist the Provincial in his government of the Province, through offering counsel and taking decisions. The Councillors may have been elected because they represent a variety of views or priories or interests, but they are not members of the Council as the representatives of any group or ideology. The development of any faction within the Council would undermine its service of the Province. Its role is to help the Provincial to implement the decisions of the Chapter and to seek the common good. This demands a profound respect for confidentiality; otherwise the Provincial will not be able to receive the support that he needs.

In his implementation of the decisions of the Chapter, and his pursuit of the common good, the Provincial will sometimes have to take decisions that are painful. I have already written of the pain sometimes involved in making assignations (3.1, *supra*, pp. 153-156). Yet a Province cannot be governed on the basis of waiting for the brethren to volunteer for ministries. Asking for volunteers may look like respect for the brethren's freedom, but, except in very special circumstances, it is a misinterpretation of the nature of the freedom with which we have given ourselves to the mission of the Order. It also undermines the freedom of the Province effectively to make and implement decisions. Finally, it rests upon the assumption that the best judge of what a brother is capable of is that brother himself. We may be radically mistaken. Sometimes a brother may consider himself to be the true successor of St Thomas whereas he is more of a dumb ox. More often, brothers underestimate of what they are capable. I trust my brethren to know what I am best able to do. It is part of the confidence that knits the Order together.

A Provincial or the Master of the Order may also have to cassate an election. This too can be painful. It may look as if we are undermining the democratic rights of the brethren to choose their own superior. Yet sometimes this must be done, precisely because these superiors have themselves been democratically elected to have care of the common good of the Province or the Order. It would undermine democracy if they were to refuse to bear the responsibility for which they have been elected. There are moments in this process. The community votes; the superior must decide whether to confirm or cassate; the brother elected must accept or refuse; the superior must decide whether to accept the refusal or to insist. At each moment we must be allowed to exercise the responsibility that is properly ours, without interference or pressure, so that we may discover what is indeed for the common good.

THE MASTER OF THE ORDER AND THE GENERAL COUNCIL

The general government of the Order relates to the other levels of government in accordance with the principles suggested in pages 101 to 104, above – itinerancy, mutual support, and the pursuit of the wider common good.

Strengthening the brethren

The primary task of the Master of the Order and the General Council is to support the brethren, and indeed the whole Dominican Family. Everywhere I go on my travels I meet brothers and sisters preaching the gospel with wonderful courage, often in situations of poverty and violence. This is an inspiration to me and the Council.

The principal way in which the Master of the Order strengthens the brethren is through visitations, trying to meet every brother. This is a privilege and a joy. The programme is so full that there is little time left for anything else. Between last November and this May, I have been in Rome for less than four weeks. I was not able, as I had hoped, to visit the brethren and sisters in the Great Lakes region of Africa to offer a support that they need. A question that I shall put to the General Chapter of Bologna is whether we should not rethink how visitations are done so that the Master of the Order has the freedom to respond to the needs of the Order in other ways.

When a Province is going through a profound process of renewal or facing a time of crisis, then an occasional visitation is not enough. Increasingly the General Council sees the need to accompany some Provinces of the Order as they face difficult challenges. We have to support them so that they may have the strength and courage to take the hard decisions necessary for their renewal. The *Socius* of the Master for that Province will often have a demanding role, accompanying the brethren as they face the challenges of rebuilding Dominican life and government.

It is rarely necessary for the Master of the Order directly to intervene in the government of a Province. When he does, it may be hard for the brethren to bear. It may appear as if their democratic right to make decisions about their life and mission has been superseded. Yet any such intervention is always an attempt to strengthen the brethren, and to help them to be renewed in their freedom and responsibility. If government at the provincial level becomes weak or even paralysed, then the

Master may have to intervene directly so that the brethren may once again be free to face the future. This is often the issue when we have to examine the unification of Provinces.

The Wider Common Good

The Master of the Order has to promote the unity of the Order in its common mission. We see this common mission most clearly in the establishment of new foundations, in the renewal of the Order where it is weak, and in the houses directly under the Master's jurisdiction.

One of the hardest tasks of the Master of the Order is to find brethren for this common mission. Humbert of Romans wrote to the Order in the thirteenth century that one of the main obstacles to the mission of the Order was 'the brothers' love of their native land, the lure of which so often ensnares them, their nature not yet having been graced, that rather than leave their own land and relations and forget their own folk, they wish to live and die among their own family and friends, not recalling that in similar circumstances the Saviour did not permit himself to be found even by his own mother.'[26] Some things do not change!

Truthfully, I can say that many brethren, especially the young, have a deep and growing sense of this common mission of the Order to which we are called. Some Provinces are profoundly generous in giving their brethren to the common mission of the Order. For example, we have found brethren to help us rebuild the Order in the ex-Soviet Union. Yet often it is difficult to find the brethren who are needed, for example, to support the brethren in Rwanda and Burundi in this time of suffering. We need brethren for the foundation of the Order in Western Canada. We need brethren to renew and sustain our international centres of study.

26. Humbert of Romans, in Tugwell, op. cit., p. 498.

How are we to deepen our participation in the common mission of the Order? It asks of us that we grow together in the grace and truth of the Incarnate Word.

We are called to the utter gracious generosity of the Word. This is not just the generosity of a Province giving a brother who is free, or even asking for volunteers. Often it is precisely the brethren who are not free who are needed. It implies the redefinition of the priorities of the Province in the light of the needs of our common mission. For example, in Latin America, we are trying to renew the Order by asking the stronger Provinces to work closely with Provinces where we are weaker. We are moving to a sort of partnership, whereby a Province may be asked to accompany another entity. We are asking these Provinces to redefine their mission in the light of the needs of the Order.

It demands of us that we live in truth. First of all the truth of what it means to be a Dominican brother. We have made our profession to the Master of the Order for the Order's mission. Of course the mission of each Province is an expression of that mission. But sometimes we must express our deepest identity as Dominicans by being released for the mission beyond the boundaries of our Province.

It asks of us that together we truthfully seek to know what are our resources for the common mission. This requires of us great mutual trust. When the Master of the Order asks a Provincial whether there is a brother suitable for some task in our common mission, there may sometimes be an understandable instinct to protect the Province's interests. We need, if we are to discern the common good, a deep trust and transparency, so that we may dialogue about how best to meet the needs of the Order while respecting the situation of the Province. In the past it was common for Masters of the Order simply to assign brethren out of their Provinces, even against the will of the Provincials. It is still sometimes necessary to do this, just as a Provincial may sometimes have to assign a brother from one convent to another, despite the superior's resistance. But ultimately our common mission demands of us trust and mutual confidence, grace and truth.

THE INCARNATION OF DOMINICAN GOVERNMENT
IN DIFFERENT CULTURES

The Word became flesh in a particular culture. Yet the Word transforms what it touches, the leaven of new life. A new form of community is born, and the flesh becomes word and communion.

So too Dominican government bears the marks of the time and place of its birth, a particular moment in European history. We were born in a time of experimentation with new forms of democratic institutions, and of intense intellectual ferment. How is this form of government to become flesh and blood in the Order in the coming years, when two thirds of all those in formation come from non-Western cultures? How is it to become incarnate in Western culture as it is today, with its strengths and weaknesses, its love of freedom and its temptation to consumerism? Central to our tradition of government is the pursuit of truth through debate and dialogue. How are we to sustain Dominican government in a society in which the very idea of truth is in crisis? The incarnation of Dominican government in all these cultures is always both a challenge and a richness. It should witness to a freedom and responsibility that is deeply evangelical, but these different cultures may help us to learn what these values truly mean.

For example, African cultures can help us to understand the nature of debate, and the importance of time and patience in listening to our brothers; in North America, the immense sense of respect for the individual can deepen our understanding of Dominican freedom; in Eastern Europe, the passionate commitment to the faith can help us to understanding what it means to give one's life to the Order; in Latin America we can learn how central to our preaching is a commitment to justice.

Yet it is also true that our Dominican tradition of government offers a challenge to every culture in which we implant the Order. It may challenge the power of tribal identity in Africa; it is critical of the individualism of contemporary America; it will invite the brethren of Eastern Europe to be freed from the effects of years of communist rule and grow in mutual trust. In Latin America, the tradition of the *coup d'état* does not always help towards a deep commitment to our elected structures of government.

Often the challenge will be to understand when a culture is inviting us to a new insight and when it may deform what is properly Dominican in our government. Does the respect for the elders in African society offer us a new insight into the proper authority of each generation, or is it contrary to our democratic tradition? Does the practice of some Western Provinces of letting the brethren have private bank accounts lead to a deeper and truly Dominican sense of responsibility, or does it lead to a privatisation of life that destroys our common life?

Answering these questions will take time. General Chapters, regional meetings of brethren in every continent, and even visitations by the Master, should be of help to the brethren as we find our way towards discovering what responsibility and freedom mean in any particular society. Time, prayer, honest debate and contact with Dominicans in other cultures will be necessary if we are to arrive at a true understanding of how government is to be implemented in each society. It is good that we take this time, both for the benefit of the Order and also so that we may build communities which can offer true witnesses to brotherhood wherever we are.

CONCLUSION

I have not talked about many matters which are central to government. For example, I have not discussed government and wealth nor the importance of visitations. I have said hardly a word about the Dominican Family or regional collaboration. There is a limit to what can be written in a letter.

In St Catherine's vision, God says, 'Dominic allied himself with my Truth by showing that he did not want the sinner to die, but rather to be converted and live. He made his ship very spacious, gladsome, and fragrant, a most delightful garden' in which 'the perfect and the not-so-perfect fare well.'[27] Here the grace and truth of the incarnate Word coincide in mercy. It is this that makes the ship so spacious, a place in which we, the not-so-perfect, can be at home. This ship may steam along slowly; it is not always clear in what direction it is moving, and the crew change roles with an astonishing frequency. But it is a place in which we may hope to grow into the freedom of Dominic, hesitantly and with many mistakes, confident in God's mercy and each other's.

27. *Dialogue*, 158

THE PROMISE OF LIFE

'I have come that they may have life, and have it more abundantly.' (Jn 10:10)

When St Dominic gave the friars the habit, he promised them 'the bread of life and the water of heaven'.[1] If we are to be preachers of a word that gives life, then we must find the 'bread of life' in our communities. Do they help us to flourish, or merely to survive?

Shortly after I joined the Order, the Province was visitated by fr Aniceto Fernandez, then Master. He asked me only one question, the traditional question of all visitators: 'Are you happy?' I had expected some deeper question, about preaching the gospel, or the challenges facing the Province. Now I realise that this is the first question we must put to our brethren: 'Are you happy?' There is a happiness which is properly that of being alive as a Dominican, and which is the source of our preaching. It is not an endless cheerfulness, a relentless *bonhomie*. It entails a capacity for sorrow. It may be absent for a time, even a long time. It is some small taste of that abundance of life which we preach, the joy of those who have begun to share God's own life. We should have the capacity for delight because we are children of the Kingdom. 'Delight is the intrinsic character of the blessed life and the life which by the gift of the Holy Spirit is on the way to blessedness'.[2] When we sing to Dominic we conclude by praying: '*Nos junge beatis*: Join us to the blessed.' May we now share some glimpse of their happiness there. If we are to build communities in which there is an abundance of life, then we must recognise who and

---

1. Stephen of Salagnac 1.9, ed Thomas Kaeppeli OP *Monumenta Ordinis Pradicatorum Historica (MOPH)*, XXII Rome 1949, p. 81.
2 Cornelius Ernst OP, *The Theology of Grace*, Dublin, 1974 p. 42.

A letter to all members of the Order of Preachers, issued from Santa Sabina, Rome, on Ash Wednesday, 25 February 1998.

what we are and what it means for us to be alive, as men and women, brothers and sisters, and as preachers.

We are not angels. We are passionate beings, moved by the animal desires for food and copulation. This is the nature which the Word of Life accepted when he embraced human nature. We can do no less. It is from here that the journey to holiness begins.

Yet we are created by God in his image, destined for God's friendship. We are *capax Dei*, hungry for God. To be alive is to embark on that adventure which leads us to the Kingdom. We need communities that will sustain us on the way. The Lord has promised: 'I will take out of your flesh the heart of stone and give you a heart of flesh' (Ezek 36:26). We need brothers and sisters who are with us as our hearts are broken and made tender.

Every wise person has always known that there is no way to life that does not take one through the wilderness. The journey from Egypt to the Promised Land passes through the desert. If we would be happy and truly alive, then we too must pass that way. We need communities which will accompany us on that journey, and help us to believe that when the Lord leads Israel into the wilderness it is so that he 'may speak tenderly to her' (Hos 2:16). Perhaps the reason why so many people have left religious life in the last thirty years is not because it is any harder than before, but because we have sometimes lost sight of the fact that these dark nights belong to our rebirth as people who are alive with the joy of the Kingdom. So our communities should not be places in which we merely survive, but places where we find food for the journey.

To use a metaphor which I have developed elsewhere,[3] religious communities are like ecological systems, designed to sus-

3. 'The Identity of Religious Today. Address to the Conference of Major Superiors of Men, USA', 1996. Published as 'Religious Vocations: Leaving Aside the Usual Signs of Identity', pp. 191-209 *infra*.

tain strange forms of life. A rare frog will need its own ecosystem if it is to flourish, and make its hazardous way from spawn to tadpole to frog. If the frog is threatened with extinction, then one must build an environment, with its food and ponds and a climate in which it can thrive. Dominican life also requires its own ecosystem, if we are to live fully, and preach a word of life. It is not enough to talk about it; we must actively plan and build such Dominican ecosystems.

This is, in the first place, the responsibility of each community. It is for the brethren and sisters who live together to create communities in which we may not just survive but flourish, offering to each other 'the bread of life and the water of heaven'. This is the fundamental purpose of the 'community project' proposed by the last three General Chapters. This will only happen if we dare to talk together about what touches us most deeply as human beings and as Dominicans. My hope is that this letter to the Order may open up discussion of some aspects of our Dominican life. I look at the apostolic life, the affective life, and the life of prayer. These are not three parts of each life (Contemplative life, 7 a.m.-7.30 a.m.; Apostolic life, 9 a.m.-5 p.m.; Affective life ?). They belong to the fullness of any life that is truly human and Dominican. Nicodemus asks how one can be reborn. This is our question too: how can we help each other as we face transformation, so as to become apostles of life?

Not every community will be able to renew itself and attain the ideal envisaged by our Constitutions and recent General Chapters. A Province will therefore have to evolve a plan for the gradual renewal of communities in which the brethren may flourish. It is to these communities alone that young brethren should be assigned. They will carry the seeds for the future of Dominican life. Unless a Province plans the building of such communities, then it dies. A Province with three communities where the brethren flourish in their Dominican life has a future, with the grace of God. A Province with twenty communities where we just survive may well have none.

THE APOSTOLIC LIFE

A LIFE TORN OPEN

The Dominican life is in the first place apostolic. This may easily be understood to mean that a good Dominican is always busy, engaged in 'apostolates'. Yet the apostolic life is not what we do so much as what we are, those who are called to 'live the life of the apostles in the form conceived by St Dominic'.[4] When Diego met the Cistercian delegates sent to preach to the Albigensians he told them 'go humbly, following the example of our loving Master, teaching and acting, travelling on foot without silver and gold, imitating the life of the apostles in everything'.[5] To be an apostle is to have a life, not a job.

And the first characteristic of this apostolic life is that it is a sharing of the life of the Lord. The apostles are those who accompanied him 'during all the time that the Lord Jesus went in and out among us' (Acts 1:21). They were called by him, walked with him, listened to him, rested and prayed with him, argued with him, and were sent out by him. They shared the life of the one who is Emmanuel, 'God with us'. The culmination of that life was the sharing of the Last Supper, the sacrament of the bread of life. Though one left early because he had too much to do.

The apostolic life is therefore for us more than the various apostolates that we do. It is a way of life. Yves Congar OP wrote of preaching that it is a 'vocation that is the substance of my life and being'.[6] If the demands of the apostolate mean that we have

4. *LCO*, Fundamental Constitution IV.
5. Cernai 21, quoted by Tugwell (ed), *Dominic*, London, 1997, p. 125.

no time to pray and eat with our brothers, to share their lives, then
how ever busy we may be, we will not be apostles in the full sense
of the word. Meister Eckhart wrote: 'People should not worry so
much about what they should do; rather about what they should
be. If we and our ways are good, then what we do will be radiant.'[7]
Dominic was a preacher with all his being.

But this apostolic life necessarily tears us apart. This is its pain
and the source of its fertility. For the Word of God, whose life the
apostles share, reaches out to all that is farthest from God and
embraces it. According to Eckhart, the Word remains one with
the Father while boiling over into the world. Nothing human is
alien to him. The life of God is stretched open to find a space for
all that we are; he becomes like us in all things but sin. He takes
upon himself our doubts and fears, he enters into our experience
of absurdity, that wilderness in which all meaning is lost.

So for us to live the apostolic life fully is to find that we too are
torn open, stretched out. To be a preacher is not just to tell people
about God. It is to bear within our lives that distance between the
life of God and that which is furthest away, alienated and hurt.
We have a word of hope only if we glimpse from within the pain
and despair of those to whom we preach. We have no word of
compassion unless somehow we know their failures and temptations as our own. We have no word which offers meaning to
people's lives, unless we have been touched by their doubts, and
glimpsed the abyss. I think of some of my French brethren, who
after a day of teaching theology and doing research, take to the
pavements at night, to meet the prostitutes, to hear their woes and
sufferings, and to offer them a word of hope. No wonder that,

6. 'What Is My Licence to Say What I Say?', *Dominican Ashram*, March. 1982, p.
   10.

7. *Die deutsche Predigten und lateinischen Werke*, Stuttgart 1936, vol V, p. 197.

from the beginning, we Dominicans have a bad reputation! It is a risk of the vocation. Jordan of Rivalto, in the fourteenth century, tells people not to be too hard on the friars if they are bit 'grubby'. It is part of our vocation:

> Being here among the people, seeing the things of the world, it is impossible for them not to get a bit dirty. They are men of flesh and blood like you, and in the freshness of youth; it is a wonder that they are as clean as they are. This is no place for monks! [8]

So the apostolic life does not offer us a balanced and healthy 'lifestyle', with good career prospects. For it unbalances us, tips us into that which is most other. If we share the life of the Word of God in this way, then we are hollowed out, opened up, so that there is the space and the silence for a new word to be born, as if for the first time. We are people of faith who reach out to open our hearts to those who do not believe. Sometimes we ourselves will be unsure of what it all means. We are like the apostles, who were summoned by Christ, and who walked to Jerusalem with him, knowing that he alone had the words of eternal life. And yet they argued as to who was the greatest, and often had no idea where they were going.

So the apostolic life invites us to live a tension. We have promised to build our lives with our Dominican brothers and sisters. 'For us henceforth to be human, to be ourselves is to be one of the preaching brethren, we have no other life-story.' [9] Here is our home and we can have no other. But the impetus of the apostolic life propels us into different worlds. It has taken many of our brothers into the industrial world, to the world of factories

8. *Prediche del Beato Giordano da Rivalto*, ed. A. M. Bisconi e D. M. Manni, Firenze, 1739, p. 9.
9. Herbert McCabe OP, *God Matters*, London, 1987, 'On Being Dominican', p. 240.

and trade unions. It takes others into universities. It takes us into the cyberworld of Internet. A new project of the French Dominicans, *Jubilatio*, carries us into the world of the young. A project in Benin takes us into the world of ecological farming. We are present in the worlds of Islam and Judaism. This tension may tear us open, so that the only life we have is not built or planned by us, but received as a daily gift, 'bread of life' that Dominic promised.

WORK IN CONTEMPORARY SOCIETY

In our contemporary society, this tension can easily become a simple division. We can become people with two lives, our lives as Dominicans in our communities and the lives we live in our apostolates. This is because of the way that work is perceived today. If this happens, then the beautiful, painful, fertile tension at the heart of the apostolic life is broken, and we may become simply people with jobs who happen to go back to religious hotels at night. Let us see why this is a particular challenge we must face today.

The fragmentation of our lives. Contemporary western society fragments life. The weekday is separated from the weekend, work from leisure, the working life from retirement, at least for those lucky enough to have a job. You can be a history teacher in the day and a parent at night and a Christian on Sunday. This fragmentation can make it hard for us to live unified and whole lives. Dominicans preach in an almost infinite variety of ways. We are parish priests and professors, social workers and hospital chaplains, poets and painters. How do we live these apostolates as friars, members of our communities, vowed brethren and sisters? I remember being very moved talking to a young Dominican journalist who shared with me the difficulties of living in the world of the media. In the day he lived in one world, with its moral assumptions, its 'lifestyle'. At night he came back to his religious community. How was he to be one person, friar and journalist? When we come back to the community at night, then like everyone else in society we will want to shut off the burdens of the day. What we do at work is 'another life'.

The professionalisation of work. Increasingly work is professionalised. For the preaching of the gospel we will often become qualified professionals. One can even get a diploma in preaching or a doctorate in pastoral studies. None of those whom Jesus called had graduated in 'apostleship'! There is nothing wrong with this professionalisation. We must be as qualified and professional as those with whom we work. Yet we must be aware of the seductions of becoming a 'professional'. It grants status and position. It locates us in a stratified society. It gives identity and invites us to a way of life. We may bring in a salary to the community. How is this doctor, professor, pastor, to be a mendicant, an itinerant friar or sister? Does our profession confine us to a narrow path, with only the prospect of promotion? Does it leave us free for the unexpected demands of our brethren and of God.

The work ethic. Finally, in western society, the work ethic has triumphed. It is what justifies our existence. Salvation not by works but by work. The unemployed are excluded from the Kingdom. Whatever we may preach, surely the hectic activism one so often encounters in the Order may suggest that sometimes we too believe that we can save ourselves by what we do. We praise Dominic as *Praedicator Gratiae*, 'preacher of grace', but though we may preach that salvation is a gift, is that how we live? Do we live as those for whom life, and the fullness of life, is a gift? Is that how we regard our brethren? Do we compete to show how busy and therefore important we are?

THE WILDERNESS OF MEANINGLESSNESS

So to be a preacher is to have one's life prised open. We have somehow to share in the Exodus of the Word of God, who comes forth from the Father to embrace all that is human. Sometimes this Exodus may carry us into the wilderness, with no apparent way through to the Promised Land. We may be like Job who sits upon the dung heap and proclaims that his Redeemer lives. Only sometimes we merely sit upon the dung heap. If we let ourselves be touched by the doubts and beliefs of our contemporaries, then we may find ourselves in a desert in which the gospel makes no sense any more. 'He has walled up my path' (Job 19:8).

The fundamental crisis of our society is perhaps that of meaning. The violence, corruption and drug addiction are symptoms of a deeper malady, which is the hunger for some meaning to our human existence. To make us preachers God may lead us into that wilderness. There our old certainties will collapse, and the God whom we have known and loved will disappear. Then we may have to share the dark night of Gethsemane, when all seems absurd and senseless, and the Father appears to be absent. And yet it is only if we let ourselves be led there, where nothing makes any sense any more, that we may hear the word of grace which God offers for our time. 'Grace shows itself where we break through despair into the affirmation of praise.'[10]

Faced with void, we may be tempted to fill it, with half-believed platitudes, with substitutes for the living God. The fundamentalism which we so often see in the Church today is perhaps the frightened reaction of those who stood on the edge of that desert, but did not dare to endure it. The desert is a place of terrifying silence, which we may try to drown by banging out old formulas with a terrible sincerity. But the Lord leads us into the

10. Cornelius Ernst OP, op. cit., p. 72.

wilderness to show us his glory. Therefore, says Meister Eckhart, 'Stand firm, and do not waver from your emptiness'.[11]

COMMUNITIES OF APOSTOLIC LIFE

How can our communities sustain us in this apostolic life? How can we support each other when a brother or sister finds themselves in that wilderness, when nothing at all makes any more sense?

The apostle is the one who is sent. The apostles did not apply for the job! We give our lives to the Order so that we may be sent out on its mission. In most Dominican communities there is the regular rhythm of going out in the morning and coming back at night. But we are not just going out to work, like a professional leaving his house. It is the community that sends us. And 'on their return the apostles told him what they had done' (Lk 9:10). Do we listen to what our brethren have done in the day when they come home in the evening? Do we give them the chance to share the challenges that they meet in their apostolates? We are out there, in the parish or the classroom, for them, on their behalf, representing them. The community is present here in this brother or sister.

How can the prayers that we share together, morning and evening, be not just the common fulfilment of an obligation but part of the rhythm of the community that sends out and receives back its members? Do we pray for and with our brothers in their apostolates? If not, then how can our community be said to be apostolic? It may became just a hostel.

The General Chapter of Caleruega has given excellent and clear suggestions as to how communities may plan and evaluate the common mission of the community, so that the brethren

11. *Sermons and Treatises*, trans. M. O'C. Walshe, vol I, London, 1979, p. 44.

grow in a real sense of collaboration. I strongly urge all communities to fulfil these recommendations (No. 44).

In our communities we should be able to share both our faith and our doubts. For most of us, especially many who are joining the Order today, it is not enough just to recite the Psalms together. We need to share the faith that brought us to the Order and which sustains us now. This is the foundation of our fraternity. Perhaps we can only do this tentatively, shyly, but even so we may offer our brothers and sisters 'the bread of life and the water of heaven'. General Chapters frequently recommend that there be preaching at every public liturgy. This is not only because we are the Order of Preachers, but also that we may share with each other our faith.

We must also be able to share our doubts. It is above all when a brother enters that wilderness, when nothing makes sense any more, that we must let him speak. We must respect his struggle and never crush him. If a brother dares to share these moments of darkness and incomprehension, and we dare to listen to him, then it may be the greatest gift that he could ever give. The Lord may lead a brother into the dark night of Gethsemane. Will we go to sleep while he struggles? Nothing binds a community more closely together than a faith that we struggled to attain together. This may be in a theological faculty or a poor *barrio* of Latin America. In wrestling together to make sense of who we are and to what we are called in the light of the gospel, then we shall surely be astonished by the God who is always new and unexpected. We may even be surprised to encounter and discover each other, as if for the first time.

THE AFFECTIVE LIFE

IN THIS IS LOVE

In this is love, not that we loved God but that he loved us and sent his Son to be the expiation of our sins. Beloved, if God so loved us, we also ought to love one another (1 Jn 4:10 f).

All apostolic life is a sharing in that redemptive love of God for humanity. If it is not, then our preaching will be at best a job, and at worst an exercise in manipulation of others, the propagation of an ideology. Perhaps in some countries the churches are empty because the preaching of the gospel is seen as an exercise of control rather than the expression of God's boundless love. So to become alive, abundantly alive as preachers, means discovering how to love well. 'My vocation is Love.'[12]

But one could put it the other way around. For us Dominicans, learning how to love is inseparable from being caught up in the mystery of God's redemption of humanity. This is our school of love. Today religious formators all over the world are beginning to face the question of 'affectivity', a word I dislike. How can we form those who join the Order so that they may love well and fully, as chaste religious? Most of us had little or no formation in facing our emotions, our sexuality, our hunger to love and be loved. I do not remember ever receiving any formation in this area. It seemed to be assumed, or perhaps hoped nervously, that a good run and a cold shower would solve the 'problem'. Alas, I cannot run and I dislike cold showers!

In this letter I will not discuss issues relating specifically to formation and affectivity, since I hope there will be a letter to the Order on the topic of formation soon.[13] I will just say this: it is not enough to hope that all will be well if we recruit well-balanced

12. St Thérèse of Lisieux, *Manuscrits autobiographiques*, Paris, p. 226.
13. See 'Initial Formation', *infra*, pp. 160-188.

young men and women, free of obvious emotional disorders. Would well balanced people lay down their lives for their friends? Would they leave the ninety-nine sheep and go and look for the one that is lost? Would they eat and drink with prostitutes and sinners? I fear that they may be too sensible. Commenting on St John's gospel, Augustine wrote 'Show me a lover, and he feels what I am saying.'[14] It is only those who are capable of love who can possibly understand the passion of the apostolic life. Unless we let ourselves be caught on the wave of that immense love, then all our attempts to be chaste may end up in being exercises in control. We may succeed, but at the risk of great damage to ourselves. We may fail, at the risk of terrible damage to others. So unless our apostolic impulse and our capacity for love are deeply integrated, then they become a matter of either controlling others or myself. But Jesus let go control of his life, and placed it in our hands.

'GREATER LOVE HAS NO ON THAN THIS, THAT HE LAY DOWN HIS LIFE FOR HIS FRIENDS' (Jn 15:13)

Loving humanity may be very admirable but it may seem like a pale and abstract substitute for that deep and personal love for which we sometimes hunger. Is it really enough? And we may feel this all the more in contemporary society in which the dominant model of love is the passionate sexual love of a man and woman. When we feel this urgency, then can we be satisfied with loving humanity?

That passionate, spousal love is indeed a deep human need, and I shall say something about it later. It may also be an image of our relationship with God, for example in the medieval commentaries on the Song of Songs. But there is another comple-

14. *In Jn* 26.

mentary tradition which is perhaps more typically Dominican. It is at the heart of John's Gospel. 'Greater love has no one than this, that he lays down his life for his friends.' So this is what the mystery of love looks like, someone giving away their life for their friends. Here we see a love that is profoundly passionate, in Jesus' relationship with the disciples, with the prostitutes and publicans, the sick and the lepers, and even the Pharisees. It is a passion whose consummation is the passion that leads to Golgotha. Is not this as passionate as any love affair?

Our society may find our way of loving incomprehensible, since we have apparently rejected the typical experience of love, the sexual union with one other person. We may feel that sometimes ourselves, that we have missed out on 'the big experience', and that we have not lived. But St Thomas Aquinas taught that at the heart of the life of the God who is love is friendship, the unutterable friendship of the Father and the Son, which is the Spirit. For us to live, to become unutterably alive, is to find our home in that friendship and to be transformed by it. It will overspill into all that we do and are. As Don Goergen OP wrote, 'Celibacy does not witness to anything. But celibates do.' [15] We witness to the Kingdom if we are seen to be people whose chastity liberates us for life.

Our communities should be schools of friendship. When he was dying, St Hyacinth repeated the words of St Dominic to the brethren, 'Have goodness and gentleness (*dulcedo*) of heart. Keep love of God and fraternal charity.' [16] Are we always sufficiently good and gentlehearted towards each other? In religious life there has often been a fear of friendship, but perhaps this has not

15. 'Calling Forth a Healthy Chaste Life', *Review for Religious*, May-June 1998, p. 264.
16. D. A. Mortier OP, *Histoire des maitres generaux de l'ordre des Frères Prêcheurs*, vol. I Rome, 1903, p. 528.

been so present in the Dominican tradition. From the beginning
there have been profound and loving friendships: of Dominic for
his brethren and sisters; of Jordan of Saxony for his beloved
Diana and for Henry; of Catherine of Siena and Raymond of
Capua. I remember an old Dominican saying in Chapter when I
was young, 'I have nothing against particular friendships; it's
particular enmities to which I object!' This friendship is never
exclusive, but profoundly transformative, painfully and slowly
liberating us from all that is dominative or possessive, all that is
patronising or contemptuous. If it is a sharing in the life of the
Trinity, then it will be a love that lifts the other to equality and sets
them free. As Bede Jarrett, the English provincial, wrote in 1932,
'Oh dear friendship, what a gift of God it is. Speak no ill of it.
Rather praise its Maker and Model, the Blessed Three-in-one.'[17]
If it is truly a friendship which is of God, then it will propel us out
into the mission of preaching the good news.

The culmination of our loving will be a dispossession. Those
whom we love we must let go; we must let them be. Does my love
for another give them freedom to make their own lives and leave
me free for the mission of the Order? Does my love for this
woman, for example, help her to grow in her love for her
husband, or am I tying her life to mine, and making her dependent? This painful but liberating dispossession invites us to become peripheral to the lives of those whom we love. We should
find that we disappear from the centre of their lives, so that they
may forget us and be free, free for someone else, free for God.
This is the hardest thing of all, but I firmly believe that it can give
us more joy than we can ever say or imagine. It is when our sides
are opened up, so that living water may flow out.

17. *The Letters of Bede Jarrett OP*, ed. Bede Bailey, Aidan Bellenger and Simon
    Tugwell, Bath, 1989, p. 182.

One of the beautiful examples within our Dominican tradition is surely that of the love between Blessed Jordan of Saxony, Dominic's successor as Master of the Order, and the Dominican nun, Blessed Diana d'Andalo. Clearly they loved each other deeply. How many Masters of the Order have written with such openness to a woman? 'Am I not yours, am I not with you: yours in labour, yours in rest; yours when I am with you, yours when I am far away?'[18] And it is clear that she taught him much about how to love. But in his letters Jordan is always giving her away to the Lord. He is the Bridegroom's friend, whose role is to bring the bride to the bridegroom:

> 'Think on him.' What is lacking to you because I cannot be with you, make up for in the company of a better friend, your Bridegroom Jesus Christ whom you have more constantly with you in spirit and in truth, and who speaks to you more sweetly and to better purpose than Jordan.[19]

We even have to be dispossessed, in a sense, of our own families. We will rightly love them and delight in their love for us, but once we make our profession in the Order we should be free to go where the mission of the Order needs us, even if it is far from the homes of our family. That is part of our poverty. Now our first belonging is to the Order and the preaching of the gospel.

SEX, BODIES AND DESIRE

An unattainable ideal?

This is a beautiful ideal, but it may seem remote and unattainable. As we struggle with sexual desire, with fantasies and possessiveness, then this selfless friendship may seem beyond our

18. Letter 46, trans. from G. Vann OP, *To Heaven with Diana*, London, 1959, p. 120.
19. Letter 48, ibid, p. 28.

reach. The media assure us every day that this ideal is 'unrealis-
tic'. But God does not transform humanity by inviting us to
labour up to heaven. The divine life comes to where we are, flesh
and blood. Jesus summons Zacchaeus to come down from the
tree and join him on the ground. The Word becomes bodily,
takes upon himself our desires, our passion, our sexuality. If we
would meet the Lord and be healed, then we too must become
incarnate, in the bodies that we are, with all our passions, with
our hurts and hungers.

We start from who and what we are. When we are clothed in
the habit, we bring to the Order this person, who is the fruit of a
history, and carries its wounds. This is the person whom the Lord
has called, and not some ideal human being. We come with the
scars of past experience, perhaps with the unhealed memories of
failures in love, of abuse, of sex. Our families have taught us to
love; they may also have inflicted wounds on us that will take
time to heal. To grow in this Christ-like love takes time, and this
time is given. It is a gift, and God always gives his gifts through
time. He took centuries to form his people, preparing the way for
the birth of his Son. God gives us life patiently, not in an instant.
If we accept his gifts, we must accept the way God gives: 'not as
the world gives do I give unto you' (Jn 14:27). Accepting this gift
of time is perhaps especially important in our society, in which
adolescence is prolonged, and it is only late that most of us arrive
at maturity. We must start with our desires, our hungers, our
bodies. We are neither angels nor beasts, but flesh and blood and
spirit, destined for the Kingdom. But, as Pascal said, if we make
the mistake of thinking that we are angels, then we will become
beasts.

Desire
'I will take out of your flesh the heart of stone and give you a

heart of flesh' (Ezek 36:26). If our hearts are to become flesh then we must let our desires be transformed.

What are the desires that shape our heart, and which we hide from others and perhaps even from ourselves? 'None of us is so self-transparent as to know quite where, in fact, our hearts are set.'[20] Until we look squarely at our desires in the face and learn to desire well, then we shall be subject to their control and so their prisoner. This is especially hard in a society which is dedicated to the cultivation of desire. Our society is dying not of famine but of an excess of desire. Every advertisement encourages us to desire more, endlessly, infinitely. The world is being consumed by a voracious, unmeasured desire, that may consume us all. Unrestrained sexual desire is merely one symptom of how we are taught to see the world, as there to be taken and consumed.

In the first place, that love which is friendship invites us to see others without seeking to possess them. We delight in them without seeking ownership. It is hard to attain this liberty of heart if we remain captivated by the culture of the market, in which everything is there to be acquired and used, even other people. Thus true friendship asks of us that we break with the dominant culture of our time. We have to learn to see aright, with clarity, with eyes that do not devour each other and the world. St Thomas wrote *'ubi amor, ibi oculus'*. 'Where love is, there is the eye.'[21] He says that when we lust we see the other as the lion sees the stag, as a meal to be devoured. Love is therefore inseparable from a true poverty of heart. As William Blake asked, 'Can that be Love that drinks another as a sponge drinks water?'[22]

So the healing of desire implies a different way of being in the world, true poverty. And what sort of sign would chastity be if we

20. Nicholas Lash, *The Beginning and the End of Religion*, Cambridge, 1996, p. 21.
21. *Sentences* 3 d 35, 1,2,1.
22. *Vision of Albion* 7.17.

remain just as acquisitive in other ways? As Don Goergen OP wrote, 'If I partake of consumer society, defend capitalism, tolerate machismo, believe that Western society is superior to others, and am sexually abstinent, I am simply witnessing to that for which we stand: capitalism, sexism, Western arrogance, and sexual abstinence. The latter is hardly deeply meaningful and understandably questioned.'[23]

We also need to see sexuality clearly and free ourselves from the sexual mythology of contemporary society. We have to demythologise sex. On the one hand a sexual relationship is usually seen as the culmination of all our hungers for communion and the only escape from loneliness. It has been called the last remaining sacrament of transcendence, the only sign that we exist for another, or even that we exist at all. To be without a sexual relationship is therefore to be half dead. On the other hand, sexuality is trivialised. An English *madam* recently declared that sex is of no more importance than having a cup of tea. It is this combination of the deification of sexuality and its trivialisation that makes celibacy so hard to bear. We are both told that we must have it, and that it is ours to have without a moment's thought. The re-education of our human hearts demands that we see sexuality clearly. It is indeed a beautiful sacrament of communion with another, the gift of oneself, and so it can never be trivialised. Yet there are other ways in which we may love fully and completely and so its absence does not condemn us to isolation and loneliness.

Finally, faced with the insatiable desires of the market place, we are invited not to repression, but to hunger for more. We are passionate people, and to kill all passion would be to stunt and wither our humanity. It would make us preachers of death.

23. art. cit., p. 263.

Instead we must be liberated into deeper desires, for the boundless goodness of God. As Oshida, the Japanese Dominican, says,
we beg God to make himself irresistible. Our desires may go
astray not because we ask for too much, but because we have
settled for too little, for tiny satisfactions. 'The ideal is for us not
to control our appetites at all, but to allow them full rein in the
wake of an uncontrolled appetite for God.'[24] The advertisements
that line our roads invite us to struggle against each other, to
trample upon each other in the competition to fulfil our endless
desires; our God offers the satisfaction of infinite desire freely
and as a gift. Let us desire more deeply.

This transformation of desire will surely imply some asceticism. This is a conclusion which I have long resisted! Dominic
surely arrived at his freedom, his spontaneity, his light-heartedness
partly because he was a temperate man, who ate and drank little.
He feasted with his brethren but he also fasted. There is an
asceticism which is not a Manichean rejection of God's world, but
teaches us a proper pleasure in it. 'It is about giving up not desire
itself – which would be inhuman – but its violence. It is about
dying to the violence of pleasure, to its omnipotence.'[25] Temper-
ance measures our appetites against the real needs of our body,
and so rescues us from the delusions of fantasy and the tyranny of
desire.

Bodies

I cannot have a mature relationship to my sexuality until I
learn to accept and even delight in human bodies, my own and
other people's. This is the body that I have, and that I am, getting
older, fatter, losing my hair, evidently mortal. I must be at ease
with other people's bodies, the beautiful and the ugly, the sick

24. Simon Tugwell OP, *Reflections on the Beatitudes*, London, 1980, p. 78.
25. Jean-Louis Brugues OP *Les idees heureuses*, Paris, 1996, p. 56.

and the healthy, the old and young, male and female.

St Dominic founded the Order to rescue people from the tragedy of a dualistic religion, which condemned this created world as evil. Central to our tradition from the beginning is an appreciation of corporeality. It is here that God comes to meet and redeem us, becoming a human being of flesh and blood like us. The central sacrament of our faith is the sharing of his body; our final hope is the resurrection of the body. The vow of chastity is not a refuge from our bodily existence. If God has become flesh and blood, then we can dare to do so as well.

We discover what it means for us to be bodily in that climax of Jesus' life, when he gives his body to us: 'This is my body, given for you.' Here we see that the body is not just a lump of flesh, a bag of muscles, blood and fat. The Eucharist shows us the vocation of our human bodies: to become gifts to each other, the possibility of communion.

The immense pain of celibacy is that we renounce a moment of intense bodiliness, when bodies are given to each other, without reserve. Here the body is seen in its profound identity, not as a lump of flesh but as the sacrament of presence. This sexual act expresses, makes flesh and blood, our deep desire to share our lives. That is why it is a sacrament of Christ's unity with the Church. We religious too, in our corporeality, can make Christ present in our way. The preacher brings the Word to expression, not just in his or her words, but in all that we are. God's compassion seeks to become flesh and blood in us, in our tenderness, even in our faces.

In the Old Testament, we often find the prayer that God's face may shine upon us. This prayer was finally answered in the form of a human face, Christ's face. He looks at the rich young man, loves him and asks him to follow him; he looks at Peter in the courtyard after his betrayal; he looks at Mary Magdalene in the garden and calls her by her name. As preachers, flesh and blood, we can give body to that compassionate look of God. Our bodiliness is not excluded from our vocation.

And the man who is both a preacher and a brother can learn, painfully and probably with very uneven progress, what it means to be a face for God precisely in having a human face, a face that can smile and laugh and weep and look bored ... It is in all our uniqueness and individuality, which is eternally valid and desired by God, that we are also the revelation, the manifestation, the expression of him who is the One Word coming forth from all eternity from the silence of God.[26]

True purity of heart is not about being freed from contamination by this world. It is more about being fully present in what we do and are, having a face and a body that expresses ourselves, beyond deceit and duplicity. The pure in heart are not concealed behind their faces, watching warily. Their faces are transparent, unprotected, with the nakedness and vulnerability of Christ. They have his freedom and spontaneity. 'Only he who has a pure heart can laugh in a freedom that creates freedom in others.'[27]

Generativity

Perhaps more than anything else, I have missed not having children. And if I, as a man, feel this, then what can it mean for a woman not to have given birth? This is a fundamental desire we must recognise. Yet if our apostolic life is caught up in the fertile love of God for humanity, then we will be fruitful. Meister Eckhart says that God's love in us is green and fertile. God is in us as 'ever verdant and flowering in all the joy and the glory that he is in himself.'[28] 'God's chief aim is giving birth. He is never

26. Simon Tugwell The Way of the Preacher, London, 1979, p. 96.
27. Joseph Pieper, A Brief Reader on the Virtues of the Human Heart, San Francisco, p. 44.
28. Meister Eckhart, Walshe, op. cit., Sermon 8.

content until he begets his Son in us. And the soul too is not content until the Son is born in her.'[29]

It belongs to our love of the brethren and sisters that we help each other to be fruitful. The apostolic life is not just a matter of endless work. If our apostolates are alive with the abundance of God's own life, then we shall share in his creativity.

But to be a parent is to live through the joy and pain of letting your children go. The consummation of being a parent is to give one's children their freedom, and let them build lives which are different from what we hoped for them. We too must let go what we bring to birth. We know that we have really been fruitful when projects that we have initiated, and to which we have given our lives, take off in new directions, and are in the hands of others. That is hard, but the generosity of parents is to give their children freedom.

HOW MAY WE SUSTAIN ONE ANOTHER?

If we let the love that is God touch us, then we shall slowly become alive. It may seem safer to remain dead, invulnerable, untouchable. But is this so?

Nature abhors a vacuum. Terrible things can happen to a man with an empty heart. In the last resort it is better to run the risk of an occasional scandal than to have a monastery – a choir, a refectory, a recreation room – full of dead men. Our Lord did not say 'I am come that they may have safety and have it more abundantly'. Some of us would indeed give anything to feel safe, about our life in this world, as in the next, but we cannot have it both ways: safety or life, we must choose.[30]

If we choose life, then we shall need communities which support us as we come alive, which help us to grow in a love which is truly

29. ibid, Sermon 68.
30. Gerald Vann OP, op. cit., pp. 46ff.

holy, a sharing in the pouring forth of God's Word.

COMMUNITIES OF HOPE

Above all we should offer each other hope and mercy. Often we are drawn to the Order because we admire the brethren. We hope that we will become like them. Soon we will discover that they are in fact just like us, fragile, sinful and selfish. This can be a moment of profound disillusionment. I remember a novice complaining of this sad discovery. The novice master replied to him, 'I am delighted to hear that you no longer admire us. Now there is a chance that you might come to love us.' The redemptive mystery of God's love is to be seen not in a community of spiritual heroes, but of brothers or sisters, who encourage each other on the journey to the Kingdom with hope and mercy. The risen Lord appears in the midst of a community of timid and weak men. If we wish to meet him we must dare to be there with them. Jordan of Saxony wrote to the brethren of Paris, who were clearly just like us: 'It cannot be that Jesus will appear to those who cut themselves off from the unity of the brotherhood: Thomas, for not being with the other disciples when Jesus came, was denied sight of him: and will you think yourself more holy than Thomas?'[31]

Above all we will need our communities if we fail in love. We may fail because we enter a time of sterility when we feel ourselves to be incapable of any love, when our hearts of flesh have been replaced by hearts of stone. Then we will need them to believe for us that:

> Hidden within the deepest
> self – no matter how
> treacherous one has been

31. ibid, p. 157.

or how corruptible – hidden
within the deepest self
the seed of love remains.[32]

Our communities must be places in which there is no accusation, 'for the accuser of our brethren has been thrown down' (Rev
12:10). We may sin and feel that we have destroyed our vocations,
and that we must leave the Order in shame. Then our brothers
and sisters may have to believe for us in God's mercy when we
may find it hard to believe ourselves. If God can make the dead
tree of Golgotha flower, then he can bring fruit out of my sins. We
may need our brothers to believe, when we cannot, that some
failure is not the end, but that God in his infinite fertility can
make it part of our journey to holiness. Even our sins can be part
of our fumbling attempts to love. All those years of Augustine's
sexual adventures were perhaps part of his searching for the One
who was most beloved, and that chastity was not the cessation but
the consummation of his desire.

COMMUNITY AND SEXUAL ORIENTATION

It is here that cultural differences can be seen most clearly.
Great delicacy is needed if we are to avoid either scandalising or
wounding our brothers and sisters. In some cultures, the admis-
sion of people of homosexual orientation to religious life is
virtually unthinkable. In others it is accepted without question.
Anything that is written about this topic is likely to be scrutinised
to see whether one is 'in favour' or 'against' homosexuality. This
is the wrong question. It is not for us to tell God whom he may or
may not call to religious life. The General Chapter of Caleruega
affirmed that the same demands of chastity apply to all brethren
of whatever sexual orientation, and so no one can be excluded on
this ground. There was much debate at Caleruega over this

32. Paul Murray OP, 'A Song for the Afflicted ' unpublished poem.

question, and I am sure that it will continue.

How can our communities support and sustain brethren as they confront the question of their sexual orientation? First we must recognise that it touches deeply our own sense of who we are. This is therefore a sensitive and important question for many young people who join the Order, for two reasons. First of all there is often a profound hunger for identity. For many young people the overriding question is: 'Who am I?' Secondly, because of the prolonged adolescence which characterises many cultures today, the question of sexual orientation is often not resolved until late. Sometimes we receive requests from brethren for dispensation because only late in life have they realised that they are fundamentally heterosexual and so able to marry.

If a brother comes to believe that he is homosexual, then it is important that he knows that he is accepted and loved as he is. He may live in terror of rejection and accusation. But this acceptance is bread for the journey as he moves to discover a deeper identity, as a child of God. For none of us, heterosexual or homosexual, can find our deepest identities in our sexual orientation. Who we are most deeply, we must discover in Christ. 'Beloved, we are God's children now; it does not appear what we shall be, but we know that when he appears we shall be like him, for we shall see him as he is' (1 Jn 3:2). By our vows we commit ourselves to follow Christ, and to discover our identity in him. It belongs to our poverty that we are carried beyond these small identities.

At the root of all other possessiveness is the ultimately possessive desire to be a self: the desire that there should be at my centre not that unnameable abyss into which as into a vacuum, the nameless God is inevitably drawn, but an identity I can own, an identity which is defined by my ownership of it.[33]

---

33. Rowan Williams, *Open for Judgement*, London, p. 184.

Any brother who makes his sexual orientation central to his public identity would be mistaking who he most deeply is. He would be stopping on the roadside when he is called to walk to Jerusalem. What is fundamental is that we can love and so are children of God, not to whom we are sexually attracted. But it does not only concern an individual's personal sense of identity. We have an identity as each other's brothers and sisters. We are responsible for the consequences for our brethren of how we present ourselves, especially in an area as sensitive as that of sexual orientation.

So, every brother should be accepted as he is. But the emergence of any sub-groups within a community, based on sexual orientation, would be highly divisive. It can threaten the unity of the community, it can make it harder for the brethren to practise the chastity which we have vowed. It can put pressure on brethren to think of themselves in a way that is not central to their vocation as preachers of the Kingdom, and which perhaps they may eventually discover to be untrue.

FALLING LOVE

However much we present friendship as a supreme revelation of that love which is the life of God, yet we may fall in love, and this may be one of the most significant experiences of our lives. One of the first public questions that I was ever asked after my election as Master, at a meeting of a great crowd of Filipino Dominican students, was: 'Timothy, have you ever fallen in love?' And the second question was: 'Was this before or after you joined the Order?' If it happens after we have joined, then we will indeed need the support and love of our communities.

For a brother or sister who has professed their lives to the Order, to fall in love is almost certainly a moment of crisis. But as fr Jean-Jacques Perennes often reminds us in the General Council, a crisis is a moment of opportunity. It can be fruitful. Any experience of love can be an encounter with the God who is love. Falling in love can be the moment when our egocentrism is torn open, and we discover that we are not the centre of the world. It can demolish, at least for a time, that self-preoccupation that kills us. Falling in love is 'for many people the most extraordinary and revealing experience of their lives, whereby the centre of significance is suddenly ripped out of the self, and the dreamy ego is shocked into an awareness of an entirely separate reality.'[34]

Once we have gone through this profound 'unselfing', then we cannot just go on living as if nothing had happened. We cannot pretend that we have never met this person, and that we can return to our old life as if nothing had happened. And this may be one reason why if a brother falls in love he may ask for a dispensation from his vows, for that old life to which he pledged himself is over.

When Thomas Merton, an American Cistercian, was at the height of his fame as a spiritual writer, he fell utterly in love with a nurse who had cared for him in hospital. He wrote in his diary that he was 'tormented by the gradual realisation that we were in love and I did not know how I would live without her.'[35] As Othello says faced with the loss of his beloved Desdemona, she is 'where I have garner'd up my heart, where I must live or bear no life, the fountain from which my current runs, or else dries up.'

Then we cannot imagine a life apart from the person we love and so we have to pray for the gift of a life that indeed we cannot imagine, a life which can only come as a gift from God. On the

34. Iris Murdoch, *The Fire and the Sun: Why Plato Banished the Artists*, Oxford, 1979, p. 36, quoted by Fergus Kerr OP, *Immortal Longings: Versions of Transcending Humanity*, Indiana, 1997, p. 72

35. John Howard Griffin, *Thomas Merton: The Hermitage Years*, London, 1993, p. 60.

cross, Jesus awaits no imaginable life, only the inconceivable and abundant life which the Father will give him. Then we cannot make a life. It must be given.

It is so very hard to let ourselves go into the hands of the Father at this moment, trusting that this death will give way to resurrection. We will need our friends and brothers and sisters as never before, who may have to believe for us, when we cannot, that in this desert we may meet the Lord of life. Possibly we have never before felt so alive, so vital. We may feel that this love is what we have been looking for all our lives. How can we take the risk of losing it? We may become dried up, bad-tempered and frustrated! At this moment we have to trust that if we remain faithful to our vows then God will be faithful too. We will receive life abundantly. Merton's biographer says that finally Merton's experience of falling in love gave him 'an inner liberation, which gave him a new sense of sureness, uncautiousness, defencelessness in his vocation and in the depths of himself.'[36]

It may seem as if I am suggesting that such an experience is almost a necessary step on the road of our spiritual development. This is not what I am saying at all. 'Greater love has no one than this, that he lay down his life for his friends.' As religious we pledge ourselves to receive the fullness of life in mystery of that unpossessive friendship. Also we priests and religious can inflict terrible damage on ourselves and others when we fall in love. We may be seen by others as 'safe' and consider ourselves to be safe too. We can easily abuse others by indulging in a form of 'emotional tourism', which leaves us free to return back to our community when things become dangerous but possibly leaving the other person damaged, and their trust in the Church and even God, undermined for ever.

36. Griffin., op. cit., p. 87.

THE WILDERNESS OF LONELINESS

In our growth as people capable of love, we may sometime have to pass through the wilderness. This may be because we feel ourselves incapable of love, or because we fall in love, or perhaps we fail in our vows. If the apostolic life leads us to the bewilderment of Gethsemane, where life loses all meaning, then crisis in love may confront us with the solitude of the cross.

The experience of loneliness reveals a fundamental truth about ourselves, which is that alone we are incomplete. Contrary to the dominant perception of much of western society, we are not self-sufficient, self-contained beings. Loneliness reveals that I cannot be alive, I cannot be, by myself. I only exist through my relationships with others. Alone I die. This loneliness reveals a void, an emptiness at the heart of my life. We may be tempted to fill it with many things – food, drink, sex, power or work. But the emptiness remains. The alcohol or whatever is merely a disguised thirst for God. I suspect that we cannot even fill it with the presence of other people. A room full of lonely people changes nothing. 'The awfulness of this loneliness shows itself precisely in the fact that all share it and none can relieve it.'[37] When Merton fell in love, then he discovered that what he was looking for was perhaps not his beloved, but a solution to the hollow at the centre of his heart. She was 'the person whose name I would try to use as magic to break the grip of the awful loneliness of my heart.'[38]

Ultimately I suspect that this loneliness must not simply be endured. It must be lived as an entry into the loneliness of Christ in his death, which bears and transforms all human loneliness. 'My God, my God, why have you abandoned me?' If we do that, then the veil of the temple will be torn in half and we shall

37. Sebastian Moore OSB, *The Inner Loneliness*, London, 1982.
38. op. cit., p. 58.

discover the God who is at the heart of our being, granting us existence in every moment: '*Tu autem eras interior intimo meo.*' 'You are closer to me than I am to myself.'[39] If we take upon ourselves the cross of loneliness and walk with it, then it will be revealed that the modern perception of the self is not true. The deepest truth of ourselves is that we are not alone. At the deepest point of my being is God giving me the abundance of life. St Catherine describes herself in the *Dialogue* as 'dwelling in the cell of self-knowledge in order to know better God's goodness toward her.' Profound self-knowledge reveals not the solitary self of modernity but the one whose existence is inseparable from the God who grants us life in every moment.

If we can enter this desert and there encounter God, then we will become free to love unpossessively, freely, without domination or manipulation. We will be able to see others not as solutions to my needs or answers to my loneliness but simply there, to be delighted in: 'Therefore stand still and do not waver from your emptiness'. It was at the foot of the cross, where Jesus gave his mother and the beloved disciple to each other, that the community of the Church was born

THE LIFE OF PRAYER

I have called you friends, for all that I have heard from my Father I have made known to you (Jn 15:15).

The person who is touched by the abundance of life loves unpossessively, spontaneously, joyfully. His heart of stone becomes a heart of flesh. This deep transformation of our humanity implies, according to our tradition, both study and prayer. Jordan of Saxony tells us that they are both as necessary to us as food and drink. Through study we remake the human heart. We discover

39. St Augustine, *Confessions* 3. 6 11.

that 'intellectual illumination which breaks forth into the affection of love'.[40] Both study and prayer belong to the contemplative
life to which every Dominican is called. I will share a few
thoughts about prayer and the fullness of life.

COMMUNITIES OF THE WORD

At the end of most visitations, the visitator will make some
edifying remarks about the need to pray more. We will nod
sagely and make vague resolutions. Does one have the impression that what is at issue is how these dry bones shall live?

When a child is born, its parents immediately begin to talk to
it. Long before it can understand, a child is fed with words,
bathed and soothed with words. The mother and father do not
talk to their child so as to communicate information. They are
talking it into life. It becomes human in this sea of language.
Slowly it will be able to find a place in the love that its parents
share. It grows into a life that is human.

So too we are transformed by immersion in the Word of God,
addressed to us. We do not read the Word so as to seek information. We ponder it, study it, meditate on it, live with it, eat and
drink it. 'These words which I command you this day shall be
upon your heart; and you shall teach them diligently to your
children, and shall talk of them when you sit in your house, and
when you walk by the way, and when you lie down, and when
you rise.' (Deut 6:6f). This word of God works in us, making us
human, bringing us to life, forming us too in that friendship
which is the very life of God. As Jordan wrote to Diana in his
Christmas letter of 1229, 'Read over this Word in your heart, turn
it over in your mind, let it be sweet as honey on your lips; ponder
it, dwell on it, that it may dwell with you and in you for ever.'[41]

40. *Summa Theologiae* 1, q. 43, a 5, ad 2.
41. Letter 41, trans G. Vann, op.cit., p. 112.

Some friends of mine adopted a child. They found him in a vast hospital ward in Saigon, an orphan of the Vietnamese war. For the first months in the ward no one had had the time to look or speak to him. He grew up unable to smile. But his adoptive parents talked to him and smiled at him, with a labour of love. I remember the day on which he first smiled back. The Word of God nurtures us, so that we come alive, human, and even able to smile back at God. A community that offers life will be one in which we find that Word of God treasured and shared. It is not enough just to say more prayers. These may stifle us, especially if recited at great speed. When Dominic prayed he relished the word of God, 'savouring the words of God in his mouth and, as it were, enjoying reciting them to himself' (fifth of the Nine Ways of Prayer of St Dominic), like someone enjoying a good French wine. Albert the Great says that we need 'to be nourished often by the charm [again *dulcedo*] of the word of God.' [42]

As the child is fed by the words of its parents, then it makes the liberating and terrifying discovery that it is not the centre of the world. Behind the breast there is a mother. Everything is not at its command. It discovers itself as part of the human community. In the conversation of our parents, we discover a world in which we may belong. So, too, as we are nourished by the Word of God, we are led into a larger world. The Good Shepherd, who has come that we may have life and have it more abundantly, is the one who opens the gate, so that we may come out and find large open spaces. In prayer we make an exodus, beyond the tiny shell of our self-obsession. We enter the larger world of God. Prayer is a 'discipline that stops me taking myself for granted as the fixed centre of a little universe, and allows me to find and lose and re-find myself constantly in the interweaving patterns of a world I

42. A sermon, *Recherches de Theologie Ancienne et Medievale* 36 1969, p. 109.

did not make and do not control.'[43]

The child ripens in the conversation of its parents, and discovers that it is not alone. So too we are caught up into God's friendship, and are healed of self-obsession and begin to glimpse the real world. Yeats wrote, 'We had fed the heart on fantasies; the heart's grown brutal from the fare.'[44] Prayer heals our hearts of fantasies. St Thomas says that praying the Our Father 'gives shape to our whole affective life.'[45] Praying that God's will be done and that the Kingdom come, our hearts are remade.

As we are liberated from our self-obsessed fantasies and enter God's larger world, we discover that others suffer violence and sorrow. fr Vincent de Couesnongle talked of 'the contemplation of the street'. For Dominic, the afflicted and the oppressed 'form part of the *"contemplata"* in *"contemplata aliis tradere"* ... The wound of knowledge that opens up Dominic's mind and heart in contemplation, allowing him with an awesome unprotectedness to experience his neighbour's pain and his neighbour's need cannot be accounted for simply by certain crowding memories of pain observed or by his own natural sympathy.'[47] It is, fr Paul Murray says, a 'contemplative wound'. That is why the contemplative life is at the heart of any search for a just world. Contemplation makes us capable of seeing selflessly.

COMMUNITIES OF CELEBRATION AND SILENCE

As a child grows up, it will stop screaming and become capable of both speech and silence. It will learn both to talk and to hear. So too for us, building communities of prayer implies more than

43. Rowan Williams, op.cit., p. 120.
44. 'Meditations in Time of Civil War', *Collected Poems*, London, 1969, p. 230.
45. II II, q. 83, a. 8.
46. Master of the Order 1974-1983; died July 1992.
47. Paul Murray OP, 'Dominicans Grounded in Contemplative Experience', a talk given at River Forest, Chicago, June 1997.

adding another psalm to Vespers. We have to create environments in which we can both speak and hear, rejoice and be silent. This is the ecosystem that we need if we are to flourish.

In the Dominican tradition, speaking to God is above all else asking for what we want. This is not infantile but realism. It shows that we are waking up from the little fantasy world of the market, in which everything is for sale, and recognising that in the real world everything is a gift from the one who is the 'the source of all that is good for us' (II II, q. 83 a. 2, ad 3). When we begin to ask, then we are on the way to adulthood. When we pray together, then do we dare to ask from God what we most deeply desire? Or do we merely recite a few petitions from the breviary?

The exodus from the Egypt of self-obsession is a moment of ecstasy. We are liberated from the dark and cramped little world of the ego. Like Miriam after the crossing of the Red Sea we will surely be exuberant. We exult in having entered the wide open spaces of God's friendship. David danced wildly before the ark; Mary exulted in the Lord, and the marvellous things he had done for her. The prayer of the preacher should surely be exultant, ecstatic. We are called 'To praise, to bless, to preach'. When the psalms say 'Let us sing a new song to the Lord', then let us do so! Dominic was exuberant in his prayer. He used his whole body, stretching out his arms, lying on the ground, genuflecting and making a lot of noise. The whole body is saved by grace and so prays. Some of my most beautiful memories of praying are with the brethren. I think of the ecstatic Eucharist celebrated in Haiti, in the midst of poverty and violence, of the dance and song of our Zulu sisters in South Africa, of the marvellous and passionate singing at the Easter Vigil in Krakow, of fire crackers and gongs one year later in Taiwan. Do we celebrate the liturgy, and exult together in the Lord who has done marvellous things for us? Do we regard it merely as an obligation to be fulfilled? It is an obligation indeed, that most solemn obligation which comes from friendship. We delight to do things for our friends.

Eckhart wrote that 'the very best and noblest attainment in this life is to be silent and let God work and speak within.'[48] There is no friendship without silence. Unless one has learnt to stop, be quiet and listen to another, then one remains locked in one's own little world, of which one is the centre and the only real inhabitant. In silence we make the wonderful and liberating discovery that we are not gods, but just creatures.

There are different types of silence. There is the silence of the women at the tomb, who 'said nothing to anyone because they were afraid' (Mk 16:8). It is the silence with which we exclude the utterly unexpected, the new, the unthinkable. It is the silence by which I shut out unwelcome words which may rob me of peace of mind. And then there is the silence of the disciples on the road to Emmaus, as they listen to the Lord as he expounds the scriptures to them. Then they say nothing, but afterwards they exclaim 'Did not our hearts burn within us, as he talked to us on the road, while he opened to us the scriptures?' (Lk 24:32) Paul Philibert OP has called prayer our openness to God's secret initiatives.[49] In that vulnerable silence we let him do new and unexpected things. We are open to be astonished by the novelty of the God of surprises: 'Behold I make all things new' (Rev 21:5).

This is the silence that prepares the way for a word of preaching. Ignatius of Antioch said that the Word came out from the silence of the Father. It was a strong, clear, decisive and truthful Word, because it was born in silence. He 'was not Yes and No; but in him it was always yes. For all the promises of God find their Yes in him' (2 Cor 1:19f). Often our words lack authority, because they are yes and no; they hint and nudge; they are coloured by

48. *Sermons and Treatises*, trans. M O'C Walshe, vol I, London, 1979, p. 6.
49. *Living in the Meantime*, New York, 1994, p. 126.

innuendoes and ambiguities, they carry little arrows and small resentments. We must create that silence in which true words can be conceived and shared.

How can we rediscover such a silence in ourselves and in our communities? In my experience there is no way other than simply taking the time to be silent in God's presence every day (cf LCO 66.11). This is the discipline that I have sought and evaded, attained and let slip ever since I joined the Order. In it I spend most of the time thinking of food and faxes. For this contemplative silence we need each other's support. We need communities which help us to grow in tranquil silence. A Buddhist monk told Merton, 'Before you can meditate you've got to learn not to slam doors'. Anyone who lives near me knows that I have not mastered that art yet! Each community needs to reflect upon how it can create times and places of silence.

This is not the depressing silence of the morgue which one sometimes found in the past, the silence which shuts out other people. We hunger for a silence which prepares for communication rather than refuses it. It is the comfortable silence which comes before and after we share a word, rather than the awkward silence of those who have nothing to say to each other. When I was a child, my younger brother and I often went into the woods, to look for animals and birds. The secret was learning to be silent together. It was a communion in shared attentiveness. Maybe we can find that, as we listen together for the word that may come.

THE WILDERNESS OF DEATH AND RESURRECTION

Jesus summons us to have life and to have it abundantly. This is the good news that we preach. Yet we have seen that in answering that summons we may find ourselves led into the wilderness. As preachers of the word, we may discover that we have no word to offer, that nothing makes sense anymore. As those who preach the love of God, we discover that we are desolate, alone and abandoned. As those who are invited to find ourselves in God's own life, we will be confronted with our mortality.

We are creatures and not gods, and we must die. Then we may cry out like the Israelites to Moses, 'Is it because there are no graves in Egypt that you have taken us away to die in the wilderness?' (Ex 14:11) Then we must 'stand firm and not waver in our emptiness', trusting that life will be given.

How are we to sustain and encourage each other as we face mortality? First we must stimulate each other with the freedom of Jesus. Knowing that the Son of man must die, he turned his face to go to Jerusalem. This is a freedom that I have seen sometimes in the brothers and sisters, giving away their lives. In the years before he was assassinated, fr Pierre Claverie OP, Bishop of Oran in Algeria, took the road to Jerusalem, as he refused to give in to threats and leave his people. In 1994 he said in a sermon, 'I have struggled for dialogue and friendship between people, cultures and religions. All that probably earns me death, but I am ready to accept that risk.' [50]

Jesus' freedom in the face of death found its culmination in the night before he died, when he took his body and gave it to his disciples, a gesture of astonishing liberty. This is what it is given to us to do together, in the face of mortality. I remember one Easter morning at Blackfriars, joyfully celebrating the Eucharist with a brother dying of cancer. All of the community was crammed in his room. Afterwards we drank champagne in honour of the resurrection. I remember celebrating the Eucharist with the brothers and sisters in Iraq a few weeks ago, as we waited for the military attack that would surely come. The Eucharist

50. Sermon after the death of Br Henri and of Sister Paule-Helene, *La Vie Spiri-tuelle*, October 1997, p. 764.

should not be the centre of our common life because we feel that we are united, or even so that we may come to feel so. It is the sacrament of that abundant life which is purely a gift, the 'bread of life' which Dominic promised we would find in the Order. We receive it together, offering each other food for the wilderness.

We live out the meaning of that Eucharist in setting each other free, infecting each other with Christ's immeasurable freedom. It may be in the small freedom of forgiveness freely given, or letting ourselves break some old pattern of life, of taking a risk. We let go. As Lacordaire wrote, 'I go where God leads me, uncertain of myself but sure of him'. In all these ways we let ourselves be caught up in the sweep of the Spirit coming forth from the Father and the Son, crying within us 'Abba Father'. As Eckhart says, 'We do not pray, we are prayed'. Yet it is also our entry into freedom and spontaneity, when we become most alive. We let ourselves be caught by the movement, like a dancer who gives in to the rhythm, and finds in it grace and freedom.

Wisdom danced in the presence of God while she made the world. St Thomas says that the contemplation of the wise person is like play, because it is pleasurable and because it is done for its own sake, like a dance. 'Unmitigated seriousness betokens a lack of virtue, because it wholly despises play which is as necessary for a good human life as is rest.' [51] The abundance of life leads us into that playfulness of those who have laid down the burden of being little gods. We can drop that terrible seriousness of those who believe that they carry the world upon their shoulders. Then our communities may indeed be places in which we will begin to know the happiness of the Kingdom. Saint Dominic, *Nos junge beatis*. Join us to the blessed, and may we share some glimpse of their happiness there now.

51. *Eth ad Nic* iv ib 854.

INITIAL FORMATION

Our brothers and sisters in initial formation are a gift of God to the Order, and we honour the Creator in welcoming his gifts. This we must do by giving you the best possible formation. The future of the Order depends upon it, which is why every General Chapter of the Order spends so much time discussing formation. Over the last few years the Order has produced excellent documents about formation, and so rather than write a long letter on formation and repeat all that has been said, I have thought it better to collect these documents together so that you and your formators can easily study them. But I do wish to share just a word addressed directly to you, my brothers and sisters who are at the beginning of your Dominican life, knowing that some of your formators may be looking over your shoulder. I shall talk in terms of the formation of the brothers, since that is what I know about more. I hope that it will also be relevant to the experience of our sisters.

One of my greatest pleasures during my visits to the Order has been the meetings with you. I have been moved by your enthusiasm for the Order, your desire to study and to preach, your true Dominican joy. But formation will also entail moments of pain, disorientation, discouragement, and a loss of meaning. Sometimes you will wonder why you are here, and whether you should remain. Such moments are a necessary and painful part of formation, as you grow as a Dominican. If they did not happen, then your formation would not be touching you deeply.

Formation in our tradition is not the moulding of passive matter, so as to produce a standard product, 'A Dominican'. It is our accompaniment of you as you freely respond to the threefold

---

A letter to brothers and sisters in initial formation, issued from Santa Sabina, Rome, on the feast of Blessed Jordan of Saxony, 14 February 1999.

call that you receive: from the Risen Lord who invites you to follow him, from the brethren and sisters who invite you to become one of them, and to the demands of the mission. If you respond fully and generously to these demands, then you will be changed. It will ask of you death, trusting in the Lord who gives resurrection. This will be both painful and liberating, exciting and frightening. It will form you as the person whom God calls you to be. This is a process that will continue throughout your Dominican life. The years of initial formation are just the beginning. I write this letter to you to offer some encouragement on the journey. Do not give up when it is hard!

I shall take as my text to explore this theme – the meeting of Mary Magdalene, the patroness of the Order, with Jesus in the garden (Jn 20:11-18).

'WHOM DO YOU SEEK?'

When Jesus meets Mary Magdalene, he asks her: 'Whom do you seek?' Our life in the Order begins with a similar question, as we lay stretched out on the floor: 'What do you seek?' It is the question that Jesus put to the disciples at the beginning of the gospel.

You have to come to the Order with a hunger in your heart, but for what? Is it because you have discovered the gospel recently and wish to share it with everyone? Is it because you met a Dominican whom you admired and wish to imitate? Is it to run away from the world with all its complications, from the pain of forming human relationships? Is it because you have always wished to be a priest, and yet feel that you need a community? Is it because you wonder about the meaning of your life, and wish to discover it with us? Whom do you seek? What do you seek? We cannot answer that question for you, but we can be with you as you face it yourself and help you to arrive at an honest answer.

During our Dominican life, we may answer that question differently at different moments. The reasons that brought us to the Order may not be the reasons why we stay. When I joined the Order I was drawn above all by the hunger to understand my faith. The motto of the Order, *Veritas*, attracted me. I doubted whether I would ever have the courage to preach a sermon. Later I stayed because this desire caught hold of me. Sometimes we may not be at all clear why we are still here and for what we long. We may cling to no more than a vague feeling that this is where we are called to be. Most of us stay in the end because, like Mary Magdalene in the garden, we are looking for the Lord. A vocation is the story of a desire, a hunger. We stay because we are hooked by love, and not by the promise of personal fulfilment or a career. Eckhart says:

> For love resembles the angler's hook. The angler cannot get the fish till it is caught on the hook. He who hangs on to this hook is caught so fast that foot and hand, mouth, eyes and heart, and all that is this person's belongs only to God. Just watch for this hook, so as to be blessedly caught, for the more you are caught, the more you are free.[1]

Perhaps you will discover that you are indeed searching for the risen Lord, but that you are called to find him in another form of life, perhaps as a married disciple. Perhaps God called you to the Order for a while, to prepare you to be a preacher in another way.

The joy of this Easter meeting is at the heart of our Dominican life. This is a happiness which we share in our preaching. But we grow in this happiness only by passing through moments of loss. The one whom Mary Magdalene loves has disappeared. 'Sir, if you have carried him away, tell me where you have laid him, and I will take him away.' She grieves for the loss of the person she

1. M. Walshe, *Meister Eckhart*, Vol. 1, London, pp. 46-47.

loves. Sometimes entry into the Order may be marked by that same experience of desolation. Perhaps you joined full of enthusiasm. You were going to give yourself to God, have hours of ecstatic prayer. But God appears to have slipped away. Praying becomes the tedious repetition of long psalms at the wrong times, with brethren who sing badly. We may even think that it is the brethren who are to blame for God's disappearance, with their lack of devotion. Why do they not even turn up to Office? Their teaching may seem to undermine the faith that brought me here. The Word of God is dissected in their lectures, and we are told that it is not literally true. Where have they buried my Lord?

'Jesus said to her, "Mary". She turned and said to him in Hebrew "Rabboni" (which means Teacher).'

We have to lose Christ if we are to find him again, astonishingly alive and unexpectedly close. We have to let him go, be desolate, grieve for his absence, so that we may discover God closer to us than we could ever have imagined. If we do not go through that experience, then we will be stuck in a childish and infantile relationship with God. It belongs to our formation that we may become disorientated, like Mary confused in the garden, not knowing what is happening. Otherwise we can never be surprised by a new intimacy with the risen Lord. And it must happen again and again as the angler reels us in. The lost Lord appears and speaks to her, and then tells her to let him go again: 'Do not cling to me'.

When they seem to have taken away the body of the Lord, do not give up and go away. When Jesus disappeared, then Peter, like a typical man, went back to work. That may be a temptation, to go back to take up again our old lives. Mary did not give up but went on looking, even if only for a dead body. If we endure, then, like her, we shall be surprised. I remember a long period of desolation, during the years of simple profession. I did not doubt the existence of God, but God seemed unimaginably distant, and nothing much to do with me. It was years later, after solemn profession, in the garden of Gethsemane in Jerusalem one summer, that the void was filled. I may have to endure that absence again one day, and then maybe it will be you, my brothers and sisters, who will help me carry on until the next surprise encounter.

Jesus says to her just one word, her name: 'Mary'. God always calls us by name. 'Samuel', God called three times in the night. Who we are, our deepest identity, we discover in responding to the call of our name. 'The Lord called me from the womb, from the body of my mother he named my name' (Is 49:1). So our Dominican vocation is not a matter of finding a job, or even a useful service of Church and society. It is my 'Yes' to the God who summons me to be, 'Yes' to the brethren with whom I live, and 'Yes' to the mission upon which I am sent. I am summoned into life, like one who was called out of the tomb by a voice shouting, 'Lazarus, come forth'.

So we can say that the fundamental goal of formation is to help us become Christians, to say 'Yes' to Christ. If it does not do that, then we are playing games. But does that mean that becoming a Dominican is unimportant, a mere incidental? No, because it is Dominic's way of following Christ. Perhaps the earliest name for Christianity was 'The Way' (Acts 9:2). When Dominic took to the roads in the south of France, he discovered a way to the Kingdom. The Order offers us a way of life, with its common prayer, its form of government, its way of doing theology and being a brother. When we make profession, then we trust that this strange way of life can lead us to the Kingdom.

So I do not wait to be a good Christian before I become a preacher. Sharing the word of God with others is part of my search for the Lord in the garden. When I struggle to find a word

to preach then I am like Mary Magdalene begging the gardener
to tell me where they have put the body of my Lord. If I can share
my wrestling with the word, then I can share also that moment
of revelation when the Lord speaks my name. I must dare to look
into the tomb and see the absence of the body if I am also to share
the subsequent encounter. To be a preacher is to share all the
moments in that drama in the Easter garden: desolation, interro-
gation, revelation. But if I speak as someone who knows it all,
untroubled by doubt, then people may be very impressed by my
knowledge, but they may feel it has little to do with them.

'GO TO MY BRETHREN'

Jesus calls Mary Magdalene by name, and sends her to his
brethren. We respond to God's call by becoming one of the
brethren.

Becoming a brother is more than joining a community and
putting on a habit. It implies a profound transformation of my
being. Being the blood brother of someone is more than having
the same parents; it implies relationships which have slowly
formed me to be the person that I am. In a similar way becoming
one of Dominic's brothers will ask of me a patient and, sometimes
painful, transformation of whom I am. There will be times,
perhaps prolonged, of death and resurrection.

It is true that most Dominican brethren are priests, and that we
belong to 'a clerical institute', but ordination does not make us
any the less brethren. During my years of formation I came to
love being one of the brethren. I wished for no more. I accepted
ordination because my brothers asked it of me, and for the sake
of the mission. I came to value being a priest, because the
communion and mercy that are at the heart of our fraternal life
found sacramental expression for the wider Church. But I was
just as much a brother as before. There is no higher title in the

Order. This is one reason why I believe that the promotion of the vocation of the co-operator brethren – a term that I have never liked – is so important for the future of the Order. They remind us of who we all are, Dominic's brothers. There can be no second class brethren in the Order.

When I was a student, I remember the visit of a priest from another province to our community in Oxford. When he arrived, there was a Dominican sweeping the hall. The visitor asked him, 'Are you a brother?' 'Yes' he replied. 'Brother, go and get me a cup of coffee.' After his coffee, he told the brother to take his bags to his room. And finally the visitor said, 'Now, brother, I wish to meet the Father Prior'. He replied, 'I am the Prior'.

DIFFERENT VISIONS OF BEING A BROTHER

To be a brother is to find that you belong with us. You are at home with the brethren. But we Dominicans may have many different conceptions as to what it means to be a brother.

One of the shocks of joining the noviciate may be to discover that my fellow novices may have come with very different visions of the Dominican life than my own. When I joined I was powerfully attracted not only by the search for *Veritas*, but also by Dominic's poverty. I imagined myself in the streets begging for my bread. I soon discovered that most of my fellow novices considered that to be foolish romanticism. Some of you will be drawn because of a love of study; others because of a desire to struggle for a more just world. You may be scandalised to see other novices unpacking enormous quantities of books or a CD-player. Some of you may wish to wear the habit for twenty-four hours a day and others will remove it as soon as possible. We easily trample on each other's dreams.

Often there is such a tension between generations of brethren. Some young people who come to the Order these days value highly the tradition and the visible signs of Dominican identity: studying St Thomas, the traditional songs or anthems of the Order, wearing the habit, celebrating our saints. Often brethren of a previous generation are puzzled by this desire for a clear and visible Dominican identity. For them the adventure had been to leave behind old forms that seemed to stand between us and preaching the gospel. We had to be on the road, with the people, seeing things through their eyes, anonymous if we were to be close. Occasionally this can lead to a certain misunderstanding, even a mutual suspicion. The Provinces which are thriving today are often those which have succeeded in getting beyond such ideological conflicts. How can we build a fraternity which is deeper than these differences?

First of all, we may come to recognise the same deep evangelical impulse in each other. In the habit or out of the habit, we preach the same Risen Lord. I have always found myself at home with the brethren, whether sitting with a few brethren by a river in the Amazon reciting the psalms in our shirtsleeves, or celebrating an elaborate polyphonic liturgy in Toulouse. Besides the objective demands of the vows and the Constitutions, one recognises certain family resemblances: a quality of joy; a sense of the equality of all the brethren; a passion for theology, even of quite contradictory tendencies; a trust in our democratic tradition; a lack of pretension. All these hint at a way of life we share, however great the superficial differences.

Secondly, our different visions of the Dominican life may be formed by different moments in the history of the Church and the Order. Many of us who became Dominicans at the time of the Second Vatican Council, grew up in a confident Catholicism, sure of its identity. Our adventure was to reach out to those far from Christ by overthrowing the barriers. What drives brothers and sisters of that generation is sometimes the desire to be close to the invisible Christ who was present in every factory, in every *barrio*, every university. Visible identity was suppressed for the sake of the preaching. Our worker-priests, for example, were a sign of the God who is close even to those who appear to have forgotten his name.

Many who come to the Order today, especially in the West, have made a different pilgrimage, growing up far from Christianity. Perhaps now you wish to celebrate and affirm the faith you have embraced and come to love. You wish to be seen as Dominicans, for that too belongs to the preaching. It can be just the same evangelical impulse which leads some brethren to put on the habit and others to take it off.

This tension is ultimately fruitful and necessary for the vitality of the Order. Accepting the young into the Order challenges us. Just as the birth of a child changes the life of the whole family, so each generation of young who come to us change the brotherhood. You come with your questions to which we have not always got the answers, with your ideals, which may reveal our inadequacies, your dreams which we may not share. You come with your friends and your families, your cultures and your tribes. You come to disturb us, and that is why we need you. Often you come demanding what is indeed central to our Dominican life, but which we may have forgotten or belittled: a more profound and beautiful common prayer; a deeper fraternity in which we care more for each other; the courage to leave behind our old commitments and take to the road again.

Often the Order is renewed because the young come to us and insist on trying to build the Dominican life that they have read about in books! Go on insisting!

It is easy for us who came before you to say, with some irritation: 'You are joining us; we are not joining you.' This is indeed true, but only half so. For when we joined the Order, we gave ourselves into the hands of the brethren who were still to come. We pledged obedience to those who were not born. It is true that we do not have to re-invent the Order in each generation, but part of Dominic's genius was to found an Order that has adaptation and flexibility as part of its being. We need to be renewed by those who have been caught by enthusiasm for Dominic's vision. We must not recruit you to fight our old battles. We have to resist the temptation to box you into the categories of our youth, and label you as 'conservatives' or 'progressives', just as you have to refrain from dismissing us as relics of 'the seventies'.

You too will be challenged by those who came before you, or at least I hope so. Accepting that there are different ways of being a Dominican does not mean that anyone can just invent his own interpretation. I cannot, for example, decide that for me the vows are compatible with keeping a mistress and a sports car. Our way of life includes certain inescapable and objective demands, which ultimately must invite me to undergo a profound transformation of my being. If I avoid that, then I will never become one of the brethren.

Above all, different conceptions of being a Dominican should never really divide us because the unity of the Order does not lie in a common ideological line, even a single spirituality. If it had, then we would have splintered long ago. What holds us together is a way of life which allows for great diversity and flexibility, a common mission, and a form of government that gives a voice to each person. The Dominican lion and the Dominican lamb can live together and enjoy each other's company.

At the beginning of the life of the Order, *The Lives of the Brethren* was written to record the memory of the first generation of our brothers. We are bound together as a community by the stories of the past as well as by the dreams of the future. Visible

signs of Dominican identity do have their value and say something important of who we are, but they should not become the
battle standards of different parties. The Dominicans whose
memory we rightly treasure were often those who were so caught
up in the passion for preaching that they did not have time to
reflect too much about their identity as Dominicans. As Simon
Tugwell wrote, 'throughout the whole story, when the Order has
been most true to itself, it has been least concerned with being
Dominican'.[2]

Formation should indeed give us a strong Dominican identity,
and teach us about our history and our tradition. This is not so
that we can contemplate the glory of the Order, and how important we are, or were, but so that we can take to the road and walk
together after the poor and itinerant Christ. A strong sense of
identity frees us from thinking about ourselves too much, otherwise we will be too self-preoccupied to hear the voice which asks
us: 'Whom do you seek?'

So brotherhood is based on more than a single vision. It is built
patiently, by learning to listen to each other, to be strong and to
be fragile, learning fidelity to each other and love of the brethren.

TALKING AND LISTENING

We know that we are at home when we can talk easily with
each other, confident that our brothers will at least try to understand us. This is probably our expectation when we join the
Order. Jesus says to Mary Magdalene, 'Go to my brothers and say
to them, I am ascending to my God and your God, to my Father
and your Father'. She is commissioned to share her faith in the
risen Lord, even though her brothers may regard her as deluded.
So we build a common home in the Order by daring to share what

2. Simon Tugwell 'Dominican Spirituality' in *Compendium of Spirituality* ed. E
    De Cea OP, New York, 1996, p. 144.

brought us here. Sometimes it will be hard. We probably came expecting to find like-minded people, with the same dreams and the same way of thinking. But we may discover that others have come to the Order by such different paths that we cannot recognise ourselves in what they say. We may hesitate to expose what is most precious, our fragile faith, to criticism and examination. Sharing our faith demands of us great vulnerability. Sometimes it may be easier to do so with people with whom we do not have to live.

One of the main challenges for the formators is to build up trust so that you may dare to talk freely. Martin Buber wrote that, 'The decisive thing is whether the young people are ready to talk. If someone treats them with trust, shows them that he believes in them, they will talk to him. The first necessity is that the teacher must arouse in his pupils that most valuable thing of all – genuine trust'.[3] Just as important is that you trust each other. You may even at times have the courage to share your doubts.

Contemporary western culture systematically cultivates suspicion. We are taught to probe beneath what others say to what is not acknowledged, concealed and even unconscious. In the Church this can sometimes take the form of hunting for error, scanning statements for heresies. Is this brother a true disciple of St Thomas Aquinas or of liberation theology? Is he one of us? It is easier to discover how a brother is wrong and has denied a dogma of the Church, or some ideology of my own, than to hear the little grain of truth that he may be struggling to share with us. But such suspicion is subversive of fraternity. It comes from fear and only love casts out fear.

Learning to listen to each other charitably is a discipline of the mind. Benedict Ashley wrote, 'There has to be a new asceticism

3. *Encounter with Martin Buber*, Aubrey Hodes, London, 1972, p. 217.

of the mind, for nothing is more painful than to maintain charity alive in the midst of genuine argument about serious issues.'[4] Loving my brother is not just a pleasant warm emotion, but an intellectual discipline. I have to restrain myself from dismissing what my brother has said as nonsense before I have heard what he is saying. It is the mental asceticism of opening one's mind to an unexpected insight. It will involve learning to be silent, not just while I wait for him to stop speaking, but so that I may hear him. I must still the defensive objections, the urge to stop him before he says another word. I must be quiet and listen.

Conversation builds a community of equals, and that is why we must build the community of the Dominican Family by taking the time to talk with our sisters and lay Dominicans, and discover the pleasure of it. Conversation builds the larger home of Dominic and Catherine. It 'demands equality between participants. Indeed, it is one of the most important ways of establishing equality. Its enemies are rhetoric, disputation, jargon, and private language, or despair at not being listened to and not being understood. To flourish, it needs the help of midwives of either sex ... Only when people learn to converse will they begin to be equal.'[5] One of the challenges for us brethren is to let the sisters form us as preachers. The most profound formation is always mutual.

BEING STRONG AND WEAK

We belong and are at home when we find that we are stronger than we ever believed, and weaker than we dared to admit. And these are not contrary qualities, for they are signs that we are beginning to be conformed to the strong and vulnerable Christ.

We are formed in the first place as Christians. In our tradition

4. *The Dominicans*, Collegeville, 1990, p. 236.
5. Theodore Zeldon, *An Intimate History of Humanity*, London, 1995, p. 49.

this means not so much the progressive submission to commandments, to tame our unruly natures, as the growth in virtue. Becoming virtuous makes us strong, single-hearted, free and able to stand on our own two feet. As Jean Luis-Bruguès OP has written, virtue is an apprenticeship in humanity. 'It is in the passage from virtuality to virtuosity.'[6]

Becoming a brother means that we receive our strength from each other. We are not soloists. It is a strength that makes us free, but with each other not from each other. In the first place we become strong because we have confidence in each other. At the origin of our tradition is Dominic's endless confidence in the brethren. He trusted the brethren because he trusted in God. As John of Spain wrote, 'He had such confidence in God's goodness that he sent even ignorant men to preaching saying, "Do not be afraid, the Lord will be with you and will put power in your mouths".'[7]

So the first task of your formator is to build up that trust and confidence. But it is also the responsibility that you have for each other, for it is usually those in formation who form each other most. You have the power to undermine a brother, sap his confidence, make fun of him. And you have the power to build each other up, to give each other strength, to form each other as preachers of God's strong word.

It is said in our Constitutions that 'the primary responsibility for his own formation lies with the candidate himself' (LCO 156). We should not be treated as children, incapable of making decisions for ourselves. We grow into brethren, equal members of the community, by being treated as mature adults. In Dominic's day, there was no sign of the traditional monastic *circator*,

6. *Les idées heureuses,* Paris, 1996, p. 24.
7. Bologna Canonization Process 26.

whose job was to go around snooping, seeing whether everyone was doing what they ought. But this is a responsibility that we do not exercise alone. If we are brothers, then we will help each other into the freedom to think, to speak, to believe, to take risks, to transcend fear. We will also dare to challenge each other.

As we grow as brethren, then we will be strong enough to face our weakness and fragility. This is, in the first place, what a friend of mine has called 'the wisdom of creatures'.[8] This is the knowledge that we are created, that our existence is a gift, that we are mortal and live between birth and death. We wake up to the fact that we are not gods. We stand on our own two feet, but our feet are a gift. We will also discover that we have not joined the communion of saints, but a group of men and women who are weak, irresolute, and who must constantly pick themselves up after failure. I have written elsewhere about how this can be a moment of crisis in a brother's formation.[9] The heroes whom a novice had loved and admired turn out to have feet of clay. But this has always been so. That is one reason why we have as Patroness of the Order Mary Magdalene, who, according to tradition, was a weak and sinful woman, but who was called to be the first preacher of the gospel.

More than five hundred years ago Savonarola wrote a letter to a novice who had clearly been scandalised by the sins of the brethren. Savonarola warns him about people who join the Order hoping to enter paradise right away. They never last. 'They wish to live among the saints, excluding all wicked and imperfect people. And when they do not find this, they abandon their vocation and take to the road ... .But if you wish to flee from all the wicked, then you must leave this world.'[10] This confron-

8. Rowan Williams, *Open to Judgement*, London, 1994, p. 248.
9. The Promise of Life especially at pp. 144-145.
10. Letter to Stefano di Codiponte, 22 May 1492.

tation with fragility is often a wonderful moment in the maturing of a vocation. This is when we discover that we are able to give and to receive the mercy which we asked for when we joined the Order. If we can do this, then we are on the road to becoming a brother and a preacher. One of the fears that may inhibit us from trusting in this mercy is the worry, that if the brethren were to see what we are really like, then they might not vote for us for profession. We may be tempted to conceal who we are until we are safely and securely inside, professed and ordained and invulnerable. To accept this would be to settle for a formation in deceit. Formation would become a training in concealment, and this would be a travesty for an Order whose motto is *Veritas*. We must believe in our brethren enough to let them see who we are and what we think. Without such transparency there is no fraternity. This does not mean that we must stand up in the refectory and proclaim our sins, but we cannot create a mask behind which we hide. We dare to embrace such vulnerability because Christ has done so before us. It prepares us to preach a trustworthy and honest word.

FIDELITY AND LOVE OF THE BRETHREN

Finally, there is a quality to brotherhood which is elusive and hard to describe, which I shall call fidelity, according to Peguy 'the most beautiful of words'. At the heart of our preaching is God's fidelity. God has given his word to us, and it is a Word made flesh. It is a word in which we can trust, and which makes of the history of humanity a story which goes somewhere rather than just a succession of random events. It is the strong and solid word of the one who said 'I am who I am'. That is a fidelity which we must seek to embody in our lives. The married couple is a sacrament of God's fidelity, who has joined himself irrevocably to us in Christ. It belongs also to our preaching of the gospel that we are faithful to each other.

What does that mean? In the first place, it is fidelity to the commitment we have made to the Order. God has given us his Word made flesh, even though it led to a senseless death. We have given God our word, even when our promise may appear to ask of us more than we may think possible. I remember, when I was Provincial, talking with an old brother who came to tell me that he was dying of cancer. He was a loveable and good man, who had lived through difficult and uncertain moments in his Dominican life. He told me, 'It looks as if I am going to fulfil my ambition of dying in the Order'. It may look a small ambition, but it is an essential one. He had given his word and his life. He rejoiced that, despite everything, he had not taken back this gift.

Secondly it means that our common mission has priority over my private agenda. I have my talents, my preferences and dreams, but I have given myself to our shared preaching of the good news. This common mission may require of me that I accept some unwanted burden for a while, like being a bursar, a novice- or student-master, or Master of the Order, for the common good. A bus may look much like a common room. It is filled with people who sit together, talking or reading, sharing a common space. But when the bus route departs from the direction of my own journey, then I will leave that bus and continue on my own way. Do I regard the Order as much like a bus, on which I stay only as long as it carries me in the direction I wish to go?

Fidelity also implies that I will stand up for my brethren, for their reputation is mine. In the Primitive Constitutions, and until recently, one of the tasks of the novice master was to teach the novices to 'suspect the good'.[11] One must always give the best possible interpretation of what the brethren did or said. If a

11. Tugwell, op. cit., p. 145.

brother comes back regularly late at night then rather than imagine the terrible sins he may have committed, one must assume that, for example, he had been out visiting the sick. Savonarola writes to that judgmental novice: 'If you see something that does not please you, think that it was done with a good intention. Many are, in themselves, better than you imagine'. This is more than the optimism of the unworldly. It belongs to that love which sees the world with God's eyes, as good. St Catherine of Siena once wrote to Raymond of Capua, reassuring him that he must trust in her love for him, and when we love someone we give the best interpretation to what they do, trusting that they always seek our good: 'Beyond the general love, there is a particular love which expresses itself in faith. And it expresses itself in such a way that it can neither believe or imagine that the other could want anything except our good.'[12]

If my brother is condemned as bad or unorthodox, then fidelity means that I will do everything I can to stand by him, and give the best possible interpretation to his views or actions. It was because of this mutual fidelity that the foreword of the Constitutions of 1228 ruled, as to be observed 'inviolably and unchangeably in perpetuity', that one never can appeal outside the Order against the decisions that the Order made. It should be virtually unimaginable, therefore, that a brother might publicly accuse or disassociate himself from one of his brethren.

This fidelity implies that I will not only stand up for my brother but to him. If he is my brother, then I must care what he thinks, and dare to disagree with him. I cannot leave it just for the superiors, as if it were not my responsibility. But I must do so to his face and not behind his back. We may fear to do this,

12. Mary O'Driscoll OP, *Catherine of Siena: Passion for the truth, Compassion for Humanity*, New City, 1993, p. 48.

expecting hostility and rejection. But, in my experience, if one makes it clear that one is speaking out of a love of the truth and of one's brother, then this has always led to a deepened friendship and understanding.

So these are some of the elements of being formed as a brother: talking and listening to each other; learning to be strong and weak; growing in mutual fidelity. All this belongs to what is most fundamental, which is learning to love the brethren. We Dominicans, with our robust approach to each other, may hesitate to use such language. It may sound sugary and sentimental. Yet it is the ultimate basis of our fraternity. This is what we are required to do by the one who calls us: 'This is my commandment, that you love one another as I have loved you' (Jn 16:12). This is the fundamental commandment of our faith. Obedience to it forms us as Christians and as brethren. St Dominic said that he had learnt 'more in the book of Charity than in the books of men'.[13] It means that ultimately we see each other as a gift from God. My brother or sister may irritate me; I may be totally opposed to their opinions, but I come to delight in them, and see their goodness.

There is a fundamental relationship between love and vocation. It has brought many of you to us. Jesus looked at the rich young man and loved him, and called him to follow him, just as he looked at Mary Magdalene and called her by her name. Stephen of Spain tells us that he went to confession to Dominic, and 'he looked at me as if he loved me.'[14] Later that evening Dominic summoned him and clothed him in the habit. Love is, as Eckhart said, the angler's hook that catches the fish and will not let it go. I must confess that I decided to join the Order before

13. Gerald de Frachet 82.
14. Testimony of brother Stephen of Spain at the Canonization Process of St Dominic.

I ever met a Dominican, drawn by the ideal that I had read about. Perhaps that also can be a blessing!

There is nothing sentimental about this love. Sometimes we have to work at it, and struggle to overcome prejudice and difference. It is the labour of becoming one of the brethren. I remember that once there was a brother with whom it was hard for me to live. Anything that either did or said appeared to irritate the other. One evening we agreed to go out to the pub together, a very English solution. We talked for hours, learned about each other's childhood, and struggles. I could, for the first time, see through his eyes and see myself as I must appear to him. I began to understand. That was the beginning of friendship and fraternity.

'I HAVE SEEN THE LORD'

Mary Magdalene goes to her brothers and says, 'I have seen the Lord'. She is the first preacher of the resurrection. She is a preacher because she is capable of hearing the Lord when he calls, and of sharing the good news of Christ's victory over death.

So becoming a preacher is more than learning a certain amount of information, so that you have something to say, and a few preaching techniques, so that you know how to say it. It is being formed as someone who can hear the Lord, and speak a word that offers life. Isaiah says, 'The Lord called me from the womb, from the body of my mother he named my name. He made my mouth like a sharp sword, in the shadow of his hand he hid me.' (49:1f). All of Isaiah's life, from the very beginning, shaped him as someone who is ready to speak a prophetic word.

The Order should offer you more than a training in theology. It is a life that forms you as a preacher. Our common life, prayer, pastoral experiences, struggles and failures, will make us capable of attention and proclamation in ways that we cannot anticipate.

One of my predecessors, as Provincial, was a brother called Anthony Ross. He was famous as a preacher, an historian, a prison reformer, and even a wrestler! One day, shortly after he was elected Provincial, he suffered a stroke and was reduced almost to silence. He had to resign as Provincial and learn to speak again. The few words he could manage had more power than anything he had said before. People came to confession to him, to hear his simple healing words. His sermons of half a dozen words could change people's lives. It was as if that suffering and that silence formed a preacher who could give us life-giving words as never before. I went to see him before I left for the General Chapter of Mexico, from which, to my great surprise, I did not come back to my Province. His last word to me was 'Courage'. The greatest gift we can give to a brother is such a word.

A COMPASSIONATE WORD

Mary Magdalene announces to the disciples, 'I have seen the Lord'. This is not just the statement of a fact, but the sharing of a discovery. She has shared their loss, their puzzlement, their grief, and so now she can share with them her encounter with the Risen Lord. She can share the good news with them because it is good news for her.

The Word that we preach is a word who shared our humanity, and is 'not a high priest unable to sympathise with our weaknesses, but one who in every respect has been tempted as we are, yet was without sin.' (Heb 4:15). Preaching will demand of us that we became incarnate in different worlds, whether that of the contemporary youth-culture or a Micronesian island, the world of drug addicts or business managers. We have to enter a world, learn its language, see through its inhabitants' eyes, get under their skin, understand their weaknesses and their hopes. We must, in some sense, become them. Then we can speak a word that is good news to them and to us. This does not mean that we must agree with them. Often we may need to challenge them. But we must feel the pulse of their humanity before we can do so.

It is the tradition of the Church to sing the praises of God at dawn. We go on being watchmen waiting for the dawn, so that we can share our hope with others who see no sign of the sun rising. It is because I have somehow glimpsed their darkness, and maybe known it as my own, that I can share a word about the 'loving kindness of the heart of our God, who visits us like the dawn from on high'.

Often we can do this because of who we are and what we have lived. Mary Magdalene searched for the body of the Lord with a tenderness which she had learned in a life that was marked, according to the tradition, by its own failures and sins. It was this life that prepared her to be the person who searched for the man she loved and recognised him when he called her by name. One of the most precious gifts you bring to the Order is your life, with its failures, its difficulties, its dark moments. I can even look back at some sin and see it as a *felix culpa*, because it has prepared me as someone who can speak a word of compassion and hope for others who are living the same defeat. I can share with them the rising of the sun.

In other areas we need a formation in compassion, an education of the heart and the mind that breaks down everything within us that is stony-hearted, priggish, arrogant and judgmental. One of the most useful things that I ever did in my rather unusual noviciate, was to visit regularly the sexual offenders in the local prison. They are perhaps the most despised people in our society. The revelation was that really we were no different from each other. We can listen to the gospel together. So our formation should wear down our defences against those who are different, and unattractive, those whom our society despises: the beggars, the prostitutes, the criminals, the sort of people with whom the Word of God spent his time. We learn to receive the gifts that they can give us, if our hands are open.

The ideal preacher is one who is all things to all human beings, perfectly human. No Dominican that I know is that, and we will be faced with our limitations. For years I went one night a week to a refuge for the homeless in Oxford, to prepare the soup and to talk with them. Yet I must confess that I dreaded it. I hated the smell, and was bored by the drunken conversation; I knew that my soup was not a success and I longed to be home reading books. Yet I do not regret those hours. Maybe the wall between me and my brothers and sisters on the street was somewhat eroded.

Compassion will reshape our lives in ways that we never planned. When St Dominic was a student at Palencia he let himself be touched by compassion for the hungry and sold his books. He only stayed in the south of France and founded the Order because he was moved by the plight of the people caught in a destructive heresy. The whole of his life was moulded by response to situations he never anticipated. This merciful man was at the mercy of others, vulnerable to their needs. Learning compassion will wrestle from our hands the tight control of our lives.

A WORD OF LIFE

'I have seen the Lord.' This is more than the reporting of an event. Mary Magdalene shares with her brethren the triumph of life over death, of light over darkness. It is a word that brings the dawn that she witnessed 'very early in the morning'.

Catherine of Siena tells Raymond of Capua that we must be 'doers rather than undoers and spoilers'.[15] We are formed as

15. Mary O'Driscoll OP, op. cit., p. 48.

preachers through the ordinary conversations that we have with others, the words that we exchange in the common room and the corridors. We discover how to share a word of life in our preaching, by being formed as brethren who offer each other words that give hope, that encourage, build up and heal. If we are people who habitually offer words to other people which hurt, undermine, sap and destroy, then however intelligent and knowledgeable we may be, we can never be preachers. There is a Polish saying, *'Wystygl mistyk; wynik cynik'*, which means: 'The mystic has cooled down; the result is a cynic.' We may be the 'dogs of the Lord' but we can never be cynics.[16]

The word of the preacher is fertile. It fructifies. When Mary Magdalene met Jesus she mistook him for the gardener. Only it is not a mistake, because Jesus is the new Adam in the garden of life, where death is defeated and the dead tree of the cross bears fruit. So the natural allies of the preacher are the creative people in our society. Who are the people struggling to make sense of contemporary experience? Who are the thinkers, the philosophers, the poets and the artists, who can teach us a creative word for today. They too should help to form us as preachers

A WORD THAT WE HAVE RECEIVED

How are we to find this fresh, compassionate creative word? I confessed at the beginning of this letter that when I joined the Order I feared that I would never be able to preach. This is a fear that often is still there. It is embarrassing for a Dominican to confess that when I am asked to preach, often my first reaction still is: 'But I have nothing to say'. But what is to be said will be given, even if sometimes at the last moment. To receive the word that is given, we have to learn the art of silence. In study and in

16. Please forgive a poor joke, and look up the etymology of 'cynic'.

prayer, we learn to be still, attentive, so that we may receive from the Lord what he gives us to share: 'What I received from the Lord, is what I also delivered to you.' (1 Cor 11:23)

Being still is for many the hardest part of formation. Pascal wrote 'I have discovered that the unhappiness of human beings comes from just one thing: not knowing how to remain quietly in a room'.[17] Ultimately the preacher must love 'the pleasures of solitude' because that is when we receive gifts. We have to nail ourselves to our chairs, not so that we may master knowledge, but so that we may be ready and alert when it comes unexpectedly, like a thief in the night. Finally we may come to love this silence as the deepest centre of our Dominican lives. It is the time of gifts, whether in prayer or study.

It demands discipline. 'Truly, you are a God who lies hidden' (Is 45: 15). To detect God's coming, we need ears that are acute, like those of a hunter. Eckhart asks: 'Where is this God, whom all creatures seek, and from whom they have their being and their life? Just like a man who hides himself, and who coughs and so gives himself away, so is God. No one is capable of discovering God, if he did not give himself away.' But God is there, discreetly coughing, giving tiny hints to those who are able to hear if they are silent. Often, later in your Dominican life, you will be overwhelmed by demands on your time. Now is the time to establish a habit of regular silence in the presence of God, to which you must cling all your life. It can make the difference between mere survival and flourishing as a Dominican.

Often people come to the Order with a new-found enthusiasm to share the good news of Jesus Christ. You may wish to take immediately to the streets, to storm the pulpit, to share your discovery of the gospel with the world. It can be frustrating to join

17. *Pensées*, no. 205.

the Order of Preachers and then find that for years you are tied to hours of boring study, reading dry books written by dead men. We yearn perhaps to be on the road preaching the gospel, or sent on the missions. We may be like those young men of whom Dostoyevsky wrote in *The Brothers Karamazov*, 'who do not understand that the sacrifice of one's life is in most cases perhaps the easiest of all sacrifices, and that to sacrifice, for instance, five or six years of their life, full of youthful fervour, to hard and difficult study, if only to increase tenfold their powers of serving truth so as to be able to carry out the great work they have set their hearts on carrying out – that such a sacrifice is almost beyond the strength of many of them'.

It is right that from the beginning we find ways of sharing the good news with others, but the patient apprenticeship of silence is inescapable if we are to communicate more than just our own enthusiasm. Dominic's memory was a 'kind of barn for God, filled to overflowing with crops of every kind'.[18] We need the years of study to fill the barn. It is true that Matthew 10:19 tells us that we must not think beforehand what we are to say, but Humbert of Romans informs those in formation that this text only applied to apostles![19]

A SHARED WORD

A year ago I was walking through the tiny back streets of Ho Chi Minh City, Vietnam, when I came across a little square, dominated by a statute of St Vincent Ferrer. Standing on his pedestal, he looked the model preacher, the solitary speaker lifted up above the crowd. We may wish to be preachers like that, individual stars, the focus of attention and admiration.

18. Jordan of Saxony, *Libellus*, 7.
19. 'Treatise on the Formation of Preachers' in *Early Dominicans: Selected Writings*, trans. Simon Tugwell OP, p. 205.

The word of the preacher is not his. It is a word that we have received not only in the silence of prayer and study but from each other. And so a community of preachers should be one in which we share our deepest convictions, as Mary Magdalene shared her faith in the Risen Lord with her brethren. In the Order's General Council we gather every Wednesday to read the gospel together. Our sermons are the fruit of our common reflection. Modern conceptions of authorship may make us possessive of our own ideas, and we may think that any brother who uses them is committing robbery. But it is the rich who believe firmly in private property. We share what we have received and as mendicant friars we should not be ashamed to beg an idea off anyone.

Our formation should also prepare us to preach together, in a common mission. Jesus sent out the disciples two by two. It is tempting to claim an apostolate as my own and to guard it jealously from the other brethren. This is my responsibility, my care, my glory. If I do that, then it may be that all that I preach is myself. Humbert of Romans tells us to beware of people 'who realise that preaching is a particularly splendid kind of job and set their hearts on it because they want to be important'.[20] If we give in to this temptation we may come to think that we are the good news for which everyone is hungering. The most enjoyable teaching that I have ever done was when I taught doctrine at Oxford with two other brethren. We prepared the course together, and went to each other's lectures. We tried to teach the students by introducing them into our discussions. The idea was that by entering our conversation they could discover a voice of their own, rather than be passive recipients of instruction.

Each brother speaks for the whole community. The most

20. *Early Dominicans*, p. 236.

famous example of this was in the early days of the conquest of the Americas. When Antonio Montesino preached against the injustices done to the Indians, the city authorities went to the Prior to denounce him. But the Prior replied that when Antonio preached it was the whole community who spoke.

All this goes against the grain of an individualism which is characteristic both of modernity and often of Dominicans. Indeed individualism is often claimed with some pride as a typically Dominican characteristic. It is true that we have a tradition which cherishes the freedom and the unique gifts of each brother. Thanks be to God. Planning common projects in the Order can be a nightmare. But we are preaching brothers and our greatest brethren, though often pictured alone, usually worked in the common mission: Fra Angelico was not a solitary artist but trained brethren in his skills; St Catherine was surrounded by brothers and sisters; Bartolomeo de Las Casas worked with his brethren in Salamanca for the rights of the Indians. Congar and Chenu flourished as members of a community of theologians. Even St Thomas needed a team of brothers to write down his words.

So our formation should liberate us from the debilitating effects of contemporary individualism, and form us as preaching brothers. We will be much more truly individual and strong if we dare to do that. In some parts of the world, which have been more affected by this individualism, this may be the great challenge for your generation: to invent and launch new ways of preaching the gospel together. This you can do. There are many young in formation, one in six of the brethren and over a thousand novices this year for the nuns and sisters. Together you can do more than we can begin to imagine now.

CONCLUSION

In 1217, shortly after the foundation of the Order, St Dominic scattered the brethren, because 'stored grain rots'. He sent them on their way without money, like the apostles. But one brother, John of Navarra, refused to leave for Paris unless he had money in his pocket. They argued, and finally Dominic gave in and gave him something. This incident scandalised some of the other brethren, but perhaps it is a good image of our formation. I am not suggesting that your formators should give in to your every request, but that our formation should be both exigent and compassionate, idealistic and realistic. Dominic invites John to be confident, not with an arrogant self-confidence, but confident in the Lord who will provide for him on the journey, and in his brother who sends him. When he sees that he has not got that far as yet, then he has mercy on him.

I pray that your formation may help you to grow in Dominic's confidence and joy. The Order needs courageous and joyful young men and women who will help us to found the Order in new places, refound it in others, and develop new ways of preaching of the gospel. Sometimes, like brother John, your confidence may falter. You may doubt your strength to set out on the journey, or even whether it is worth while to do so. May such dark and uncertain times become part of your growth as Christians, preachers, brothers and sisters. When you feel lost and unsure, may you hear a voice, unexpectedly close, saying, 'Whom do you seek?'

The Identity of
Religious Life

Head of Dominic
after thirteenth century wooden figure
of Saint Dominic in Prouille

Drawing by Sister Mary Ansgar Sheldon OP

RELIGIOUS VOCATIONS:
LEAVING BEHIND THE USUAL
SIGNS OF IDENTITY

Many years ago I remember going to my first meeting of the Conference of Major Superiors for England and Wales. I nervously put on my habit and went down to face the crowds. And on the staircase I was stopped by a fierce sister whom I had never met before. She looked at me witheringly and said: 'You must be insecure if you have to wear that thing!'

WHERE HAVE ALL THE VOCATIONS GONE?

We religious have been worrying about our identity for a long while now. Who are we? How do we fit into the fabric and structure of the Church? Are we clerical, lay or some special hybrid of our own? I believe that no answer will be helpful unless we start from the fact that we share a crisis of identity with most people of our time. What makes us special? Well, it is certainly not having a crisis of identity. That is just part of the common lot we share with others. It is only worth reflecting upon if it helps us to live the good news for all those other sorry souls who are haunted by the same question, Who am I?

Please forgive me if I share with you a few over simplistic observations upon why this question of identity is an obsession of modernity. We have seen a profound social transformation this century and especially since 1945. In Europe, and I suppose in the States too, we have seen the weakening of all sorts of institutions that gave people an identity, that defined a profession, a role, a vocation. The universities, the medical and legal professions, the trade unions, the Churches, the press, various crafts – all these

Keynote address to the assembly of the (US) Conference of Major Superiors of Men, Arlington, VA, 8 August, 1996.

institutions offered people not just ways of earning a living, a job to do, but a way of being a human being, a sense of vocation. To be a musician, a lawyer, a teacher, a nurse, a carpenter, a plumber, a farmer, a priest, etc., was not just to have a job; it was to be someone; one belonged to a body of people with institutions that defined appropriate conduct, that shared a wisdom, a history and a solidarity.

What we have seen over the last years is the corrosive effect of a new and simpler model of society, for we have all found ourselves members of the global market, buying and selling, being bought and sold. The basic institutions of civil society that sustained the professions and vocations have lost much of their authority and independence. Like everything else, they must submit to market forces. In England even a football team exists now less to play football than to make a profit.

It became less and less clear that one could choose what to do with one's life. One had to satisfy the demands of supply and demand. It was not just we religious who lost a sense of vocation; the whole idea of a vocation became problematic. Nicholas Boyle, an English philosopher, wrote, 'There are no vocations for anyone any more; society is not composed of people who have lives which they commit in this or that particular way, but of functions to be performed only as long as there is a desire to be satisfied.'[1] All these professions and crafts and skills were like little ecosystems that offered different ways of being a human being. They have weakened and crumbled. Like the fragile habitats of rare toads or snails, society is becoming homogenised. All one is left with is the individual and the state, or even the consumer and the market. Much simpler but more lonely and vulnerable.

1. 'Understanding Thatcherism', *New Blackfriars*, 1990, p. 320

In the Church I suspect that we have suffered from the blowing of this same cold wind which left us also with a simpler and less confident community. For the Church too is part of civil society. We had been a complex society, with all sorts of institutions which gave us identity. We too had universities, hospitals, schools, professions and above all religious orders, which offered people vocations, identities which were shored up, respected and honoured.

The Church had all sorts of hierarchies and structures that counterbalanced each other. To be a mother superior or a Catholic headmistress was to be someone to be reckoned with! Priests quailed as they rang the doorbell. But to some extent our Church has gone through a similar transformation to the rest of society. And what we were left with was not just the individual consumer and the state or the market, but the individual believer and the hierarchy. We have lost confidence in other identities. And that is perhaps one reason why the question of priesthood, and who is allowed to be one, is such a hot issue for us. Because if you cannot get a foot on that ladder, then you cannot be anyone that really matters.

Who are we religious? How do we fit into the fabric and the structure of the Church? We often try to answer by placing ourselves in terms of the hierarchy. Are we lay or are we clerical, or somewhere halfway between the two? Or we may answer by placing ourselves over against the hierarchy, as the prophetic individuals shaking our fists at 'the institutional Church'. But that is the wrong sort of map. I think that it is rather as if one were to look for the Rockies on a map that gave the boundaries of the states of America. Are they in Colorado or are they in Wyoming? Why cannot we see the mountains?

That map of the Church which is the hierarchy is a good and valid one. We are all on it somewhere. Some of us religious are lay, some priests and some even bishops! But we cannot use it for locating religious life. It does not show us up for who we are, just as the Rockies are not on that map which is of the state boundaries. And you cannot even get clues as to where they are. Where there are no towns there could well be some mountains. But you need another sort of map if you are to see them clearly.

People often complain of the clericalization of the Church. It seems paradoxical that at the Second Vatican Council we proclaimed a new theology of the Church; we discovered a theology of the laity; we were all part of the People of God on pilgrimage to the kingdom. But the Church seemed in fact to grow ever more clerical. Instead of putting this down to a sinister plot, I believe that we should see this in the context of the profound transformation of western culture. In the world of the global market, there is no real place for people to have vocations, whether to teach, to nurse or to be a religious. A job is just a response to a demand. And so when the Catholic Church entered the modern world with a bang, when Pope John XXIII threw open the windows, a cold wind blew down all sorts of fragile vocational identities within the Church as well.

Faced with the clericalization of the Church, there are of course steps that can be taken to open up positions of influence to lay people and women, to loose the dominance of a clerical caste. But that is the subject of another lecture. What I am saying here is that it would be a mistake to think that the answer for our crisis of identity is to abolish all hierarchy and go for a Church which is more like our liberal, individualistic society. That would not give us what we want. What we can see in our own society, on the streets of our great urban wildernesses, is that individualism is cruel. It makes urban deserts in which few can really flourish.

Mary Douglas, an anthropologist, argues that women, for example, would do even worse in a more individualistic society.

She wrote, 'The processes of individualism downgrade the economically unsuccessful, and cannot but create derelicts and beggars. Members of an individualist culture are not aware of their own exclusionary behaviour. The condition of the unintentionally excluded, for example beggars sleeping on the streets, shocks visitors from other cultures.'[2]

According to Mary Douglas, a healthy society is one that has all sorts of counterbalancing structures and institutions that give a voice and authority to different groups so that no one way of being human dominates and no single map tells you how things are. Perhaps what we want is not to reproduce the homogenised desert of the consumer world, but to be more like a rain forest, which has all sorts of ecological niches for different ways of being a human being. In that sense we do not want less hierarchy but more. We need lots of institutions and structures that recognise and give a voice and authority to all those various ways of being a member of the people of God, such as women, married couples, academics, doctors and religious orders. In the Middle Ages it was more like that. The emperor and the nobility, the great abbeys of men and women, the universities and the religious orders, all provided alternative *foci* of power and identity. We had many more maps upon which people could find themselves.

I read once in Cardinal Newman, and I have never again been able to find where, that the Church flourishes when we give recognition to different forms of authority. He names specifically tradition, reason and experience. Each demands respect and needs institutions and structures to sustain it. Tradition is sustained by the bishops, reason by universities and centres of study, and experience by all sorts of institutions from religious orders to

2. Mary Douglas, *In the Wilderness: The Doctrine of Defilement in the Book of Numbers,* Sheffield, 1993, p. 46.

married life where people hear the Word and reflect upon it in their lives.

What we want then is not the individualism of the modern urban desert, but something more like a rain forest, with all sorts of ecological niches for strange animals that can thrive and multiply and give praise to God in a thousand different voices.

Who are we religious and what is our vocation in the Church? The answer to that question matters, but not just because it may give us the confidence to carry on and even attract some new vocations. It is important because to address it we must reflect upon that crisis of identity which afflicts most people today; no one is created by God just to be a consumer or a worker, to be sold and bought in the marketplace like a slave. If we can recover a confidence in our vocation, then we may be able to show something of the human vocation. The issue which we have to address touches upon what it means to be a human being.

IDENTITY AS VOCATION

I read the other day about a thirteen-year-old American boy called Jimmy, who got into trouble because he and his family insisted on his right to wear an earring to school. And they did so on the grounds that 'each person has the right to choose who he is.' Of course, in a way one wants to cheer on Jimmy. In a sense he is right. It belongs to being someone, having an identity, that one can make significant choices and say, 'This is me. I will wear those earrings.' But one cannot choose to be absolutely anyone. If I were to decide to put on earrings, leathers and drive around Rome on a motorbike, I expect that my brethren would object and say. 'Timothy, that simply is not you.' At least I hope they would! I can no more decide to be a punk than I can decide to be Thomas Aquinas.

To be someone is to be able to make significant decisions about one's life, but these somehow must hang together, make a story. To have an identity is for the choices that one makes throughout one's life to have a direction, a narrative unity.[3] What I do today must make sense in the light of what I did before. My life has a pattern. Like a good story. One of the reasons why the professions and crafts were so important to human identity was that they gave a structure to large chunks of a person's life. To be a musician or a lawyer or a carpenter is not just something that one does; it is a life, from youth to old age, relaxing and working, in sickness and in health.

But our vocation as religious brings to light the deepest narrative structure of every human life. During my first class as a novice, the novice master drew a large circle on the board and told us: 'Well, lads, that's all the theology you need to know. All comes from God and all goes to God.' It turned out to be a bit more complex than that! But the claim of our faith is that every human life is a response to a summons from God to share the life of the Trinity. This is the deep narrative in every human life. I discover who I am in answering that call. What he said to Isaiah he says to me: 'The Lord called me before I was born. He named me from my mother's womb.' A name is not a useful label but an invitation. To be someone is not to choose an identity off the supermarket shelf (Hell's Angel, pop star, Franciscan); it is to respond to the one who summons me to life: 'Samuel Samuel,' calls the voice in the night. And he answers, 'Speak Lord, your servant is listening.'

Jimmy, I hope now with his earrings, is partially right. Identity is about making choices. But it is not just a matter of choosing who you will be, as one chooses the colour of one's socks; the

---

3. See Alasdair MacIntyre, *After Virtue. A Study of Moral Theory*, London 1981, Chapter 15.

choice is to respond to that voice that summons one to life. Identity is a gift, and the story of my life is made up of all those choices to accept or refuse that gift.

Paul writes to the Corinthians, 'It is God who has called you to share in the life of his Son, Jesus Christ our Lord; and God keeps faith' (1 Cor 1:9). What I wish to suggest to you is that religious life is a particular and radical way of saying yes to that call. In a very stark and naked way, it makes plain the plot of every human life, which is the answering of a summons. In our odd way of life we make explicit what is the drama of every human search for identity, as every human being tries to catch the echo of the voice of God calling him or her by name. Other Christian vocations, such as marriage, also do this, but differently, as I will suggest below.

LEAVING ALL

When we religious discuss our identity, you can be pretty sure that before long the word 'prophetic' will occur. And this is understandable. Our vows are in such a direct contradiction with the values of our society that it makes sense to talk of them as prophetic of the kingdom. The apostolic exhortation *Vita Consecrata* uses the term. I am delighted when other people use that term of us, but I am reluctant for religious to claim it for ourselves. It could carry a hint of arrogance: 'We are the prophets.' Often we are not. And I suspect that true prophets would hesitate to claim that title for themselves. Like Amos, they tend to reject the claim and say, 'I am neither a prophet nor the son of a prophet.' I prefer to think that we are those who leave behind the usual signs of identity.

The rich young man asks Jesus, 'What do I still lack?' 'Jesus said to him, "If you wish to be perfect, go, sell your possessions and give to the poor, and you will have treasure in heaven; then come and follow me." When the young man heard this, he went away with a heavy heart: for he was a man of great wealth' (Mt 19:20-22).

In the first place, our vocation shows something about the human vocation by what we leave behind. We give up many of the things that give identity to human beings in our world; money, status a partner, a career. In a society in which identity is already so fragile, so insecure, we give up the sorts of things to which human beings look for security, the props of our unsure sense of who we are. We ask incessantly the question, 'who are we?' But we are those who give up the usual markers of identity. That is who we are! No wonder we have problems! We do this so as to bring to light the true identity and vocation of every human being. First of all, we show that every human identity is gift. No self-created identity is ever adequate to who we are. Every little identity which we can hammer out in this society is just too small. And second, we show that human identity is not finally given now. It is the whole story of our lives, from beginning to end and beyond, that shows us who we are.

St John writes 'Dear friends, we are now God's children; what we shall be has not yet been disclosed, but we know that when Christ appears we shall be like him for we shall see him as he is' (1 Jn 3:2). Throwing away the props is a sign that all human identity is a surprise, a gift and an adventure.

Let me flesh this out with a few simple examples. This is not, of course, intended to be a complete theology of the vows, but a few suggestions as to how they touch the question of human identity.

OBEDIENCE

In the Dominican Order, when you make profession you put your hands into the hands of your superior and you promise obedience. I suppose that in all our congregations, in one way or another the crunch comes when you put your self into the hands of your brothers and sisters and say, 'Here I am; send me where you will.'

Erik Erikson defined a sense of identity as 'a feeling of being at home in one's body, a sense of knowing where one is going and an inner anticipated recognition from those who count.'[4] Well, obedience neatly wipes out that sense of knowing where you are going. One is given the glorious liberty of not knowing where one is headed. The religious is a person who is liberated from the burden of having a career.

A career is one of the ways that human beings tell the longer story of their lives and so glimpse who they are. A career, for those lucky enough to have one, gives a sequence and a structure to the stages of a person's life as they move up the ladder, whether it is in a university, the army or the bank. We do not have that. However many times we might be elected to office, we go up no ladder. When I made profession on September 29, 1966, my career ended. I am and can only ever be a friar. I believe that there is a legal document in France which includes in the list of those 'without profession' priests and prostitutes. I remember as a university chaplain my role was to be the one person on the campus without a role – who 'loitered with intent,' as the English police say when they arrest suspicious characters.

And we are not only at the summons of our brothers and sisters to go where we are sent. We are obedient to the voices of those who call upon us in various ways. I remember a French Dominican who came to Oxford to learn Bengali. He had been a worker priest for sixteen years, making cars for Citroen, or more often

4. Quoted by Theodore Zeldin, *An Intimate History of Humanity*, London 1995. p. 380.

than not, leading strikes and making sure that cars were not produced! But now Nicholas and his Provincial came to the conviction that his life had entered a new stage, and that he would go to Calcutta and live with the very poorest people. And I remember asking him what he intended to do there. And he replied that was not for him to say. They would tell him what he was to do.

The summons may come via the most surprising people. Our brethren in Vietnam have suffered many years of persecution, imprisonment and often having to hide among the people. One of them, a lovely man called Francis, after hiding for a while was finally caught by the police and imprisoned. And he said to his captors: 'We should thank you. For we Dominicans had been living together, but when you came for us you sent us among the people.'

The vow of obedience summons us beyond all the identities that a career could ever give us, and so beyond all the identities that we could ever construct. It points to an identity which is open to all those whose lives go nowhere, who never have a career, who never hold down a job or pass an exam or be a success. Our renunciation of a career is a sign that all human lives do ultimately go somewhere, however much they may appear to come to a dead end, for there is a God who faithfully summons each of us to life.

Every year the Justice and Peace Commission of the Irish Conference of Major Religious Superiors produces a critique of the government's budget, and ministers tremble as they await it. But one day, after a particularly savage report, the prime minister, Charles J. Haughey, dismissed it, saying that it was hard to take seriously criticisms made by a group that called itself both major and superior. They took note and changed their name to the Conference of Religious. Not that I am dropping a hint!

CHASTITY

The vow of chastity can be so hard to live because it touches so many aspects of our identity. I presume that this will be treated at length by the other speakers, and so I will only say a brief word.

For most human beings the most fundamental sign of their identity is that there is another person for whom they are central: their husband, wife or partner. This we do not have. However many people I may love and who may love me, I do not and cannot define myself by such a relationship. That is such a loss, such a deprivation that I do not believe it can be lived fruitfully unless one's life is deeply nurtured by prayer.

One of the most painful things, at least for me, is that one gives up the possibility of having children. In some societies that means that one can never be accepted as a man. I remember the desolation of a newly ordained priest who went to celebrate the Eucharist at a convent in Edinburgh. When the front door was finally answered the sister looked at him and said. 'Oh, it's you, Father: I was expecting a man.'

It also reminds me of an American brother, one of whose names was Mary, following a pious Irish custom. He was sounding off about how the world was filled with weirdoes and perverts these days. And a brother put down the paper he was reading and said: 'Come on; why do you think you're so normal. You are called Mary, and you are wearing a skirt.'

One gives up father, mother, brother, sister, the whole defining network of human relationships that gives one a name and a place in the world.

I visited Angola during the civil war. I shall never forget a meeting with the postulants of the brothers and sisters in the capital, Luanda. They were cut off from their families by the conflicts which surrounded the city, and they were faced with a moral dilemma. Should they try to cross the war zone to find their families and support them during this terrible time, or should they remain with the order? For Africans, with their deep sense of family and tribe, this was a terrible situation. And I shall never forget the young sister who stood up and said, 'Leave the dead to bury the dead; we must stay to preach the Gospel.'

So then, our lives are marked by a great absence, a void. But this makes no sense unless it is lived joyfully as part of a love story that is the deep mystery of every human life. It must either be lived passionately as a sign of that love of God which calls every human being to the fullness of life, or else it is barren and sterile.

Everyone is summoned by that love, even those whose lives seem barren of affection, who have no spouse, no family, no children, no tribe, no clan, the utterly alone.

POVERTY

The vow of poverty, of course, goes to the heart of what gives people identity in the world of the global market. It is the renunciation of the status which comes with income, the ability to be someone who buys and sells. It calls us to be a real counter-sign in our culture of money. Of course we are not often that. As I write these words high on a hill above the Tiber in our enormous old priory of Santa Sabina, I can see a little shack on the bank of the river where a family is living and hanging out their washing. If it rains and the river rises, their house will be swept away. I look at them, and I blush to think how they see us.

But everywhere during my travels I have come across communities of men and women religious, of all congregations, sharing the lives of the poor, who are living signs that no human life is destined to end on a rubbish dump, that every human being has the dignity of a child of God. This Christmas I celebrated the midnight Eucharist with one of our brothers, Pedro, who literally lives on the streets of Paris. He celebrated the feast with a thousand tramps in a big tent, on an altar made of cardboard boxes to symbolise that Christ was born that night for everyone who lives in cardboard boxes under the bridges of Paris. When he pulled the cork of the bottle of wine for the Offertory, cheers rang out from around the congregation!

In each of these vows we see how some pillar of human identity is left behind, surrendered. We give up the usual things that tell us who we are and that we matter and that our lives are going somewhere. No wonder we get unsure about our identities. But maybe our freedom is not to even care about who we are. We should be much more interested in who God is. As Thomas Merton once wrote:

> You have called me here not to wear a label by which I can recognise myself in some category. You do not want me to be thinking about what I am, but about who you are. Or rather, you do not even want me to be thinking about anything much, for you would raise me above the level of thought. And if I am always trying to figure out what I am and where I am and why I am, how will that work be done?[5]

In his autobiography *The Long Walk to Freedom*, Nelson Mandela describes his great pride and joy when he bought his first house in Johannesburg. It was not much, but he had become a man. A man must own land and beget children. But because of his struggle for his people, he hardly lived in that house or saw his family. He made an option for something very like our vows. He wrote:

> It was this desire for the freedom of my people to live their lives with dignity and self-respect that animated my life, that transformed a frightened young man into a bold one, that drove a law-abiding attorney to become a criminal, that turned

5. Thomas Merton. *Epilogue Meditation Pauperis in Solitudine*

a family-loving husband into a man without a home, that forced a life-living man to live like a monk. I am not more virtuous or self-sacrificing than the next man, but I found that I could not even enjoy the poor and limited freedom I was allowed when I knew my people were not free. Freedom is indivisible – the chains on any one of my people were the chains on all of them, the chains on all my people were the chains on me.[6]

Mandela lost his wife, his family, his freedom, his career, wealth and status from a great hunger for the liberation of his people. His imprisonment was a sign of the hidden dignity of his people, which would one day be revealed. Few religious communities are quite as tough as Robben Island, but we too leave behind much that could give us identity as a sign of the hidden dignity of those who have died in Christ. For as Paul writes to the Colossians: 'You died: and now your life lies hidden with Christ in God. When Christ who is our life is revealed, then you too will be revealed with him in glory' (3:3).

On Easter morning, Peter and the beloved disciple sprint to the empty tomb. Peter just sees a loss, the absence of a body. The other disciple sees with the eyes of one who loves, and he sees a void filled with the presence of the Risen One. Our lives too may seem to be marked by absence and loss but those who see with the eyes of love may see them filled with the presence of the risen Lord.

I do not wish to make an exclusive claim for our vocation as religious men and women. All human vocations – as doctors, teachers, social workers, etc, – say something about that human vocation which is to answer the call of the God who summons us to the kingdom. What is specific about our vocation is that it

6. Nelson Mandela, *The Long Walk to Freedom*, London, 1994, p. 750

shows this universal destiny through a leaving behind of other identities. The apostolic exhortation *Vita Consecrata* speaks of us as 'eschatological symbols.' And that is surely true. Besides, it appeals to me. It would be nice to be able to put on your passport application, under 'profession', 'eschatological symbol'. But one could argue that even more than us, it is matrimony that is the eschatological symbol. It is the consummation of love, this sabbath of the human spirit when two people rest in mutual love, that gives us a symbol of the Kingdom for which we long. Perhaps we are a sign of the journey and the married couple of the destiny.

AN ECOLOGY FOR FLOURISHING

I have tried to give a definition of the identity of religious life. It is a paradoxical definition because it defines us as those who give up identity as understood by our society. But we cannot stop here – much as you may wish to! In our society, which is hostile to the whole idea of vocation and which is subverting the sense of identity and vocation of every human being, a neat definition is not enough. It would be like trying to comfort tigers threatened with extinction with a nice definition of tigerhood.

In this human desert which is the global marketplace, we need to build a context in which religious can actually flourish and be vital invitations to walk in the way of the Lord. What a particular religious order or congregation does is to offer such a context. In today's world we may be tempted to think of religious orders as being like competing multinationals: Do you buy high octane Jesuit gas or green, lead-free Franciscan gas? But the image that comes more readily to my mind is of each institute as being like a mini-ecosystem which sustains a weird form of life. To flourish as a butterfly you need more than a nice definition; you need an ecological context that will get you from egg to caterpillar, and from cocoon to butterfly. Some butterflies need nettles, ponds and some rare plant: otherwise they cannot make it. For another form of butterfly the presence of sheep droppings seems to be vital. Each religious congregation differs in offering a different ecological niche for a strange way of being a human being. I shall resist the temptation to think which forms of butterflies our various orders bring to mind, for the moment anyway!

A religious order is like an environment. Building religious life is like making a nature reserve on an old building site. You have to plant a few nettles here, dig a pond there and so on. What do our brothers and sisters need to flourish on that journey as they leave behind career, wealth, status and the assurance of a single partner? What do they need as they make that hard pilgrimage from noviciate to grave? Each congregation will have its own requirements, its own ecological necessities, its own identity.

And this brings me to an apparent paradox: I have defined the identity of religious life as being in the giving up of identity, leaving behind the props and markers that tell people who they are. And yet our orders and congregations do offer us identities. We each have our distinctive styles. That is why you have all those terrible jokes about Jesuits, Franciscans and Dominicans changing light bulbs!

I remember that when I told a Benedictine great-uncle of mine that I intended to become a Dominican, he looked hesitant and said: 'Are you sure that that is a good idea? Aren't they supposed to be rather intelligent?' And then he paused and said, 'No, come to think of it, I have known lots of stupid Dominicans.'

But the paradox is only apparent. Each congregation does offer an identity, but it is a particular way of walking after the Lord, a particular way of self-forgetfulness. A Carmelite should be happy to be one, not because it gives her or him status, but because it is a particular way of giving it up. I need to delight in my order, with its stories, its saints, its traditions, so that I can grow in the courage to give up all that our society finds important. I love the story of Blessed Reginald of Orleans, one of the earliest friars, who said when he was dying that being a Dominican had gained him no merit because he had enjoyed it so much. I need stories like that to encourage me to flourish as a poor, chaste and obedient friar, to rejoice in it as a liberty :and not a prison. I need stories like that to liberate me from self-preoccupation.

That is why I have great sympathy with the young religious who today often demand clear signs of their identity as members of a religious order. The adventure for my generation, who grew up with a strong sense of Catholic and even Dominican identity, was to cast off the symbols that set us apart from others, like the habit, and immerse ourselves in modernity, let ourselves be tested by its doubts and share its questions.

And this was right and fruitful. But the young who come to us today often are the children of that modernity, and they have been haunted by its questions since childhood. They have sometimes other needs, clear signs of being a member of a religious community, to sustain them in this very odd way of being a human being.

A final remark: We need an environment in which we are sustained in personal growth. The fact that we are called to leave behind those things which our society considers to be symbols of status and identity does not mean that we are absolved from the difficulties of growing into mature and responsible human beings. We all know brothers who want ever more expensive computers while claiming that the vow of poverty excuses them from worrying about money.

What we can see with our own eyes is that giving up family and power and wealth and self-determination does not make us into wimps. No one could say that Nelson Mandela is a weak personality! But that growth into maturity will demand that we pass through moments of crisis. Do our communities sustain us then? Do they help us to live these moments of death as times of rebirth too? When an old monk was asked what they do in the monastery, he replied, 'Oh, we fall and get up, we fall and get up, we fall and get up.' We need an environment in which we can fall and get up as we stagger along to the kingdom.

CONCLUSION

Let me conclude by summing up in one minute the journey that we have made in this lecture.

The question that I was asked was this: What is the identity of religious life today? I answer this by saying that we must place this in the context of a society in which most people suffer from a crisis of identity. The global market wipes out all sense of vocation, whether you are a doctor a priest or a bus driver.

The value of being a religious is that it gives vivid expression to the destiny of every human being. For every human being discovers his or her identity in answering the summons of God to share the divine life. We are called to give particular and radical expression to that vocation by leaving behind any other identity that could seduce our hearts. Other vocations, such as marriage, give alternative expressions to that human destiny.

But I concluded that it is not enough to stop with a nice definition. We need more than that to keep us going on the journey. Each religious order or congregation should offer the necessary environment to sustain us on the way. And if we are not to be seduced by the consumer society, if we are to offer islands of a counterculture, then we must work very hard to build that environment in which our brothers and sisters can flourish as we journey.

THE BEAR AND THE NUN:
WHAT IS THE SENSE
OF RELIGIOUS LIFE TODAY?

SEARCHING FOR A STORY

I have been asked to speak about '*La vie religieuse, quel sens aujourd'hui?*' This is an urgent question for religious today because many of us wonder whether the way of life to which we have committed ourselves has any meaning at all. There are fewer vocations in western Europe than before; in France many congregations are growing smaller and some are dying out; to be a religious does not have the same status and respect that it used to have. We may appear to have lost our role in a Church that seems to have become more clerical, and our importance in a society in which lay people now do so much that before was largely done by religious. With the new sense of the sanctity of marriage we are not even considered to live a way of life that is more perfect than any other. It is understandable that many religious ask, '*La vie religieuse, quel sens aujourd'hui?*'

In this situation it would be natural to try to find the sense of religious life in something special about us, something that we do that no one else does, something that gives us our special place, our special identify. We are like blacksmiths in a world of cars, looking for a new role. I suspect that this is one reason why we religious often eagerly talk of ourselves as prophets. We claim that we are the prophetic part of the life of the Church. It gives us a role, an identity, a label. I do believe that religious life is called to be prophetic, but not as a solution to our identify crisis! Instead I would like to start elsewhere, which is with the crisis of meaning which western society is living. I believe that religious life is more important than ever before because of how we are called to face

---

An address to the Major Religious Superiors of France, October, 1998.

the crisis of meaning of our contemporaries. Our life must be an answer to the question: 'What is the sense of human life today?' Perhaps this has always been the primary witness of religious life.

How can we even begin to think about a question as large as the contemporary crisis of meaning. To say anything adequately, I would have to have studied books about modernity and post-modernity. I have not done so. My excuse is that with my life on the road, I have had no time. But the truth is that if I were to read these books probably I would not understand them. They are mainly written by clever French people and beyond the grasp of the English! Instead I will try a simpler approach. I would like to offer you the contrast between two images, two implicit stories of human life.

Every culture needs stories which embody an understanding of what it means to be a human being, what the pattern of life is. We need stories which tell us who we are and where we are going. When there is a crisis of meaning in a society, one symptom is that the stories that society tells seem no longer to make sense of our experience. They do not fit any more. When a society goes through a moment of profound change, then it needs a new sort of story to make sense of its life.

I shall argue that the basic crisis of meaning in our society is that the story which has been implicit in European culture for a few hundred years, no longer makes sense. It is a story of progress, of the survival of the fittest, of the triumph of the strong. The hero of this story is the modern self. He (and it is usually a he!) is alone, and free. This is the story that has been implicit in our novels, our films, our philosophy, our economics and our politics. But now it is ceasing to make sense of our experience. I shall take as a symbol of this story a poster of a bear that I have often seen in the posters of Rome.

So we are a society that hungers for a new story that will make some sense of who we are. I believe that the meaning of religious life lies in answering that question: 'What is the meaning of human life today?' People must be able to recognise in our lives an invitation to be a human being in a new way. For me the symbol of this other story will be of a nun singing in the dark to the paschal candle.

So I wish to offer you this contrast between two images, two stories, of a bear and a nun. I wish to contrast these two stories by looking at the three elements which are necessary for every story: a plot that evolves through time; the events that move the story forward, and the actors. If our contemporaries feel lost and confused, hungry for meaning, then it is because the stories of modernity no longer make sense of our experience of time, events and what it means to be an individual. We religious should embody another way of being alive.

PLOT AND TIME

Let me start by telling you about my bear. A year ago, the walls of Rome were covered with posters of a large and angry bear. And the inscription on the poster read '*La forza del prezzo giusto*' – 'The power of the Right Price'. As I waited for buses I had much time to contemplate this bear. It captures well the story of modernity.

In the first place this bear suggests that the basic plot of history is an irresistible progress. It is a bear of which Darwin would have been proud, a victor in the evolutionary process. Human history marches onwards. It is also a symbol of the global economy, the market-place. What drives human history forward is economics. '*La forza del prezzo giusto*' – 'The power of the Right Price'. History is the story of inevitable progress, through the liberalis-ation of the market. The best economic system must triumph. The bear is the victor.

When I was growing up (and looking at you I suspect that when many of you were growing up too), it was still just possible to believe that humanity was on the way to a glorious future. But already there were shadows. I was born a week before the end of a war that left fifty million people dead. We slowly learned of the Holocaust and of the six million Jews who died in the camps. I grew up under the shadow of the bomb. I remember my mother storing tins of food in the cellar, just in case a nuclear war started. Yet, still it was possible to cling to the idea that humanity was moving forward. Every year we saw independence given to our old colonies, medicine was wiping out diseases like TB and malaria. Surely poverty would also be ended soon. Even the planes and cars went more quickly every year. Things would go on getting better.

Today we are less sure. The gap between rich and poor goes on growing. Malaria and TB are coming back and within a year there will probably be forty million people with AIDS. Unemployment stands at twenty million in Europe alone. The dreams of a just world seem farther away. Where is humanity going? Does our history have a meaning, a direction? Or are we wandering around in circles in the desert, getting no nearer to the promised land? Even the Church, which seemed to be moving towards renewal and new life at the Second Vatican Council, now seems not to know where it is going.

At the heart of modernity there is a contradiction, and that is why its story is no longer plausible. On the one hand the bear is indeed irresistible. The global market is triumphing over all its enemies. Communism has fallen in Eastern Europe and even China looks as if it may succumb. But, on the other hand, the story is not taking us to the Kingdom. What we seeing is growing poverty and war. Even the Asian tigers are sick. The bear is irresistible but it is tearing us to pieces. So the plot of modernity contains an unbearable contradiction. We cannot find ourselves in it any more.

We cannot live without stories. As we have come to doubt the story of humanity's march forward, so other stories must fill the vacuum. They may be millenarian stories of the end of the world, stories of aliens, stories of victory in the World Cup (Congratulations, France!). Often enough, it is just what we call in English 'soap operas', trivial serials on television. Recently the final episode of a soap opera in the United States was watched by eighty million people. Restaurants closed for the night. When it was announced that a giant asteroid would hit the earth on 26 October 2028, there was less interest. Having come to disbelieve in the myth of progress we take refuge in fictions.

Maybe it was the hunger for a story that explains the extraordinary reaction to the death of Princess Diana. The English are, as you know, very unemotional, or so the French like to think! But I have never seen such grief. It was as if the story at the heart of humanity had come to an end under a bridge in Paris. Millions of people wept as if they had lost their wife or child or mother. Everywhere I go in the world, I know that eventually people will ask me about the Princess. I am prepared to answer questions about her after this lecture. In Vietnam they even told me that I looked like Prince William. I was delighted, but they are a very polite people! It was the world's soap opera. Perhaps her story appealed to so many precisely because in her we could see ourselves. She was a good but not perfect person, who really cared for others, whose life should have been wonderful, and yet inexplicably it was a failure. It was a sad and futile story, which evoked the futility that so many people feel, as they wonder where their lives are going.

In what sense can religious life suggest another plot, an alternative story?

Let me offer you another image. I celebrated Easter this year in a monastery of Dominican contemplative nuns. The monastery was built on a hill behind Caracas, in Venezuela. The church was packed with young people. We lit the Paschal Candle and placed it on its stand. And a young nun with a guitar sang a love song to the candle. The song had all the harsh passion of Andalusia. I confess that I was completely bowled over by this image, of a young nun singing a love song in the darkness to the newborn fire. This image suggested that we are caught up in another drama, another story. This is our story, not that of the angry bear, devouring its rivals.

In the first place, the nun singing in the night suggests that the basic plot of the story of humanity is longer than that represented by the bear. Out in the garden the celebrant had inscribed the candle with these words: 'Christ yesterday and today, the beginning and the end, Alpha and Omega. All time belongs to him, and all the ages. To him be glory and power through every age. Amen.'

The religious life is perhaps in the first place a living Amen to that longer span of time. It is within the stretch of the story from Alpha to Omega, from Creation to Kingdom, that every human life must find its meaning. We are those who live for the Kingdom when, as Julian of Norwich said, 'All will be well, all manner of things will be well.'

The vocation that most radically brings to light that longest story is that of the contemplative monk or nun. Their lives have no meaning at all if they are not on the way to the Kingdom. Cardinal Basil Hume is the most respected Christian in England, and partly because he is a monk. And he wrote of monks: 'We do not see ourselves as having any particular mission or function in the Church. We do not set out to change the course of history. We are just there almost by accident from a human point of view.

And, happily, we go on "just being there".[1]

Monks are just there, and so their lives have no meaning at all, except as pointing to the fulfilment of the ages, that meeting with God. They are like people waiting at a bus stop. Just being there points to the bus that must surely come. There is no provisional or lesser sense. No children, no career, no achievements, no promotion, no use. It is by an absence of meaning that their lives point to a fullness of meaning that we cannot state, as the empty tomb points to the Resurrection, or as the wobble in the orbit of a star points to the invisible planet.

Western monasticism was born in a moment of crisis. It was when the Roman Empire was slowly dying before the assaults of the barbarians that Benedict went to Subiaco and founded a community of monks. When the story of humanity seemed to be going nowhere, then Benedict founded a community of people whose lives had sense only in pointing to that ultimate end, the Kingdom.

One might say that religious life forces us to live nakedly the crisis of modernity. Most people's lives have a shape and a story which may hold the larger question at bay. A life may have its own meaning, from falling in love, marrying, having children and then grandchildren. Or maybe someone's story may find its meaning in a career, in rising up the ladder of promotion, in gaining wealth and even fame. There are so many stories that we may tell which will give a provisional pattern and a meaning to our span of years. And that is good and right. But our vows do not give us that consolation. We have no marriage to offer a shape to our lives. We have no careers. We are naked before the question: 'What is the meaning of human life?'

But it is not enough to sit and wait for the coming of the

1. *In Praise of Benedict*, Ampleforth, 1996. p. 23.

Kingdom. Sometimes the younger brethren may not agree with me, but one does have to get out of bed each morning and do something. Even monks and nuns must do something! I remember asking an especially lazy brother what he was doing one day. He replied that he was being an 'eschatological sign', waiting for the Kingdom. How do we give value to what we do now? Most of us spend our days doing useful things, teaching, working in hospitals, helping in parishes, looking after the forgotten. How do our daily lives say something about the story of humanity?

Let us return to that young nun again. It is the middle of the night when she sings that wild song. It is in the night when she praises God. Even when it is dark, between the beginning and the end, one may encounter God and praise him. Now is the hour. As he is waiting to be murdered, Jesus says to the disciples, 'In the world you have tribulation, but be of good cheer, I have overcome the world' (Jn 16:33). Now is the hour of victory and praise.

What this suggests is a new sense of time. What gives shape to time is not the story of inevitable progress towards wealth and success. The hidden shape of our lives is the growth in friendship with God, as we meet him on the way and say Amen. It is not just the end of the story which gives it meaning. The pattern of my life is the encounter with God, and my response to his invitation. This is what makes of my life not just a sequence of events but a destiny. As Cornelius Ernst OP said, 'Destiny is the summons and invitation of the God of love, that we should respond to him in loving and creative consent.'[2] Even in the dark, in despair, when nothing makes sense any more, we may meet the God of life. As a Jewish philosopher wrote: 'Every moment can be the small door through which the Messiah can enter.' The story of our lives is of this meeting with the God who comes in the night

2. *The Theology of Grace*, Dublin, 1974. p. 82.

like a lover. This we celebrate with praise.

Some of the most moving moments of the last six years have been the times when I have been able to share with my brothers and sisters in praising God in the most difficult circumstances. In a monastery in Burundi, after touring a country torn apart by ethnic violence; in Iraq, as we waited for the bombs to fall; in Algeria, with our brother Pierre Claverie before he was killed. It is central to the religious life that we sing the praises of God, even in the night. We sing the psalms, the *tehillim*, the book of praises. We measure the day with the hours of the Divine Office, the liturgy of the psalms, not just with the mechanical hours of the clock. 'Seven times a day I praise you'. Well, at least twice for most of us.

I remember a story which illustrates how the time of praise may interact with the time of the clock, the time of modernity. When one of my brethren was a child at school, a dentist came to give lessons in dental hygiene to the children. He asked the class when they must clean their teeth. There was absolute silence. He said, 'Come on, you know when you must clean your teeth. In the morning and in the evening … ' This touched a button in the minds of these good Catholic children who knew their catechism. And they all carried on 'before and after meals'. 'Excellent,' said the dentist. 'In times of temptation and in the hour of our death'. Well, if we always cleaned our teeth in the hours of temptation, we might avoid many sins!

This regular rhythm of praise is more than just an optimism that all will be well in the end. We are claiming that even now, in the desert, the Lord of life meets us and shapes our lives. In this sense religious life should be truly prophetic, for the prophet is the one who sees the future bursting into present. As Habakkuk says, 'Even though the fig tree does not blossom, nor fruit be on the vines, even though the olive crop fails … yet I will rejoice in the Lord, I rejoice in the God of my salvation.' (3:17-19)

Recently I met the Order's Promoters of Justice and Peace for Latin America. They were a new generation, not the old ones of the late sixties like me! They were young men and women who keep alive a dream. I expected that they would be discouraged, given the worsening economic situation, the growing violence, the social disintegration of the continent. Not at all! They said that it was precisely now, when all the utopias had disappeared, when the Kingdom seemed more remote than ever, that we religious have our role to play. No one else could dream now. But to fight for a more just world now, when no progress ever seems to be made, means that one has to be a person of deep prayer. As our Brazilian brother, Frei Betto has said, one has to be a mystic now to believe in justice and peace.

ACTION

There is a second contrast between the stories of bear and nun that I would like to make, and that is in terms of how things happen. What is the motive force of the story? What carries the story forward? We need both plot and action.

We have already seen that the bear represents the competitive struggle for survival. What moves history is that competition in which the weak perish and the strong thrive. Whether you are studying evolution or economics, that is just the way things happen. That is the basic assumption of the modern story. The motor which drives history is free competition, which eliminates the defective, the hopeless, the unviable.

But once again we see a contradiction. For this bear is a symbol of that freedom which is at the heart of modernity: freedom to compete in the free market, in which everyone is free to choose what they want. Yet we have seen that this freedom too is, to some extent, illusory. For we are caught in a global transformation of the world that makes us powerless, and which no one is able to halt, which is destroying communities, and devouring the planet. So at the heart of the modern story is a double contradiction. We are offered progress, and find poverty; we are offered freedom, and find ourselves powerless. What alternative story can religious life embody?

But let us look again at that young nun, singing her love song in the dark. She represents another way of telling a story. The story that she celebrates is of a man who is crushed by the strong but lives for ever. The big bears of Rome and Jerusalem devour the weak man from Galilee. What we celebrate in this story is not God's superior strength, God the bigger bear, but his utter creativity in raising Jesus from the dead.

There can be no story unless something new happens. Stories tell about how things change. But the model of change of modernity is that of the survival of the fittest. Evolution, whether biological or economic, brings change, but through the competition to survive. But our story of the nun suggests an even more radical novelty, the unimaginable gift of new life. We praise the God who says, 'Behold I make all things new.' (Rev 21:5) We religious are called to be signs of God's unspeakable novelty, his unutterable creativity.

How are we religious to be the signs of this strange story of the God of death and resurrection? The clearest sign is in the presence of all those religious who refuse to leave places of death and violence, trusting in the Lord who raises the dead. Everywhere there is violence, in Rwanda, Burundi, the Congo, Chiapas, one can find men and women religious whose presence is a sign of that other story, of which our nun sings. Naturally here in France we think of those many religious who have died in Algeria. You must all know so well those wonderful words of Christian de Cherge, prior of the Trappist monks, when he wrote his last spiritual testimony, shortly before his death. I hope you will let me repeat them yet again:

When an A-Dieu is foreseen

If it should happen one day – and it could be today – that I become a victim of the terrorism which now seems set to engulf all the foreigners living in Algeria, I would love my community, my Church, my family, to remember that my life was given to God and to this country. I ask them to accept that the one Master of all life was not a foreigner at this brutal departure. I ask them to pray for me: for how would I be found worthy of such an offering? I would like them to be able to link this death with so many other deaths, equally violent, but shrouded in indifference and anonymity …

This life lost, totally mine and totally theirs, I thank God who seems to have willed it in its entirety for the sake of that joy in everything and in spite of everything.

The preparation for such a witness is surely, that every religious community should be a place in which we learn how to come alive through death and resurrection. I had a great-aunt, who became a Sacred Heart nun. At the age of seven she startled all her numerous sisters by pinning on the nursery wall a bit of paper saying, 'I wish to be dissolved and united with Christ'. I doubt whether many candidates for religious life do that sort of thing these days, thanks be to God! But surely a religious community should be a place in which we learn to die and rise, a place of transformation. We are not the prisoners of our past. We can grow in holiness. We can die and be made new.

This is unlikely to happen if we flee from facing the death of our own institutions. Today in western Europe, many congregations, communities, monasteries and provinces must face death. There are many strategies for avoiding that truth. Perhaps we beatify the founder, start expensive building programmes, write beautiful documents about plans that we will never implement. When we send brothers or sisters to the Philippines or to Colombia or Brazil, is it because of a sudden new missionary zeal, or because we want vocations to let us survive? If we cannot face the prospect of death, then what have we to say about the Lord of life? I once had to visit a Dominican monastery in England with an old friar. The monastery was clearly nearing the end of its life, but one of the nuns said to my companion, 'Surely Father, our dear Lord would never let this monastery die!' To which he replied, 'He let his Son die, didn't he?'

One of the ways in which we live out that unimaginable story of death and resurrection is surely in bringing new life to birth in unexpected places. We must be those who go into the valley of death and show our belief in the God who raises the dead. I remember one of my Scottish brethren, who was a poet and a wrestler, an unlikely combination, but then he was an unlikely man. He started a scheme in Scotland for bringing art to prisoners. He was convinced that unless we could believe in their creativity, then they would never be healed. His first attempt was in a tough prison in Glasgow. He asked the prisoners what they would like to try: painting, poetry, sculpture, dance. You can imagine the reactions that he got! And so he rolled up his sleeves and said, 'If any of you think that art is not for real men, then I will fight him!' And he did, every one of them. And they all took poetry and painting classes! I am glad to say that this is not the only way to bring people to faith in the God who makes all things new.

Perhaps another more traditional way in which religious have always been a sign of the ever creative God is through beauty. Of this you have always been more deeply aware in France than in many other countries. A few weeks ago I met an old Dominican in Germany who is a painter and sculptor. And I asked what he most enjoyed doing. He replied that he always loved carving tombstones! There are some wounds so deep that only beauty may heal them. In the face of some sufferings hope can only be expressed by art. A beautiful tombstone can speak eloquently of the hope of resurrection of the God who can raise the dead.

Finally there is the beauty of liturgy, the beauty of the praise of God, which speaks of the God who transforms all things. It is the beauty from which we started, of a young nun singing a love song to a candle in the night. It is the beauty of a passionate song of the people of southern Spain that bowled me over. It reminds me of Neruda who said that, between the dramas of birth and death, he had chosen the guitar!

ACTOR

Finally one cannot have a story without actors, characters. Every story needs its hero. And what better image of the modern self could one find than our bear, angry and alone. But this modern self is in crisis.

Fundamental to modernity is this new sense of what it means to be a human being; a separate and autonomous self, detached and free, and ultimately alone. He is the fruit of an evolution that has gone on for centuries, in which social bonds have been dissolved, and privacy has become possible and an ideal. He has been our hero since the time of Descartes. We can see him in every American western, a lonely figure.

Part of the crisis of modernity is that this 'modern self' contains a contradiction. Because one cannot be a 'self' alone. One cannot exist as a solitary, autonomous atom. One cannot exist without community, without people to whom we talk, without what Charles Taylor calls 'webs of interlocution'.[3] This is the contra-

---

3. *Sources of the Self*, Cambridge, 1989, p. 36.

diction at the centre of the modern story, that we see ourselves as essentially solitary, and yet in fact no one can be a self outside some form of community. It is impossible to be a 'modern self' for long. The bear on the poster represents an impossible ideal. Alone it would die.

Let us return for a last time to our nun, singing to the Paschal Candle. She is not alone. Just visible in the light of the candle are the crowd of young people. The Easter Vigil is a gathering of the People of God. What is born that night is a community. We come together to remember our baptism into the body of Christ and recite together a common profession of faith. This represents another vision of what it means to be a self.

'What is the sense of human life today?' One of the ways in which religious life tries to answer that question, is by living in community. To find one's identity in this community, as a brother or a sister, is to live another image of the self, another way of being a human being. It embodies an alternative story to that of the modern hero. In the early days a Dominican community was called a *sacra praedicatio*, a 'holy preaching'. To live together as brothers 'with one heart and one mind' was a preaching, before one said a single word. Probably more young people are drawn to religious life by the search for community than for any other reason. According to the apostolic exhortation after the Synod on religious life, *Vita Consecrata*, we are a sign of communion for the whole Church, a witness to the life of the Trinity.

But if community is what draws the young to religious life, it is the difficulty of community life that makes so many give up. We aspire to communion and yet it is so painful to live. When I meet young Dominicans in formation, I often ask what they find best and worst about religious life, and they usually give the same answer to both questions: living in community. That is because we are all the children of this age, moulded by its perception of the modern self. We are not wolves in sheep's clothing. We are bears in nuns' habits!

Perhaps one could say that in religious life we live the mirror image of the crisis of the modern self. The modern self aspires to an autonomy, a freedom, a detachment that is impossible to sustain, because no one can be human alone. We need to belong to communities to be human at all, whatever we may think. But we religious live the mirror image of this drama. We enter religious life aspiring for community, longing to be truly brothers and sisters of each other, and yet we are products of modernity, marked by its individualism, its fear of commitment, its hunger for independence. Most of us are born into families with 1.5 children and it is hard to live with the crowd. And so the modern self and the religious life are alternative aspects of the same tension. The modern self dreams of an impossible autonomy, and we religious aspire to a community which is hard to sustain.

The bear cannot become the nun during the space of a year's noviciate. There is the slow education in becoming human, in learning to speak and to hear, to break the hold of self-absorption and egoism, which makes myself the centre of the world. It is the slow rebirth through prayer and conversation, that will liberate me from false images of God and the other person.

In this we live, naked, acutely, the drama of the modern Church. Never before has the Church so insistently presented herself as a community. *Koinonia* is the heart of all contemporary ecclesiologies. And yet never before has the Church, at least in Western Europe, offered so little real communion. We speak the language of communion, but it is rarely how we live. Language and reality have come apart. One of the ways in which we try to give flesh and blood to this dream of communion is surely by daring to build communities in impossible places, where everyone else has given up. So often in recent years, I have found little communities of religious, usually women, building community where everyone else seems to have despaired, where human beings are crushed and dispersed by violence and poverty. Where it seems hopeless, one can find often a few sisters, making a home with an open door.

One image will stand for so many memories. The day after I celebrated the Easter Vigil with that nun in the monastery, I went to visit a little chapel run by the brethren in Caracas, in one of the most violent *barrios* of Latin America. The chapel was filled with bullet holes. On average some twenty-eight people are murdered in the parish every weekend by gun fire. On the wall behind the altar was a fresco painted by the local children. There was a picture of the Last Supper, with Jesus eating with a circle of Dominicans, men and women. Dominic was patting his dog. But the beloved disciple, sleeping on the side of Jesus, was a local child, a kid from the streets. It was a symbol of the child who had eventually found somewhere to belong in this violent world, the promise of a home.

CONCLUSION

I must conclude. I began by asserting that we can only find the meaning of religious life if we see how it is an answer to the search for the meaning of human life. And then I suggested that one way to understand the contemporary crisis of meaning in western society is by saying that the basic story that we tell about who we are and where we are going, no longer works. This is symbolised by our beloved bear. It is a story filled with contradictions. It tells of progress but seems to be leading us to poverty. It offers freedom, and yet often we find ourselves powerless. It invites us to be the modern self, autonomous and alone, and yet we discover that we cannot be human without community.

So religious life can only respond to that hunger for meaning by embodying another story, another vision of what it is to be human, which we see symbolised in our even more beloved nun, singing to the Candle in the night. And this is a story which offers another sense of time. It is not so much the inevitable march of progress as the story of how we meet the Lord who summons us to himself. And what drives that story is not the competition of the free, but the unimaginable creativity of God who raises the dead. And the hero of this story is not the solitary hero of modernity, but the brother or sister who find themselves in community, and build community for others.

Religious life is nothing other than the attempt to live that other story, the paschal story of death and resurrection. As Bruno Chenu wrote in his excellent book, which I read too late, 'Religious endeavour to put into practice a certain baptismal logic: a life in Christ taken to its ultimate implications.'[4] The vows do not give a different, a special meaning to our lives. But they make public and explicit our rejection of the story of the bear. Obedience, for example, is a clear rejection of the image of the self as autonomous, solitary and disengaged. It is a declaration of our intention to live by that other story, to discover who we are in the common life of the brethren. It is a commitment to be liberated from the unsustainable burden of the modern and lonely self. In obedience, we also reject the image of life as the struggle to be strong, just as in poverty we publicly renounce the competitive struggle for success, the rat race of the consumerist society. In chastity we accept that the deepest fertility we can ever have is that of the creative God who raises the dead.

These vows leave us naked and exposed. They subvert any other stories that might give provisional meaning to my life and enable me to carry on for another day. We promise to give up

4. *L'Urgence prophetique, Dieu au defi de l'Historie*, Paris, p. 262.

career, financial success, any of the hiding places that might suggest that the bear is right after all. If that paschal story is not true, then our lives have no meaning at all and 'we are of all people the most to be pitied.' (1 Cor 15:19)

This is not easy. We are children of modernity and we have been formed by its stories and have shared its dreams. I know, for example, that I myself am more like the bear than the nun. My instinctive responses are more often that of the solitary self than the brother. I know that I have barely begun the process of being reborn. My imagination is but half reshaped. Waiting at the bus stops in Rome and looking at the posters, I see myself.

From this I draw two conclusions. First of all, that at least I can share with my contemporaries a struggle to lose the mask of the bear and acquire a human face. If I did not share this struggle, then I would have nothing to say in response to the question: 'What is the sense of human life today?' The religious is not a celestial being, who has escaped modernity, but one whose vows have made the tussle to be new inevitable, inescapable. We share with other people the pangs of rebirth. If we are honest about our struggles, then they may come to share our hope.

Secondly, because it is hard, then we must really dedicate ourselves to building communities in which this new paschal life is possible. A religious community needs to be more than a place where we can eat our meals, say a few prayers and come to sleep every night. It is a place of death and resurrection, in which we help each other to become new. I have come to like the idea of religious life as an ecosystem, a concept that I have developed elsewhere.[5] An ecosystem is what enables strange forms of life to flourish. Every strange form of life needs its ecosystem. This is

5. 'Religious Vocations: Leaving behind the Usual Signs of Identity', *supra*, pp. 189-209, at pp. 206-209.

especially true for the young who now come to religious life, often only recently come to faith in God. A rare frog cannot live and reproduce and have a future unless it has all the necessary elements of its ecosystem: a pond, shade, various plants, lots of mud, and other frogs. To be a religious is to choose a strange form of life, and we each will need our sustaining environment: prayer, silence, community. Otherwise we will not thrive. So a good superior is an ecologist who helps his brethren build the necessary environments in which they may thrive. But ecosystems are not little prisons which cut us off from the modern world. An ecosystem allows a form of life to flourish and react creatively with other forms of life.

We need ecosystems that sustain in us that sense of paschal-time, the rhythm of the liturgical year which carries us from Advent to Pentecost. We need communities that are marked by its rhythms, by its patterns of feasting and fasting. We need communities in which we do not simply rush through a few Psalms before leaving for work, but where we are sustained as people who even in the wilderness may finally come to praise. We need to build communities in which we can share our faith, and share our despair, so that we bring each other through the wilderness. We need communities in which we may slowly be reborn as brothers and sisters, children of the living God.

The nun sings in the dark, as Dominic sang as he walked through the south of France. This is the Christian vocation. St Augustine told us: 'Walk along the way. Sing as you walk. That's what travellers do to ease the burden ... Sing a new song. Let no one sing old songs there. Sing the love songs of your homeland ... Like travellers, sing, and they often sing at night. All the noises they hear around are frightening. Yet they sing even when they are afraid of bandits'.[6] Or bears!

6. *Enarrationes in Psalmos* 66.6

Living the Gospel Today

Blackfriars, Oxford

TRUTH AND CONFLICT
REBUILD HUMAN COMMUNITIES

Most of my adult life I have been involved in universities, as a student, a chaplain and finally as a teacher. I taught at Oxford for twelve years, as a member of Blackfriars.

Eight years ago, this happy academic life, giving tutorials and lectures and sometimes sleeping in the Bodleian Library, was brought to an abrupt end. After a few years as Provincial of England, I moved to Rome. It meant substituting airports for libraries. In my first three years as Master of the Dominican Order I visited eighty-three countries. I was confronted with a world whose violence and poverty I had never imagined. I discovered that for very many of my brothers and sisters, being a member of a religious order today means living dangerously. I shall never forget a trip to Rwanda, when the country was beginning to erupt. After a day of being confronted with so much violence, so much misery, we were reduced to silence. There was nothing to say. Thank God, literally, we were given something to do, the ritual of the Eucharist, a rite to express what we could not articulate. And then there were visits to Algeria, where our brothers and sisters live in daily danger of death. In August 1996 I stayed with brothers who work in the Amazon basin, who receive regular death threats from local landowners who openly admit that they liquidate anyone who opposes them, sometimes boiling their bodies and feeding them to the pigs. And when I met a group of brothers and sisters recently from the United States, and asked them what they believed to be the principle challenge for us in America today, they too claimed that it was violence.

Two very different lives then. It would be easy to suggest that after years of living in the ivory tower of the university I had at

An abridged text of an address delivered to the Department of Religious Studies at Yale University and published in *Priests and People*, December 1996.

last met the world as it really was, 'the real world' as some say. My reaction is different, though. I have become more than ever convinced of the importance of places of reflection and research if we are to heal our society of its violence and rebuild the human community.

BEYOND THE 'SINGLE VISION'

One root of this social crisis, and there are others, is what might be termed a crisis of truth. I wonder whether there has ever been such a violent century, with the First World War, and its millions dead, the death camps of Auschwitz and Dachau, the bombs of Hiroshima and Nagasaki, and the endless haemorrhaging of human society since then in war, poverty and starvation. There are many reasons for this, from the globalisation of the economy to the development of technology. Yet one seed of this violence is surely that we have lost confidence in our ability to seek the truth together, and so to build a common human home in which we may recognise ourselves and each other.

In this poem 'The Second Coming', Yeats describes a world that is disintegrating, and he hints at the roots of that crisis:

Turning and turning in the widening gyre
The falcon cannot hear the falconer
Things fall apart; the entire world cannot hold;
More anarchy is loosed upon the world,
The blood dimmed tide is loosed, and everywhere.
The ceremony of innocence is drowned;
The best lack all conviction, while the worst
Are full of passionate intensity

'The best lack all conviction'. George Steiner wrote a book called *Real Presences. Is There Anything in What We Say?* And the title says it all. Steiner maintains that the profound crisis which we are living has its roots in the last century, and the collapse of shared belief that our words have anything to do with how things are. They disclose nothing. The covenant between word and world is broken. He writes:

> It is this break of the covenant between word and world which constitutes one of the few genuine revolutions of spirit in western history and which defines modernity itself.[1]

And it is perhaps the temptation of those who work in academic institutions, a profound scepticism as to any truth claims. We may spot how patterns of domination may perform our perception of the world, how patriarchy and racism corrupt and betray, and yet remain uncomfortable at any more positive claim as to how things are. We may be more likely to accept the authenticity of a person that the universal veracity of a statement. To quote Yeats again, 'A man can embody the truth, but he cannot know it'.

But the other side of modernity is 'the worst' who 'are full of a passionate intensity'. I read the review of a book by Ben Kieran, who runs the Cambodian Genocide Programme at Yale. What he describes is the crucifixion of a whole country on the cross of a dogma. He quotes one person who was deported from Phnom Penh in 1975: 'if we said anything they would say that we were obstructing the wheel of history. We would lose our arms and legs' – a people literally dismembered by a vision of the world, broken on the wheel of history.

FUNDAMENTALISM

William Blake once prayed:

> May God us keep
> from single vision and Newton's sleep.[2]

1. *Real Presences: Is There Anything in What We Say?*, London, 1989, p. 93.
2. Letter to Thomas Butts, 22 November 1802 – verses composed while walking from Felpham to Havast.

In this singleness of vision which is perhaps the other side of modernity, it may find its most militant expression in religious fundamentalism. The death of the seven Trappist monks in Algeria in May, killed by Islamic fundamentalists, stands as a potent symbol for the fundamentalism that is so characteristic of nearly all religions at the end of this millennium. Christianity is not immune to it, whether a biblical fundamentalism into which Protestantism can easily fall, or the dogmatic fundamentalism of some Catholics.

But I do not believe that there is anything especially religious about fundamentalism. It is not the last resort of religion trying to hang on in a secular age. In fact this literalism seems to me to be one aspect of that scientific culture which is at the heart of modernity. After all, Blake prays for release 'from single vision and Newton's sleep'.

Religious fundamentalism may look as if it is protesting against the evils of a secular world, but it is what happens to religion when it becomes infected by that literalism which has often been so uncharacteristic of a scientific culture

The most pervasive and destructive of all fundamentalisms in this century have surely been secular. The 'single vision' of communism has been for America the great enemy for most of this century, and perhaps we are a little lost now that the enemy is barely breathing anymore. But it is mirrored in another 'single vision' which is ravaging the planet just as surely, that of the world as global market, in which we are all reduced to consumers, eating and being eaten. Admittedly we do not go out and shoot people who do not believe in free market economies, but all over the planet it is a vision of the world that is destroying human community, and leading to death.

Karl Polanyi wrote a book some fifty years ago called *The Great Transformation: the Political and Economic Origins of Our*

Time, which described the roots of this way of looking at the world. At its heart there is a fiction, which is that everything can be seen as a commodity. Human lives and labour, the land, money, can all be seen as goods produced for marketing, commodities for sale. But this is a fiction and a deception, 'the commodity fiction'.

This is the most widespread fundamentalism of our time, and held with a religious passion. In France the other day, I saw a programme about how to be nice to tourists, and in its conclusion was 'Saying *Bonjour* is a commercial act.' In England even the football teams have become merely competitors in the market, and a good year for Manchester United is one in which they make money as well as winning matches.

What I am trying to evoke, with a few broad brush strokes, is that crisis of truth which I believe lies at the heart of much of the violence of our time.

'The best lack all conviction and the worst are full of a passionate intensity'. Modernity is characterised by the scepticism of those who are tempted to disbelieve that our words can say anything, and the intolerance of those who believe that their words say it all.

Surely so much war, genocide and intolerance find their roots in the collapse of a belief that in talking to each other we may come to a common truth in which we may recognise each other. There is not much place for dialogue when we are caught between the twin temptations of relativism and ideology.

REACHING OUT FOR THE TRUTH

Whenever I set off on a trip, the hardest decision is what books to take with me. What can I read on the planes and waiting in the airports to save me from brain death? For my last trip, I decided to take Newman's *The Idea of a University*. His definition of the purpose of a university will probably seem vastly over optimistic to us. The university exists, he writes, to educate 'the intellect to ransom well in all matters, to reach out towards truth and to grasp it.'[3] There is a wonderful Victorian confidence about that statement 'to reach out towards truth and to grasp it'. It may smack of intellectual arrogance to us.

Yet what I found fascinating was Newman's description of how the university trains us to reach out for the truth. He wrote:

> We know, not by a direct and simple vision, not at a glance, but, as it were, by piecemeal and accumulation, by a mental process, by going round an object, by the comparison, the combination, the mutual correction, the continual adaptation, of many partial notions, by the employment, concentration, and joint action of many faculties and exercises of mind.[4]

The process of seeking the truth, then, is not for Newman through the direct and univocal perception of some single vision, but a much more tentative, fumbling, humble approach, trying to feel one's way through 'many partial notions'. This is evocative of what has been my own experience in trying to understand scriptural texts. You cannot march in and claim their meaning with the aid of some grand theory. Study is much more like sneaking up on the meaning of the text, trying this approach and then another, inching one's way towards understanding.

You may begin with a historico-critical approach and then a moment comes when you feel that this is not yielding anything more, and you try to slide up on the text from a sociological perspective; then maybe the time has come for a bit of literary analysis.

To take an image from Wittgenstein, you must be like a carpenter who knows when to use each tool in the bag; when to

3. *Discourse*, VL.1.
4. *Discourse*, VIL.1

use a hammer and when a chisel; when you need glue or when to use a screwdriver.

Emily Dickinson describes well how one has to slink up on the truth, aslant, rather than grabbing it by the forelocks.

> Tell all the Truth but tell it slant –
> Success in Circuit lies
> Too bright for our infirm Delight
> The Truth's superb suprise
>
> As Lightning to the Children eased
> With explanation kind
> The Truth must dazzle gradually
> Or every man be blind.[5]

Creeping up on the truth of a text, or a person, is always a matter of letting oneself be thrown by 'The Truth's superb surprise'. It is letting oneself be astonished, discovering that one did not know in advance what was to be discovered.

Perhaps the first requirement of a good university teacher is that he or she refuses to be a guru, to be the one who knows. St Thomas Aquinas strongly maintained that no one can, strictly speaking, teach anyone anything. All that the teacher can do is to accompany the students in their process of discovery.

THE ROLE OF THE UNIVERSITY

So, in an age of agnosticism and ayatollahs, the role of the university is to be the place where we learn that the truth may be sought. Truth is not to be captured with the cleanness of a single vision, but sneaked up on, through many partial notions, many inadequate theories, through all sorts of tools, and it comes to us finally as a surprise and a gift.

In that sense, it is the paradoxical role of the teacher to

5. *The Poems of Emily Dickinson*, Cambridge MA, 1963 edition, p. 792.

introduce us to the humility of learning. Not because we must learn to submit to a teacher, but because the teacher shows him or herself to be someone on the way, the doctor as fellow disciple.

I am not suggesting that universities are the only places in which we may initiated into this truth-seeking. Families, monasteries, women's groups, guilds, religious orders, schools or artists, all these should be places of learning too. But since the thirteenth century, the university has been a central place for keeping alive this hunger for truth.

Clearly, if the university assumes this role of refusing the single visions that rule this world, whether communist or consumerist, then it will need a real independence of heart and mind. I believe that we should not underestimate the potential cost of our intellectual freedom from the dominant ideologies of our society. Could we resist the subtle pressure to redefine our agenda in return for fat funding from corporations?

This is a question which Seamus Heaney puts delightfully in his poem 'Verses for a Fordham Commencement':

> Or is it a misalliance,
> Ivory towers in a world of violence
> And corporate money.
> Are college walls perhaps a door
> Shut on the workers and the poor
> While the privileged and the few ignore
> The unwashed many?

You will be relieved to know that in the end he exonerates the university.

I think that it is not coincidence that the rise to power of Mrs Thatcher and her ideology of the market saw the closure of dozens of faculties of philosophy in Britain. Philosophy does not earn money.

TALKING WITH A STRANGER

Now I would like to explore another aspect, which is that universities should be places where we can learn to talk to strangers. A consequence of the conflicting fundamentalisms of our time is that those who are different easily become not just strangers but enemies with whom it is impossible to talk.

How can we learn to talk to strangers? What conversation can we initiate with those who are different? And what role can the university play in preparing us for this dialogue?

The most dramatic experience I have had of the pain of dialogue was in Burundi some two years ago. It was during the first explosion of violence, which killed perhaps as many as a hundred thousand people. That would be as if four million people were killed in the U.S.A. Our brothers in Burundi come from both ethnic groups, and all had lost brothers and sisters and family. The struggle was to witness to the gospel by somehow staying together. I visited the country with the local superior, a Tutsi, and a member of the general council of the order, who is Hutu. Before I left we gathered everyone together to celebrate the Eucharist, the sacrament of unity. But what could we all say to each other? As in Rwanda, what was most important was what we could do, repeating the gestures performed by a man in the face of his betrayal and death. Each brother could and did talk of his suffering, of those he had lost, so that they were joined in the suffering rather than divided by it.

One of the functions of the Church, and of a religious order, is to try to be present in those places of deafness and incomprehension, to offer a space where conversations may begin. I think of an ecumenical community I visited in Belfast, which was literally on the frontier between the tribal lands of Catholics and Protestants. It was a place where quietly, slowly, a few brave souls could try to knit some common language. It was above all the women who had the courage to do this. One of our Dominican brothers, Pierre Claverie, the late Bishop of Oran in Algeria, wrote:

> The Church accomplishes its vocation and its mission when it is present in the ruptures which crucify humanity in its flesh and its unity. Jesus is dead, spread-eagled between heaven and earth, arms stretched out to gather together the children of God dispersed by the sin which separates them, isolates them and sets them over against each other and against God himself. God has placed himself in the lines of fracture born of this sin. In Algeria, we are on one of these seismic lines which divide the world: Islam/the West, North/South, rich/poor. We are truly in our place, because it is here that one may glimpse the light of the Resurrection.

(Bishop Claverie was assassinated by a bomb planted by Islamic fundamentalists in August, 1996.)

But how in these hard places can we learn to talk to strangers? I wish to suggest that the university should be one of the places in which we learn to talk to those who are different. Steiner wrote, 'Apprehension [the meeting with the other] signifies both fear and perception.'[5] The meeting of the other is a fearful moment, but it can become a matter of recognition, of understanding. Thinking can open my eyes to see the stranger and build the common human home.

Part of our apprenticeship is surely in learning to read texts written by strangers, and coming to understand them. Struggling with St Paul or Augustine, with Descartes or the texts of the French Revolution, requires of one an openness to the other. It is not unlike an education in friendship. Nicholas Lash argues this very strongly:

5. *Real Presences*, p. 139.

Good learning calls, no less than teaching does, for courtesy, respect, a kind of reverence: for facts and people, evidence and argument, for climates of speech and patterns of behaviour different from our own. Watchfulness is, indeed, in order, but endless suspicion and mistrust are not. There are affinities between the courtesy, the delicacy of attention, required for friendship; the single-minded passionate disinterestedness with which no good scholarly work can be done; and the contemplativity which strains, without credulity, to listen for the voice of God – and does not shout.[6]

The word 'disinterestedness' is worth pausing over. It suggests how the university should be the locus of an alternative perception of reality.

UNPOSSESSIVENESS

But in what sense does scholarly work offer a disinterested perception of things? It would be easy and wrong to mistake this for a distance, a disengagement from concern and commitment. That would be the 'lack of conviction' of the best. And it is surely a temptation of the academic world to fall into a sort of critical detachment which frees our hearts from risks of engagement and commitment, in the name of intellectual freedom. Faced with our messy violent world we may claim a scholarly detachment which justified keeping our hands clean.

I suspect that the disinterestedness that Lash has in mind is quite other. It is a refusal to let one's perception of anything be dominated by 'interest'. This is temptation of any single vision. The Khmer Rouge did not see its prisoners as individuals, but were interested in them merely as functions of the wheel of history, actors in the great class struggle. The consumer society

6. *Believing Three Ways in One God*, London, 1992.

will not delight in the cow for its own sake, but see it as potential profit, unless it happens to be a sad, mad English cow. In this culture of greed, then perhaps study requires of us a certain freedom from acquisitiveness. We may have to learn to see things with unpossessive eyes. It is no coincidence that when Dominic founded an order dedicated to study, he made poverty central to our way of life. The disinterestedness of the scholar is not the detachment of someone who holds back. It is more like the disinterestedness of friendship.

So learning to study the text of strangers is part of my human formation, and forms me as someone who is capable of relating to another: another time, another view, another person. The Constitutions of my Order speak of study as 'the cultivation of humanity's natural inclination to the truth.' This inclination to truth that we need to cultivate is not just a human desire to know many things, but a natural human desire to reach out to those who are different, to break the tight hold of our egocentricity. It wakens us from the illusion that we are the centre of the world. Whether we are studying the ending of Mark's Gospel or the sexual habit of a rare snail, our eyes are being opened to see what is other. Study is ecstatic.

I would even go so far as to say that study can touch and heal the deepest hunger of the human being, which is to love. The perception of the other belongs to loving them. As Simone Weil wrote: 'It is only those we love whose existence we recognise fully: *On ne reconnait pleinement l'existence que de ceux que l'on aime.*' [7]

For example, Augustine's conversion to Christianity was both a falling in love and a moment of understanding. It was an intellectual act and a transformation of his heart.

Late have I loved you, O beauty so ancient and so new; late

7. *Cahier* II, 1953, p. 227.

have I love you... I tasted you and now I hunger and thirst for you; you touched me and I have burnt for your peace.

But that falling in love came from hearing a child command him to read a text: *Tolle lege, tolle lege*, 'Take and read.' Angela Tilby said:

Without books, without reading, our understanding is uninformed, our judgements narrow.... I sometime think that God would rather we were literate than that we were indiscriminately caring. Augustine found his true self through a child's cry and a challenging text. He met the living God on the page of a book, and it broke his heart and set him free.[8]

SOCIAL BEINGS

But if universities are to train us in the delicate art of talking to strangers, then it is not enough that we struggle with texts and try to understand the dead. Ultimately a university will contribute to the building of human community and to the art of dialogue if its members are able to talk with each other. Newman once wrote that if he had to choose between a university with highly trained professors and rigorous examinations, which taught the pupils lots of facts, and one in which a lot of young people merely met and debated with each other, then he would without hesitation choose the latter. Because the primary function of a university is to teach us to be social beings, able to talk, to listen and learn from those who are different.

This is a wonderful idea. Yet in my experience this can be hard. How far are we able to argue with our colleagues, and seek the truth together? How open are we to having our favourite theories questioned? Perhaps the greatest challenge that universities

8. 'Thought for the Day', BBC Radio 4, 13 May 1996, quoted in *The Tablet*, 5 June 1996, p. 792.

face, if they are to contribute to the healing of our bruised world,
is to learn that pleasure of debate with those who are different. As
Theodore Zeldin said, in *An Intimate History of Humanity*:

> Unfortunately, though humans ruminate, cogitate, brood,
> play with ideas, dream and make inspired guesses about the
> thoughts of other people all the time, there has been no Kama
> Sutra of the mind to reveal the sensuous pleasures of thinking,
> to show how ideas can flirt with each other and learn to
> embrace.[9]

When I was a young Dominican student we still sometimes
practised a version of the medieval *dispuatio*. This was a form of
debating central to the life of the thirteenth-century university,
and it embodies a vision of what a university should be. In the
disputatio the aim was not so much to demonstrate that your
opponent was utterly and in every way wrong, and to be derided
and dismissed as a fool. Instead you had to show the limited sense
in which he was right. The aim was, through disagreement and
mutual criticism, to arrive at common truth, that was able to
accommodate what was true in each position.

Perhaps even in universities we have been seduced by a competitive form of debate., which is as blind and violent as the
struggle of the species to survive in the Darwinian jungle, or as
senseless as the struggle for mastery between Coca-Cola and
Pepsi-Cola. But we are called to be a place of counter-culture, of
a different way of relating, through which one believes that one
may learn something from those with whom one disagrees. This
requires of us compassion and vulnerability.

I wish to conclude with a poem by Czeslaw Milosz, in praise
of reason 'beautiful and invincible'. It captures something of the
vocation of the university. And this reason that it praises, is surely

9. London, 1994, p. 442.

not that arrogant reason of the single vision, which believes that
it can grasp the truth with an unhesitating clarity and arrogance,
but that more humble reason which arrives at a just perception
hesitantly, through many 'partial notions', using all the tools she
can find, delighting in debate and dialogue.

Human reason is beautiful and invincible.
No bars, no barbed wire, no pulping of books,
No sentence of banishment can prevail against it.
It establishes the universal ideas in language,
And guides our hand so we write Truth and Justice
With capital letters, lie and oppression with small.
It puts what should be above things as they are,
Is an enemy of despair and friend of hope.
It does not know Jew from Greek, or slave from master,
Giving us the estate of the world to manage.
It saves austere and transparent phrases
From the filthy discord of tortured words.
It says that everything is new under the sun,
Opens the congealed fist of the past.
Beautiful and very young are Philo-Sophia
And poetry, her ally in the service of the good.
As late as yesterday nature celebrated their birth,
The News was brought to the mountains by a unicorn and
    an echo.
Their friendship will be glorious, their time has no limit.
Their enemies have delivered themselves to destruction.

DIALOGUE AND COMMUNION

I wish to address the issue of dialogue and communion, Part III of the *Instrumentum Laboris*.

When St Ignatius of Loyola was ill, he spent his time reading adventure stories, of knights and explorers. But these left him dissatisfied. But then he asked himself: 'What if I were to do what Blessed Francis and Blessed Dominic did?', and he discovered the true adventure of following Christ. Every religious vocation is embarking on this adventure, and one cannot know in advance what it will ask or where it will take one. It may be the adventure of discovering Christ on the streets of Calcutta, the intellectual adventure of a St Thomas, or the mystic adventure of St John of the Cross.

This is an adventure that demands courage, especially today when our vows are in such direct contradiction to the values of our society, when life-long commitment is incomprehensible for many and when religious life often brings the danger of martyrdom. What many religious hope for from this Synod is that it will encourage us to have the confidence and creativity of our founders.

If we religious respond wholeheartedly, there will be inevitable moments of tension as the *Instrumentum Laboris* recognizes. A renewal of religious life, any bold experiment, will often be seen initially as threatening and suspect. When the Dominicans arrived in the University of Paris in the thirteenth century, the troops had to be called in to protect them from the diocesan clergy! One of the challenges to the Synod is to discover how we may live these moments of tension fruitfully, as part of our journey to the Kingdom, as building up the Body of Christ rather than in tearing it apart. Above all in the Church we need to strengthen

Address to the Episcopal Synod on Religious Life, Rome, November, 1994.

the climate of mutual confidence.

The *Instrumentum Laboris* asks us to confront moments of tension through dialogue: 'The difficulties which sometimes arise must be overcome by searching together for all means to bring about a sincere dialogue in charity, a charity which always looks to the good of the Church' (72). The sign of true charity is that it heals us of fear, for 'perfect charity casts out fear' (1 Jn 4:18). Fear is corrosive of all communion. Too often in the Church we are afraid, afraid of debate. There is no need for fear. From the days of Pentecost, the Church has known tensions. The community of Jerusalem, which was 'one in heart and mind' (Acts 4:32), quarrelled over the distribution of money and over interpretations of obedience to the Law. The mystery of our communion in the Spirit, of which the hierarchy is the visible sign, does not mean a seamless unanimity. Debates and arguments are the signs of a Church which is always being renewed by the Spirit. A perfect unanimity would be a sign of the immobility of death.

Gaudium et Spes speaks of the Church's mission of dialogue, which requires of us 'mutual esteem, reverence and harmony, and acknowledgement of all legitimate diversity' (92). Dialogue is fruitful when it is the struggle to learn from each other. The medieval *disputatio* practised by St Thomas was based on the assumption that one's opponent is always, in some sense, right. It is easy to identify another person's errors. Do we have the courage to hear what they may teach us? The struggle of true dialogue is like Jacob wrestling with the angel, leaving one wounded and blessed. This demands of us vulnerability. In many religious congregations there is the practice of the Chapter, in which one learns the mutual obedience of listening to one's brother or sister. Even though this is only one model of obedience, and evolved in a very specific context, yet it is a rich tradition that has much to offer the Church.

Above all we can only live these hard moments of discernment fruitfully if we have a profound humility. We are called to give ourselves totally to that Absolute who is God, but who is beyond all words, and whose truth we never master. So any debate or argument within the Church should be characterised by an immense humility before the mystery of God and our salvation, with what St John of the Cross calls 'the emptiness of faith'.

Throughout the world we can see today a crisis of powerlessness. Two thirds of all human beings live in political and economic situations in which they have no say over their lives, and where they feel doomed to a terrible passivity. Often women feel themselves voiceless and weak. Even in the rich countries most people's lives are subjected to the all-powerful market. The temptation of our age is passivity, a fatalism.

But Peter says to the cripple in the Temple, 'Stand up and walk' (Acts 3:6). Peter is the one who is called to strengthen his brethren. The Church is invited to live the mystery of Pentecost as a community in which this fatalism is challenged, in which every child of God should be empowered to do more than we ever believed possible. As the Holy Father said, addressing the religious of England and Wales, the vows should 'free us from the tyranny of the consumer society'.[1] The Holy Spirit is, as St Paul says, 'no cowardly spirit' (2 Tim 1:7) and should breathe confidence into us all. May we religious have the courage to set off after Christ, as did Francis and Dominic and Ignatius and Teresa before us, doing new things and risking our lives.

1. Meeting with Religious, Roehampton, Saturday 29 June 1982.

A FERTILE CONCEPTION
– INCULTURATION

It is a great pleasure for me to have been here these last few days, listening to this debate on Inculturation in Religious Life and Formation. I want to share a few very simple reflections on the theme but with great hesitation since I am becoming one of the least inculturated people I know. I move so rapidly from one country to another that I have to look out of the window when I get up to remember where I am: 'There are coconut trees, and so it cannot be London.' In fact when I was in Chicago, one person thought from my accent that I was Irish and another that I was Australian. Here one of my own brothers has got the idea that I am American. I am starting to get worried! Secondly I have no expertise in this area. At the General Chapter of Mexico we talked much about inculturation and acculturation and deculturation and inter-culturation. Peter Lobo made some fine contributions to the debate. At the end I swore to myself that I would never again say anything about such matters. But the first lesson I have learnt as Master of the Order is that of obedience, and so here goes.

The last time that I was in England I had lunch with an aunt, and she asked me what I thought of Hans Küng. So l started to explain what I thought were his strengths and weaknesses. After five minutes she stopped me and said: 'My dear, all I want to know is this: Is he a good or is he bad?' And let's face it, in most theological debate that is what people wish to know! And if my aunt were here today, I would say to her: yes, inculturation is a good thing. In fact there can be no good theology which is not inculturated. One problem in the Church is that people often

Address delivered to the Second Joint Conference of Dominican Major Superiors and Formators at Nagpur, India, on 21 October, 1993.

think that whereas one might find inculturated theology in India
or Africa, where they live, whether it is Rome or Munich, no such
contextualization is necessary. But I would like to add three
points:

1. The Gospel should both embrace and transform any culture
in which it is planted.

2. No culture is pure and static. Every culture is in a constant
process of evolution, creating new meaning, otherwise it is dead.
The Gospel should meet a culture there where it is most creative
and fresh, like a bee seeking out the nectar of the flower.

3. Inculturation is always painful, like any process of coming
to birth. And we can only engage in it if we are prepared to
experiment and sometimes fail. This requires great mutual trust.

There are many other things that I would like to add, such as
the need for prayer and for study if the inculturation is to have
depth, but those comments will have to wait for another time.

THE GOSPEL BOTH EMBRACES AND CRITICIZES
ANY CULTURE THAT IT ENCOUNTERS

As Father Thomas Aykara said, the fundamental event of
inculturation is the Incarnation. God, the source of all, becomes
a squealing, crying, Jewish baby, who needed to have his nappies
changed, and who had to learn to walk and speak like any other
child. Often people fear that inculturation might fragment the
Universal Church and divide us from each other, and yet the one
in whom we are united, the one who overthrows the boundaries
of division, is this first century Jewish man. You cannot get more
inculturated than that. And yet at the same time one must say that
Jesus was one who threatened Jewish identity, who challenged
the Law and who welcomed the Samaritan.

He was utterly Jewish and yet he was perceived as a threat to
Jewish identity. And this must surely always be so in every

moment of inculturation. Every culture builds a home, in which the Gospel may be planted. But every home excludes a stranger, who must be welcomed and whose presence is perceived as threatening. Every culture has its Harijans.

And a culture is not only defined by whom it excludes, but by what it shuts out, by its perceptions of reality, its underlying philosophy. These too are challenged by the Gospel.

We can see the same process at work when Christianity embraces the Roman world. We adopt the language of the Romans and speak Latin; we still build our churches on the basis of their halls, even here at Nagpur; the priest wears a distant descendant of Roman clothes; we accepted much of vision of Roman law. And yet Christianity reached out beyond the boundaries of the Empire to embrace the stranger, for example the Irish! The foreigner is made at home. Every culture is both welcomed and transformed.

The Spirit is like yeast, which transforms what it meets. In France grapes become wine; in England hops become the loveliest beer; in Scotland grain becomes whisky; in Japan rice becomes saki.

And this reflects that founding act of Christ, who performed that utterly Jewish act of the Passover, the feast of the home, and yet used it to found a community in which everyone had a place – the betrayer like Judas, the denier like Peter, and all the disciples who would run away and leave their Saviour alone. It is the home in which anyone can belong.

During my travels around the Order this first year I have seen how in every continent, inculturation poses this same question: who is the stranger whom we must welcome? In Africa, for example, where tribal identity is strong, and where the Order is perceived as a tribe, the challenge is to make at home the members of another tribe, to be a tribe beyond tribalism. I went to Rwanda which has been deeply divided by conflicts between two tribes. Here our Vicariate of Rwanda and Burundi is a sign of the Gospel, for members of both tribes live together as brothers. This is an incarnation of the Gospel, in which our identity as human beings is prised open, stretched and transformed. When I went to Zaire in February it was in a state of near civil war between tribal groups. You could see both how the Church was trying to enter the extraordinary richness of that culture, and be truly Zairean. The liturgy was wonderfully African, alive and beautiful. But we also had to challenge the tribal identities and invite people to find themselves in Christ.

In Guatemala, the strangers are perhaps above all the indigenous people, living in the mountains. Here we have a wonderful experiment of inculturation, in which the sisters and the brothers are co-operating. At Coban in the mountains of Alta Vera Paz, the sisters are accepting many indigenous vocations, and seeking to evolve a way of being a Dominican that respects their customs, their lovely songs, their ways of dressing and being human. The brethren have built a study centre nearby, which is in contact with the brethren working in the indigenous villages, collecting information about their rituals and customs, so that we can find a way of evolving an indigenous way of being Dominican, for both the men and the women. The stranger is made welcome. But what is the challenge that we must put to them?

A priest who worked with the Masai in Kenya wished to have a truly inculturated Eucharist, and so he tried to make it as African as possible. And when he turned up to preside he found that gathered around the table were only the men. The women were not to be seen. So he asked: 'Where are the women?' And the men replied: 'It is not our custom to eat with the women.' Is that inculturation or a betrayal of the Gospel? No prizes for the correct answer!

In the discussion group in which I have participated at this Conference we found similar questions posed in the context of Asia. On the one hand we saw that there was much to learn from the Indian understanding of the Guru, the Master. We were reminded that becoming a Master demanded real asceticism, real renunciation, a real poverty and simplicity of life. (I was not, I might say, taking all of this personally.) Do we, who are regarded as gurus, really make that deep apprenticeship of silence and asceticism? Do the religious of Hinduism and Buddhism put us to shame? Where might one find Dominic in India if he walked the roads today? Would we meet him walking the roads with a begging bowl, like a Jain holy man? Does not this culture challenge us to rediscover our own ascetic and mendicant tradition? Yet at the same time we found that we wished to challenge some aspects of the Asian understanding of the guru. We do not expect the disciple to submit to the Master in blind obedience. As the Provincial of the Philippines said: 'The Master must teach the disciple to learn to learn, to learn creativity, originality. If he stands on the Master's shoulders it is to see further.'

I think that Western culture poses particular problems with regard to inculturation. You do not find theologians demanding that we be inculturated, adopt the norms of our society, and yet that is often what is happening. I think that this is partially because it has become not just one culture among the cultures of the world. Since the fall of Communism, it has become the one global culture which threatens to suck in and absorb all others in its vast stomach. Western consumerist capitalism is the culture which simultaneously embraces nearly everyone, and excludes the vast majority. It touches most of humanity and shuts it out from its promised land. It sells everyone a TV so that they may see paradise, and then forbids them to enter.

For me a symbol of this was a visit to Soweto a couple of years ago. I wandered about this sad and exuberant place, this great township of some two million African people, which was not until recently even marked on South African maps. And I came across a school and ambled in. And the children ran to me shouting what I thought was some obscure African word, 'ninja'. It turned out to refer to some strange turtles that are the heroes of the then latest TV series in the United States. And they had cups and T-shirts and even shoes covered with pictures of these ninja turtles. These children were offered the culture of American TV, and told they could never belong. I think also of the endless queues of people waiting in Moscow to buy a MacDonald's hamburger, a week's wages for this 'holy wafer' of Western culture.

Do we Dominicans wish to be radically inculturated into this culture? Will this add new riches to our religious life? This is a culture of wealth, not just of wealthy people but of the glory of money. Perhaps more radically than in any other society, the poor cannot properly belong since they are by definition those who have failed. Their fate is invisibility. Of course I do not for one moment deny the wonderful things that this culture has produced, and its real inventiveness; its tolerance for human difference; its love of human rights and so on. But I would still suggest that we religious must resist inculturation here and be with those who do not belong. But do we? This is a question I put to the superiors of the Dominican Leadership Conference in the United States last week. Even the language we use suggests we are sucked into an alien view of the world. The Prior Provincial becomes part of 'The Administration', a sort of Chief Executive; the brethren become 'personnel', and instead of a love of poverty we have endless discussions of budgets. Maybe the vows of our religious life are in such radical contradiction with the values of the consumerist West that we can only thrive as religious if we opt out, become out-culturated! Chastity seems puerile, poverty absurd, and obedience infantile.

I also think that it is interesting that this matter of poverty illustrates the ambiguity of the relationship of the Gospel and culture. In India there is precisely a religious tradition which respects poverty and which invites us to embrace it; in the West there is a culture of wealth which we are invited to refuse.

Inculturation is then both an embrace and a challenge. And it must be so, for the identity to which we are called as Christians is beyond our naming. Who we are is a mystery hidden in God. For, as St John says: 'My children, we know that we are God's children now, but we do not know what we are to be. We know that when Christ appears, we shall be like him.' (1 Jn 3:2)

INCULTURATION AND CREATIVITY

I was fascinated by the argument between Professor Pawar and Mataji the first evening. Being a good Dominican I love an argument. It was wonderful to hear someone challenge our assumption that inculturation was a good thing. We seemed to be faced with a dilemma: to inculturate and risk assimilation or to stick to our own traditions and culture and go on being foreigners. Do you do what the Buddhists do or follow the Roman rubrics? What a sticky spot to be in! It is my own view that this is a false dilemma, for it only faces us if we make the mistake of thinking of culture as something frozen, stuck, immobile, like a pure white ice cream in a cultural deep freeze. Here you have some set and eternal thing which is Indian culture, whose practices you either adopt or remain a foreigner.

Perhaps the magic of Indian culture for me is precisely its complexity and fluidity, forever old and new. This is symbolised by what I have heard from the window of my room. In the

evening I heard the sound of the music of some Hindu festival –
maybe it was for the festival of the goddess – and mixed with the
beat of the drums was the rhythm of one of those endless trains
on that network of railway lines holding the subcontinent together.
And then in the early hours I have heard another train, whose
hooter strangely resonated with the early morning call to prayer
of the mosque, perhaps played on a tape recorder. Every culture
is alive in a constant state of transformation, of meeting other
cultures and absorbing or rejecting them, of remembering old
ways and inventing new ones. Any culture which is worthy of the
name is complex and fertile.

Think of Jewish culture. The whole history of that culture is
one of interaction, of the absorption and rejection and
transformation of ideas from Egypt, Canaan, Babylon, Assyria,
Persia, Greece and Rome. There never was a pure Jewish culture
which you could pop into the deep freeze, any more than there is
a pure English or Indian or Japanese culture. If there were they
would be brain dead. They bubble away like Irish stews constantly
evolving.

How does the Incarnation, that epitome of inculturation, take
place? It is through the most acutely creative moment of human
life, in the conception of a child. God pitches his tent among us by
meeting us in our most deeply creative moment. God becomes
one of us at the moment that we make something new, present in
the fertility of a woman. And it is always so in any true moment
of inculturation for a culture is most alive, most itself, where it is
most creative, just as a tree is most alive at the tips of its branches.
And the challenge of inculturation is to be there, sharing in its
inventiveness, sharing its exploration. The choice is not to adopt
a given Buddhist or Hindu ceremony or carry on with a Roman
one: 'Do we say the Rosary or sing a mantra?' We enter it as it
makes things new, for then something may be born which is

utterly Indian and utterly Christian.

The most wonderful example of that was given to us in the Indian dance of the life of Jesus that we saw the other night. I think that this was more than a synthesis of the Indian and the Christian. It was mating which brought to birth a child which was completely of both its parents. What it meant to be Indian was extended and deepened in that dance, and what it meant to be Christian was expanded. Such moments make us more Catholic. When I saw those wonderful finger movements I understand what it might mean to celebrate that the 'finger of God is upon us'. Never have I seen the mystery of the Resurrection so beautifully evoked. Afterwards I asked myself why. Why was I so touched? I think that it is because for us the Resurrection is the Resurrection of the Body, and so it is most radiantly evoked in the dance of the bodies, expressed in the stretching of our bodiliness. The dancers said that their dance is prayer. One might say that our bodiliness is made prayerful. What better way to evoke the Resurrection in which the Body of Christ is utterly transformed into perfect praise?

Let me give you another example: Everywhere I went in Central America earlier this year I was struck by the thriving popular culture. Our Dominican students wrote poems, painted, composed music. When I asked the pre-novices in El Salvador to tell me about their society, they spontaneously composed five little plays, including one about the visitation of a contemplative monastery of Dominican nuns by the Mother General, 'Mother Timotea'. Here one could imagine an inculturation of the Gospel, because here there was the fertility doing something new. The example I loved most was that of a Haitian cross, painted by a peasant in our parish in the central mountains. It made the cross into a *via crucis*, along which walked a peasant, walking the way that all Haitian peasants must go, a path of suffering. But at the centre of this cross was a flowering palm tree, the dead wood bore fruit. And behind the hills one could see the glimmerings of a new dawn. Here was a symbol so old and so new, the glorious and beautiful cross, pointing one back to the flowering crosses of the Middle Ages and further, and yet so new and so of just this moment and culture. Yesterday we saw the flowering cross in the philosophy house of the Congregation of Mary Immaculate. In theology one could think of Thomas Aquinas grasping and transforming Aristotle, and giving us a theology which is utterly Aristotelian and utterly Christian.

Surely it belongs to our Dominican way to love what is simultaneously so traditional and so fresh, this beauty 'so ancient and so new' – the ever-fertile tradition. As Mataji said, quoting the Chinese proverb: 'Find your roots and then fly.' The Enlightenment because it rejected tradition, drove a wedge between our feet and our wings.

So the challenge of inculturation is surely to be there where the action is, there where there is intellectual and artistic creativity, so that we may make that which is both utterly our own and which belongs to the culture. In any culture we must seek out the thinkers, the artists, the explorers and sit at their feet so that they can help us to make something new. It does not even matter whether they are believers are not.

And this involves courage and trust. We must let people experiment, try things out and sometimes fail. We have the liberty to make mistakes. We must not fear failure. One famous theologian, I forget who, said that one cannot contribute a single theological insight unless one makes a hundred mistakes. There can be no creativity if you are afraid to play a bit – *homo ludens*, playful humanity. And you cannot play around if you are afraid of falling on your face. You cannot dance if you are always afraid of standing on another's feet.

An interesting question to ask is this: do we dare to accept young men and women who might wish to venture a bit into the unknown? What do we look for in vocations? Do we wish them to be nice and safe, people who will not rock the boat? Do we dare accept the rather difficult ones, who will certainly be a problem but who might, just might, be saints? It is good to imagine how we might have reacted if some of our great predecessors had applied to join our Province. What would we have written about them after their novitiates. St Thomas Aquinas: 'Eats and thinks too much. Refuses to join in communal sport and play basketball'; Jordan of Saxony: 'Always writing to a sister Diana; he will have problems with chastity'; Catherine of Siena: 'Too fond of the brethren, and thinks she hears voices. Bad start'; Fra Angelico: 'We can't afford the paint'; Savonarola: 'We can't afford the books; he keeps burning them'; Las Casas: 'He stirs things up too much'; Martin de Porres: 'His obsession with people at the door upsets community life. No sense of obedience and said that it was less important than charity. Troublemaker'. And what would we have said of Dominic? Would we have let him in? Would we?

You might think that we Dominicans who so care for the truth should above all fear error. On the contrary, it is because we believe that the Holy Spirit is poured upon the people of God that we can dare to risk getting it wrong, for the Church will tell us when we do. History suggests that sometimes it may say that we are wrong when we are not. That is the pain of bringing about the new. The point is that we can play with confidence. I can play with ideas and search and experiment because it does not all depend upon me. It seems to me that the adventure of inculturation is inseparable from that strong sense of our wider belonging in the Order and the Church. It is because we belong that we dare to be free. If we are neurotic about making mistakes, as religious often are, then it suggests we do not believe in Pentecost. Look at

St Peter, our rock. He hardly ever got it right, and the Church did not collapse.

LET US TALK TO ONE ANOTHER

The sort of process that I am envisaging, of being creative and imaginative, of experiment and taking risks, will of course be painful and disturbing. It will create moments of conflict and uncertainty. One person's inculturation is another person's betrayal. Just think of sexual ethics. Do the official sexual ethics of the Church represent a refusal to enter the modern world, as most of my young friends seem to think, or a prophetic stance against a degradation of the body? Should we inculturate – and have lots more sex and make many of the young feel more at home – or be a counter-culture which might exclude the young for whom this is incomprehensible, but be a witness to the Gospel? Another example: when I was a Dominican student in Paris twenty years ago, the brave and prophetic thing to do seemed to be to give up the habit, live in an ordinary flat and get a job. Today it looks rather boringly conformist.

Any experimentation, any creativity, will involve painful disagreements, dissension, mutual puzzlement. 'This is not the Order I joined', some may say. And so it has always been, ever since the beginning, ever since Peter confronted Jesus when he began to walk on the way to Jerusalem; ever since Paul confronted Peter at Antioch for refusing to eat with the Gentiles. There is nothing new in such conflicts. What matters is whether they are fertile, fruitful. Do they lead us to truth? I believe that we should never embark on such a course of experimentation, of inculturation, if we do not dare to talk to one another. And do we, do we dare to talk and listen?

One of things that has most struck me during this last year of wandering about the world, is just how much our Church is marked by silence. It is not the meditative rich silence that Mataji can teach us. It is not the silence of our contemplative nuns but the silence that comes of fear. I believe that what most afflicts us is a fear of debate. It is not that people do not make statements; there are statements about dissident theologians and statements by dissident theologians. The papers are full of denunciations and counter-accusations but this does not add up to much of a conversation. Surely we should be among those who, as at a dreadful tea party, try to get the dialogue going!

We are one of the largest and most diverse religious families in the Church. Where else could one find such a diversity of people, brethren and sisters and nuns and laity, contemplatives and actives, academics and pastoral people, progressives and conservatives. If we cannot take the risk of talking then who will? And yet sometimes at the heart even of our own communities, where three or four are gathered together in Dominic's name, there may be silence in the midst of them. As I endlessly repeat as I wander around the world: we do have a tradition of dialogue, of disputation. And, as you can see in St Thomas, this is not founded on hammering your opponent into the ground, but arguing with him so as to learn from him or her. Central to our tradition is the belief that you might argue with someone precisely because you dare to hope that he or she may teach you something. Who was that holy man who grabbed his opponent and said: 'I will not let you go until you teach me something'? We should wrestle with the other as Jacob wrestled with the angel, so that we may demand a blessing.

We must dare to raise the question of truth. It is our motto. In much of modern Western culture, this is a word which one may hardly breathe. To question the truth of another's utterance, is to put them into question, is to question their value, their right to be. If someone tells you that he/she is really a Martian who has come from outer space, then you must merely reply: 'Honey, if you are comfortable with that idea, then it's fine by me.' But we Dominicans ought to dare to raise the question of truth not because we know it all, but because we hope that together we may discover it, and so we respect the other enough to say sometimes: 'I believe you to be wrong.' It is not worth saying to anyone: 'I think that you are wrong', unless you believe that it matters what they think.

It is too easy to say in ecumenical discussions that 'we all believe the same thing deep down'. There would be no point in dialogue if it were so obviously true. The first stage of friendship is discovering how much you are alike. The second is daring to see how much you differ. The third may be the revelation that in the hidden heart of the unspeakable God, we are indeed one.

And so, to conclude, I would suggest, indeed I would argue that if inculturation is not just selecting items off some cultural supermarket shop shelf – 'I will have a Hindi *bhajan*, one item of Buddhist meditation, and a Christian Eucharist, please' – if it is a thoroughly creative business, then it asks of us a twofold courage: There is the courage to experiment, to play, to risk failure and mistakes. But there is also the equally deep courage of talking to one another, in the pursuit of truth that transcends us all. Do we dare?

INTEGRAL FORMATION

In my room in London I had a reproduction of a painting by Van Gogh which showed a mother and a father teaching a child to walk. The mother is holding up the child, while on the other side of the picture the father has his arms stretched, beckoning the child to dare to walk to him. And the child's face is filled with pleasure, eager for the adventure. All that I want to say about formation today is contained in that picture. First of all, it gives a picture of formation as learning to walk. Secondly it shows this happening in the context of community, in our case the Dominican family amid the world in which we live. And thirdly the face of this child, setting out on its first great adventure, is filled with joy which must belong to all learning.

WALKING

The parents are teaching their child one of the hardest lessons that it will ever have to learn, which is to walk on its own two feet. At this moment the parent begins to initiate the child into it most basic freedom. This is perhaps the most fundamental image of formation that we have. In the prophet Hosea, God says, 'It was I who taught Ephraim to walk, I who took them in my arms, and they did not know that I secured them with reins and led them with the bonds of love' (11:3f). God here is the loving parent, teaching the baby Israel to stand on its feet and walk, one of the first lessons of any father or mother for their children. And when Jesus begins the formation of his disciples, he invites them to walk with him to Jerusalem, to take to the road. To be a disciple is to

---

A paper read at a congress in the Pontifical University of Saint Thomas Aquinas, Rome, in November 1995. The theme of the congress was 'Integral Dominican Formation at the Service of the Church and of Society.' The full title of this paper was 'An Integral Dominican Formation'. Pope John Paul II, a past pupil, attended the closing session.

walk on the way, *ho hodos*. Interestingly, at the end of the Synod, the Pope reminded us that the word 'Synod' comes from *synhodos*, to be together on a journey. Synods are not moments for drawing discussions to an end; they belong to our journey to the Kingdom.

I would like to start this morning saying a little about learning, to stand on one's own feet intellectually, learning how to walk with one's intelligence. I know that this conference is about integral formation, but one must start somewhere and we are in a university. Also I believe that true study, according to our tradition, touches the whole of one's humanity.

The only reason for the existence of a university is that we believe that thinking is a worthwhile activity. It matters what we think and say. Our words have the power to build up or to destroy each other. This may seem absurdly obvious, and yet I am firmly convinced after two years of travelling around the world as Master of the Order, that our world suffers from a deep social and political crisis which is connected with, among other things, a loss of confidence in thought and language. At the basis of all human community is a belief that we can build human community by talking and listening to each other. The rising tide of fundamentalism, religious or political, is symptomatic of a world which has lost its confidence that it matters what one says. I remember when Damian [Byrne][1] was Master and came on visitation to my Province, we listened to a televised broadcast of a debate in Parliament. I was profoundly ashamed to listen to these politicians shouting insults at each other, with no hint that anyone might ever learn anything from their opponent.

A university is founded on an assumption that is not widely accepted in our society, and that is that the world is actually

1. Master of the Order, 1983-1992; died February 1996.

intelligible, that by thinking we can come to see things as they are. Our human words reveal reality. They cast light. And this is because our world was made by God and he gave us minds to understand it and each other. This is the basis of all human community and society. A profound scepticism can only lead to the jungle and destroy us all. So one of the most important things that a student should learn is that his intelligence is a gift from God, which, like his legs, he must dare to use. God says to St Augustine, 'Run on, for I shall hold you up. I shall lead you and carry you on to the end.'[2] So one might imagine the Rector of our University as being like the father in the picture, saying to the students, 'Come on, you can do it. Dare to think'.

But it is only worthwhile walking if one wants to get somewhere. The good teacher initiates one into not only a confidence in one's power to think but also a deep sense of one's need to do so, because we are ignorant. He or she infects us with the passion for discovery, the deep sense that we are only at the beginning of understanding anything at all. We come to learn both confidence and humility. Lessing once wrote: 'If God held all truth firmly in his right hand and in the left the singular and ever-living drive towards the truth, and he said to me "Choose!" then, even at the risk of always and eternally deceiving myself, I should throw myself humbly on the left and say, "Father, grant me this. The pure truth is reserved for you alone!" ' This may sound deeply shocking, and I hope that I never have to make the choice. I also believe it to be deeply Dominican. St Thomas, after whom this university is named, was a man who stands most obviously for a belief in human reason, and yet a deep awareness of its limitations. He is confident in the power of thought and yet he remained for ever the man of questions, asking, searching, never

2. *Confessions*, Bk VII, 16.

satisfied, eager to learn from anyone., Herbert McCabe, who
taught me most of what I know about St Thomas, wrote:

> Now, whatever his many other virtues, the central sanctity of
> St Thomas was a sanctity of mind, and it is shown not in the
> many questions he marvellously, excitingly answered, but in
> the one where he failed, the question he did not and could not
> answer and refused to pretend to answer ... 'What is God?' It
> was the intellectual sanctity of St Thomas that here accepted
> defeat.[3]

Most of us cannot remember learning to walk, but probably
the first thing that happened is that we fell on our faces. Indeed
one must fall flat on one's face several times before one can walk
gracefully, unselfconscioulsy. A university is therefore only a
place where one learns to think if it encourages one to take the
risk of falling on one's face, picking oneself up again, having
another go. Often in our Church we are too afraid of falling on
our faces, of making mistakes. But, as Meister Eckhart said, 'one
seldom finds that people attain to anything good unless first they
have gone somewhat astray.' Unless we dare to get it wrong then
we shall never get it right.

A university that is filled with a fear of making mistakes has
betrayed its vocation. We must form people who dare to think ,
to be intellectually adventurous, confident that their mistakes
belong to their journey to the truth.

COMMUNITY

The second thing that we see in this picture of Van Gogh, is
that the child learns to walk with the help of its parents. The
mother holds it up and the father dares it to walk across to be with
him. The most famous image of the thinker in our western

3. *God Matters*, London, 1987, pp. 236 f.

culture is that of Rodin's *Penseur*, the solitary figure, bent into himself, eyes shut, struggling with some deep interior truth. But I believe that Van Gogh offers us a much better picture. The child must learn to walk. It belongs, like learning to speak, to its entry into the human community. The community is there, in its parents, ready to welcome it. Study is the deeply ascetic process of peeling away the layers of self-centredness, and discovering that one is not the centre of the world, but one belongs to the community of humanity.

St Albert the Great wrote of the pleasure of seeking the truth together: *In dulcedine societatis quarens veritatem.*[4] Study is essentially the entry into a community of people who seek the truth. Central to learning to think is therefore discovering how to live with other people, how to listen to them, how to learn from them. This is perhaps the hardest task of all formation, learning how to live with those who are different, who think differently, live differently, eat differently, have a different sense of humour. Central to any true study is that deep humility which exposes one to people who are not like one. It is initiation into a conversation that began before and which will continue after we are dead. How can I possibly come to grips with a first century Jew like St Paul, if I cannot manage to understand my twentieth century neighbour just because he is French? How can I ever have a hope of understanding St Augustine, if I am locked in silence with a brother because he has different views from me about Christology?

Since the Enlightenment reason has essentially been seen in terms of mastery, domination, control, ownership. Science, which offers the basic model for all knowledge in our society, is intimately linked with our competitive, dominative society. It embodies what Augustine thought was characteristic of the earthly

4. In Libr. viii Politicorum C.G.

city, the *libido dominandi*, the hunger for power. Theology does not merely have another object of study, God and the mystery of our redemption. It invites us to study in another way, not through mastery and domination but through the entry into friendship. Aquinas argues that our relationship to God is that of friendship, *amicitia Dei*. Doing theology, exploring this relationship, then, is inseparable from learning to live in friendship, with all the attentiveness, humility and gentleness that friendship requires. It is not just about learning facts but about learning the art of friendship. That is why it is important for me that the Angelicum is known as 'the Friendly University'. This is not just because the professors like smiling at the students. It embodies a vision of what it is to study, to explore the friendship that is the secret of God's own life.

In friendship one learns to delight in those who are different. Sometimes in our Church, I have to admit that one encounters a deep fear of women. The woman is sometimes that 'Other' who is unknown and feared, who must be mastered or fled. I therefore think that if it belongs to theology that we dare to face and know the other, to enter into dialogue with those who are unlike us, then we men must do theology with women, we must make together a theology that bears the imprint of their experience; it must be a theology that is the fruit of our conversation and friendship. That is why I profoundly hope that our centres of study can become projects of the Dominican family.

Jordan of Saxony said that Dominic was able to understand the most difficult things, '*Humili cordis intelligentia*',[5] through the humble intelligence of his heart. It sums up everything that I have been trying to say so far. First of all he understood things through his intelligence. He liked to think, to argue, to debate. He stayed

5. *Libellus*, 71

up all night arguing with the innkeeper because he believed that reason mattered. But it was a humble intelligence. It was not a proud, dominative intelligence that tried to crush the other, but was attentive, open, that knew its limit, especially when faced with the mystery of God. But above all it was an intelligence of the heart, *cordis intelligentia*.

True intelligence is deeply connected with compassion, with vulnerability to the other. This is above all true of the study of theology, where we seek to understand the mystery of our redemption by the God who so loved the world that he sent his only Son to be our Redeemer. A theology that remains abstract, untouched by the sufferings of our poor violent world, has not begun its task. It is inseparable from the hunger for a just and better world. Let me remind you of the words of Blessed Hyacinth Mary Cormier which I quoted at the blessing of his sarcophagus – the study of 'the holy books of scripture demand of us that we acquire "the entrails of mercy and extend them". The world "entrails" denotes in our corporeal being that which is most sensitive, most impressionable, most vital.'[6]

Now if is of course impossible for every theologian to be engaged in continuous close contact with the sufferings of our world. One cannot write scholarly books and visit the refugee camps of Zaire and Burundi. Not even St. Thomas could have done that. Scholarship demands a certain leisure and silence. Not every Dominican need live his or her vocation in the same way. But it does raise questions about the relationship between our centres of study and the rest of the Church and the world. How do we live the community of the Order so that the scholar working on the text of St Thomas and the brother or sister working in a *barrio* in Caracas share the richness of their insights?

6. *Etre a Dieu*, Paris, 1994, p. 128.

How can they illuminate each other, while respecting the different forms that their vocations take?

So often during these last few days, we have heard that the motto of Cormier as Master of the Order was *Caritas Veritatis,* the charity of truth. Love is inseparable from telling the truth, and as he said, *'donner la vérité est la plus belle acte de charité'*, to tell the truth is the most beautiful act of charity. But the truth with which we are concerned in this university that he founded, includes the truth of our suffering, violent, crucified world. And our study has as its aim the healing of the human community and the coming of the Kingdom.

THE FACE OF THE CHILD

Finally, and very briefly, let me say something about the face of this child who is learning to walk. It is filled with joy. Learning to walk, even if you do fall flat on your face, is a pleasure! One only begins to understand theology a bit when one discovers the pleasure of it, the delight of learning. Otherwise one will finish one's studies and never open another book. An Old Testament professor may know every irregular Hebrew verb, but unless he communicates a 'delight in the law of the Lord' then he has taught nothing.

When Augustine finally turns to God he cries out famously: 'Late have I loved you, Oh Beauty so ancient and so new'.[7] Maybe what moved Augustine was not so much an intellectual conviction of the truth of Christianity – that had happened long before – but the utter beauty of our God. The child in our painting does not set out across the grass to its father because of an intellectual or moral conviction that it ought to, but for the pure pleasure of it. When we form people as Christians, then it must be in

7. *Confessions*, Bk X, 27.

revealing some sense of the beauty of Christ which shines out in all his brothers and sisters, as the poet Hopkins wrote, 'lovely in limbs and lovely in eyes not his'.

The theme of this Congress is an Integral Formation, a formation of the whole human being. One of the ways in which this may happen is in discovering the unity of the True, the Good, and the Beautiful. In our society these three have been split from each other. So often truth is just a matter of science or technology; ethics are reduced to utilitarianism, and beauty is merely a subjective sensation. For us they are ultimately one, and in discovering their unity we too are made whole.

MY BITTER-SWEET VISIT TO IRAQ

The visit to the brethren and sisters in Iraq was planned long before the crisis. It was providential that it was now that I and my regional assistant fr Daniel Cadrin could pass a week with them, as they waited for the bombers to arrive. The only way to enter Iraq during the embargo is a fifteen-hour drive from Amman to Baghdad across the desert. It is like entering a high security prison, and we wondered, as most people going to prison do, when and if we would get out again.

It took four hours to cross the frontier, even with the help of a young Iraqi Dominican who was returning home after finishing his studies in France, and the lavish distribution of cans of Pepsi Cola, which appears to be the local currency. Then as throughout the trip I was astonished by the exquisite courtesy of everyone I met. Never once was I reproached for being British, although our aircraft carrier was waiting in the Gulf to add its bombs to those of the Americans. What would it have been like for an Iraqi coming to Britain if there had been one of their aircraft carriers waiting in the English Channel?

When we arrived in Baghdad there were few signs of defensive preparation. The Iraqis discovered during the Gulf War that there is little that one can do against American bombs. The city waited, vulnerable and apparently unprotected. Even more surprising was to find the brethren building a new priory, to accommodate the postulants for the Order. It was a sign of hope to see the workmen completing a building that might be destroyed within a week. The young architect explained that the building was intentionally a symbol of what the people were suffering. It looked as if it were cracked open, fractured, and yet

---

First published in *The Tablet*, London, 28 February 1998, and reprinted with permission.

strong. He explained that it represented a people who are crucified and yet hope for healing.

Before we arrived in Iraq, I had shared in the general obsession
with news of the latest developments. In Istanbul we had listened
to every bulletin of the BBC World Service, wondering when the
denouement would come. Yet we found the people we met in Iraq
were less concerned about this. Long years of suffering the war
with Iran, the Gulf War, the seven long years of the embargo, had
pushed them to deeper levels.

A Dominican sister told us: 'We are ground down, exhausted
by years of death. Since the Gulf War, six hundred thousand
children have died of malnutrition and a lack of medicine. We
will live with death.' Somehow these years of deprivation and
isolation have eroded such minor questions as to whether one
might die next week because of a bomb from the air, or in ten
years' time from another cause. The real question was whether
after death there is life, and whether there is a God who hears us.
It was as if the embargo had sometimes seemed to shut out even
God. The nuncio, Mgr Giuseppe Lazzarotto, told me that when
he asks for support projects from international aid agencies, he is
refused unless it is for food or medicine. But, as our sisters told us:
'We are not animals such that it would be enough to have a full
stomach. What this people hunger for more than anything else is
a word of hope.'

Every Monday more than a thousand young people come to
the theology classes offered by the Dominican brethren in Baghdad. Almost as many come to the priory at Mosul, in northern
Iraq. These are Christians of every denomination, drawn to
study the Scriptures, to argue about Christology and the doctrine
of the Trinity. Meanwhile the world was waiting for the bombs
to fall. In the north of the country we found a flourishing
movement of Dominican laity, in the villages populated by

Chaldean and Syrian Christians. They gather in each other's homes every week to study the word of God. They told us that, faced with life or death, they can no longer be satisfied with superficial answers. What does God have to say to us?

I was reminded of a Dominican friar, Riccoldo da Monte Croce, who lived in Baghdad seven hundred years ago. The Dominican community had enjoyed a wonderful relationship with the Muslim community for years. But after the fall of Acre, one of the last crusader strongholds, in 1291, the Christians found themselves unwelcome. Some friars died, others went to Iran, others returned to Italy, and Riccoldo found himself alone. His Dominican habit was taken from him and he was forced to become a camel driver. He was plunged into despair, fearful for his life. In the market place he found among the sale of the booty from Acre the blood-stained habit of one of his brethren. He wrote letters to the Dominicans in Italy but no one answered, not even the Master of the Order. 'What can have happened to the Master General, that he does not answer my most sad letters?' – a common complaint in the Order I am sure.

He wrote to St Dominic, Our Lady and even the Heavenly Court, expressing his desolation and despair. 'Having had no response, I will act like someone who, in a public street, has received an intolerable injury. I will cry out "Someone help me!" Is there not anyone who can reply?' That is the silence which afflicts some Christians in Iraq.

Finally, among the books ransacked from the Acre priory he found a copy of Gregory the Great's *Moralia* , his commentary on the Book of Job. And here he discovered the answer for which he had waited. God had spoken, in the Scriptures. Here he must search for the reply to all his questions.

So too the young Christians of Iraq search the Scriptures to understand, hungry for God's word for them. Now the Dominican superior in Iraq, Fr Yussuf, is preparing the publication of the first Kurdish New Testament for the sisters who work among the Kurds on the Turkish border.

So these years of suffering have worn away any comfortable little beliefs and exposed starker alternatives, great hope and despair, sometimes the two inhabiting the same heart. Somehow the embargo with all its deprivations has brought many young Christians to a deeper knowledge, hard bought. It is as if the ground has opened under their feet, and the sky above their heads. As the French poet Victor Segalen wrote of discovering the divine name of God:

Only when there is great drought, when frostbound winter crackles, when springs, at their lowest ebb, spiral in shells of ice,

When the void gapes underground in the heart's cavern – where blood itself has ceased to flow – under the vault, now accessible, the Name can be received.

But let the hard waters melt, let life overflow, let the devastating torrent surge rather than knowledge!

It was a bitter-sweet week. We visited the maternity ward of the hospital run by our sisters in Baghdad, and rejoiced for the safe delivery of prematurely born twins. We prayed that they would not prematurely die. All over the country we found that Christian communities were weakened by emigration, especially to the United States, both paradise and enemy. Yet we met one young man who, having got as far as Morocco, decided to come back. His village is just a few miles from Ninevah. He told us that he was like Jonah. Though he tried to flee, he knew he must return and share with his people their fate and his hope in Christ.

One of the faces I will always remember is that of Sr Olga, young and strong. She is an Assyrian Christian. They are usually called 'Nestorians' by the Catholics, though this is a name that

they dislike. She felt called to religious life, although there have
been no communities of religious in her Church for centuries.
Because she trusted that we would not try to 'capture' her for the
Catholics, she asked one of the brethren to help her in this new
venture. When she made her vows to her bishop, this brother
preached, the first Catholic priest to do so in an Assyrian church
after centuries of hostility. She and her little group of novices visit
the mental hospitals and prisons of Baghdad as a sign of the God
who has not forgotten.

We feasted with our brothers. They had managed to find a few
bottles of wine. 'All this must be drunk before you leave,' said Fr
Yussuf. We knew that they had spent more than they could
afford, and that when the French Provincial came next month
there would be nothing left for him. In Mosul, we visited the
house of formation of the Dominican sisters, filled with young
postulants and novices. Since it was hard to come by the ingredi-
ents to make a cake, they performed a dance in which each one
represented some element of the cake that they would have liked
to make, the cream, the almonds, the wheat that they did not
have. Then they put on the traditional clothes of their villages and
we danced and sang until we were exhausted. It is not possible
here to discuss their perception of the political situation. I can
only say that they shared the perplexity which I have found
throughout the Arab world, that in the name of civilisation we
would even contemplate so barbarous an act as to attack this
people. How could we, in the name of peace, consider launching
a war that would probably bring devastation to the region for
years?

It seemed as if with the fall of Communism we had lost our
traditional enemy and needed another. Iraq was chosen. As in an
old fashioned Western movie, the hero must find the enemy and
kill him again and again.

When we drove back across the desert to Amman, I thought of the words of Isaiah to the exiles in Babylon: 'In the wilderness prepare a way of the Lord, make straight in the desert a highway for our God.' We followed much the same route that those exiles took when they went home, and it was certainly straight and flat. But I did not feel as if I was going home. I felt sad and almost guilty to leave these people, Christian and Muslim, to their fate.

Now it seems they have been spared attack, at least for a while. The world breathes a sigh of relief. We can think about something else now. But for the Iraqi people the old and long struggle continues to survive under the embargo, to hope for a future.

THE HIDDEN BEAUTY OF GOD

I was not pious as a child, but I do remember one moment that might be called transcendental, if that does not sound too pretentious. It happened after I had served an early morning Mass in the lovely abbey church at Downside. The place was dark, except for the candles on the side altars, where the slower priests, served by the less fortunate boys, were still celebrating the Eucharist. It was a moment of deep peace. Despite my inability to get into even the fourth cricket eleven, my looming failure of French 'O' level, and all the turmoil of adolescent emotion, I knew, suddenly and surely, that 'all shall be well, and all manner of things shall be well', as Mother Julian of Norwich wrote. It was also a moment of intense beauty. Not just the beauty of the church, which I still love deeply, but a hint of a beauty that was an invitation and a promise. I will mention a second moment, which was apparently utterly different, but a sort of deepening of the experience of that early morning in the abbey church. It happened just a few weeks ago, in an untidy overgrown cemetery near a small town called Rio Maria, in the eastern Amazon, Brazil. Some of the tombs were built like great concrete beds, floating in the dry burnt weeds. These were for the local people who had been murdered by gunmen employed by the landowners to assassinate anyone who resisted them or tried to escape slavery.

I went there with one of our brothers, Henri Burin des Roziers, a lawyer who has taken case after case of murder to court, although even when there is a conviction it is rarely enforced. Also there was Fr Ricardo Rezende, the local parish priest with whom Henri lives, and who has courageously fought

From *The Tablet*, London, 11 June, 1999. It was number six in a series of articles commissioned by *The Tablet:* 'Glimpses of Heaven'. Reprinted with permission.

this obscene slaughter for years. They have both been told that they will be murdered soon. It seems unlikely that the body-guards provided by the government can do much to save them. We prayed at the tombs of their friends, Expedito the poet, Joao Canuto, a local trade union leader and his brothers, and many more.

That cemetery is a monument to a casual cruelty, and yet, quite unexpectedly, a place of deeper peace than even that glimpsed early in the morning at Downside. This peace was pure gift, that peace which Jesus promised when he too was about to be murdered: 'Peace I leave with you; my peace I give to you; not as the world gives do I give to you. Let not your hearts be troubled, neither let them be afraid.' (Jn 14:27) It was an ugly place, old tombs caving in, and filled with the memories of uglier deaths.

Some local peasants who tried to escape enslavement were shot, boiled and fed to the pigs. Yet, inexplicably, it was a place of utter beauty. As we prayed for the dead it was as if this dirty old cemetery was the gateway to heaven, where one might see the angels of God ascending and descending upon the Son of Man.

The early Fathers taught that one way to God was through learning to grow in awareness of the divine beauty, *philokalia*. As Augustine said, in the *Exposition on the Book of Psalms*, 44, 3:

Beautiful is God, the Word with God. He is beautiful in Heaven, beautiful on earth; beautiful in the womb; beautiful in His parents' arms, beautiful in His miracles, beautiful in His sufferings; beautiful in inviting to life; beautiful in not worrying about death, beautiful in giving His life and beauti-ful in taking it up again; He is beautiful on the cross, beautiful in the tomb, beautiful in Heaven. Listen to the song with understanding, and let not the weakness of the flesh distract your eyes from the splendour of His beauty.

But it is a beauty that is often hidden. I know that to keep alive a sense of the transcendent, I need the more obvious forms of beauty to keep me going: Santa Sabina, the Dominican headquarters in Rome, in the early morning light; the frescoes of Fra Angelico; Mozart; an occasional dose of English countryside; beautiful people. But our eyes need education so as to see God's beauty when it is concealed in the apparently ugly. We need to be healed if we are to see 'God's better beauty, grace', as Hopkins said. Art can help here sometimes. Rembrandt can teach us to see the discreet beauty of the old. But compassion surely trains the eye to see the loveliness of God in unexpected places. Often on my trips I have shut my eyes from ugliness which is almost too terrible to behold: people mutilated by war in Rwanda, deformed beggars in Calcutta's railway station. I hope, with grace, to learn to see God's beauty there one day.

The passion for a just world is not just a matter of commitment to political vision. It is the hunger for a world in which the divine beauty of all God's children will be apparent, and the world will be healed of its disfigurement. It is the struggle for a world in which the transcendent splendour of God will flame out, 'like shining from shook foil', as Hopkins said.

There is a rabbinic tradition that when the Messiah comes he will sit at the city gates as a beggar, and most people will see just an ugly man: 'He had no form or comeliness that we should look at him, and no beauty that we should desire him' (Is 53:2). But those who have eyes to see will glimpse the radiant beauty of the Redeemer.

The ultimate coincidence of beauty and ugliness is in the cross. This was the most hideous event that could ever be. We have all seen crucifixions that portray the obscenity of this brutal act: the crosses of Grünewald, the crosses of the late Middle Ages with the Christ of the Black Death, the agonised Christs of Latin

America. There are also wonderful and beautiful crosses, where Christ is at peace, the radiant cross of the *Dream of the Rood*, 'most shining of crosses, compassed with light.' Has anyone ever painted a crucifixion in which the brutality is transfigured with a brilliant beauty, so that we would cry out with the centurion, 'Truly this is the Son of God'?

THE ROSARY

When I saw that I had been asked to talk about the Rosary, I must confess that I had a moment of panic. I have never read about the Rosary or reflected about it ever in my life. I am sure that most of you have much more profound thoughts about the Rosary than I have. The Rosary is simply something that I have done, without thought, like breathing. Breathing is very important to me. I breathe all the time, but I have never given a talk on it. Saying the Rosary, like breathing, is so simple. So what is there to say?

SIMPLICITY

It may seem a little strange that a prayer as simple as the Rosary should be particularly associated with Dominicans. Dominicans are not often thought of as very simple people. We have a reputation for writing long and complex books on theology. And yet, we fought to keep the Rosary ours. The General Chapter of 1574 urged the brethren to preach the Rosary. It is *'nostra sacra haereditas'*, 'our sacred inheritance'.[1] There is a long tradition of pictures of Our Lady giving the Rosary to St Dominic. But at one time, other religious orders grew jealous, and started commissioning paintings of Our Lady giving the Rosary to other saints, to St Francis and even to St Ignatius. But we fought back, and, I think in the seventeenth century, persuaded the Pope to ban the competition. Our Lady was only allowed to be shown giving the Rosary to Dominic! But why is this simple prayer so dear to Dominicans?

1. F. Baggiani, 'Statuti cinquecenteschi di Confraternite del Rosario', *Memorie Dominicane* 26 (1995), p. 221.

An address at Lourdes, in October 1998, for the ninetieth anniversary of the *Pelerinage du Rosaire,* the annual pilgrimage to Lourdes organised by the Dominicans of France.

Perhaps it is because at the centre of our theological tradition is a longing for simplicity. St Thomas Aquinas said that we cannot understand God because God is utterly simple – simple beyond all our conceptions. We study, we wrestle with theological problems, we strain our minds, but the aim is to draw near to the mystery of the One who is totally simple. We have to pass through the complexity so as to arrive at simplicity.

There is a false simplicity, which we must leave behind. It is the simplicity of those who oversimplify, who have too easy answers to everything, who know it all in advance. They are either too lazy or are incapable of thought. And there is the true simplicity, the simplicity of heart, the simplicity of the clear eye. And that we can only arrive at slowly, with God's grace, as we draw near to God's blinding simplicity. The Rosary is indeed simple, very simple. But it has the deep and wise simplicity for which we hunger, and in which we will find peace.

It is said that when St John the Evangelist became an old man, he became utterly simple. He liked to play with a dove, and all that he would say to people, when they came to see him, was 'Love one another'. You and I would not get away with that! People would not believe us. It is only someone like St John, who wrote the richest and most complex Gospel of all, who can arrive at the true simplicity of wisdom and say no more than just: 'Love one another'. Just as it is only a St Thomas Aquinas, after he has written his great *Summa Theologiae,* who can say that all that he had written is 'as straw'. Yes, the Rosary is very simple. But perhaps it is an invitation to find that deep simplicity of true wisdom. It was said of Lagrange, one of the founders of modern biblical scholarship, that he did three things every day: he read the newspapers, studied the Bible, and prayed the Rosary!

I would also like to suggest that not only is the simplicity of the Rosary good and deep simplicity, but also that it has many characteristics which are truly Dominican.

THE ANGEL AS A PREACHER

The Hail Mary begins with the words of the angel Gabriel, 'Hail Mary, full of grace, the Lord is with you.' Angels are professional preachers. It is their whole being to proclaim the good news. The words of Gabriel are the perfect sermon. It is even short! He proclaims the essence of all preaching, 'The Lord is with you'. Here we see the heart of our vocation, to say to each other: 'Hail Daniel, Hail Eric, the Lord is with you'. That is why Humbert of Romans, one of the earliest Masters of the Order, said that we Dominicans are called to live like angels. Though I have to say that, in my experience, most Dominicans are not especially angelic!

Last December, I was in Ho Chi Minh City, visiting the Province of Vietnam. After the day's work was over, my *socius* and I loved to go and get lost in all the back streets of the city. Part of the fun was to escape the Government spy who was sent to see what we were up to. We spent hours wandering around the maze of tiny streets, filled with life – people gambling, eating, talking, playing billiards. Many of the houses had images of Buddha. And then one evening, we went around the corner into a little square, and there, right in the middle, was an enormous statue of a Dominican with wings. It was St Vincent Ferrer, who is always represented as an angel. He was the great preacher. He was seen as the angel of the Apocalypse, announcing the end of the world. Well, no preacher can get everything right! So Gabriel the archangel is a good model for us Dominicans.

And there is another way in which the Hail Mary is like a sermon. Because a sermon does not just tell us about God. It starts from the Word of God which is addressed to us. Preaching is not just the reporting of facts about God. It gives us God's Word, which breaks the silence between God and us.

The opening words of the prayer are words that are addressed to Mary by the angel: 'Hail Mary, full of grace'. The beginning of everything is the Word which we hear. St John wrote 'In this is love, not that we loved God but that he loved us, and sent his Son to be the expiation for our sin.' (1 Jn 4:10) In fact in the time of St Dominic the *Ave Maria* only consisted of these words of the angel and those of Elizabeth. Our prayer was the words given to us. It was only later, after the Council of Trent, that our own words to Mary were added.

So often we think of prayer as the effort that we make to talk to God. Prayer can look like the struggle to reach up to a distant God. Does he even hear us? But this simple prayer reminds us that this is not so. We do not break the silence. When we speak we are responding to a word spoken to us. We are taken into a conversation that has already begun without us. The angel proclaims God's word. And this creates a space in which we can speak in turn: 'Holy Mary, Mother of God'.

So often our lives are afflicted by silence. There is the silence of heaven, which may at times seem closed to us. There is the silence which may appear to separate us from each other. But the Word of God comes to us in good preaching, and breaks open those barriers. We are liberated into language. We find words come, words for God and words for each other.

Perhaps we can say even more. Meister Eckhart once said that 'We do not pray, we are prayed'. Our words are the reverberation, the prolongation of the Word spoken to us. Our prayers are God praying, blessing, praising in us. As St Paul wrote, 'When we cry "Abba, Father" it is the Spirit himself bearing witness with our spirit that we are children of God ... ' (Rom 8:14) The greetings of the angel and Elizabeth to Mary are continued in the words that we address to her. The second half of the prayer echoes the first. So the angel spoke 'Hail Mary, full of grace', and this becomes, in our mouths, the same greeting, 'Holy Mary'. Elizabeth says 'Blessed is the fruit of your womb', and we say 'Mother of God'. We are caught up into God's speaking. Our prayer is God speaking within us. We are caught up into the conversation that is the life of the Trinity.

So, I would suggest that this simple prayer of the Hail Mary is like a tiny model sermon. It proclaims the good news. But like all good sermons, it does more than that. It does not simply give us information. It offers a word from God, a word that echoes in our words, a word that overcomes our silence and gives us a voice.

A PRAYER FOR HOME AND A PRAYER FOR THE JOURNEY

There is another way in which this prayer is very Dominican. And that is because it is a prayer for the home, and a prayer for the road. It is a prayer which builds community and also which propels us on our journey. And that is a tension which is very Dominican. We need our communities. We need places in which we are at home, with our brothers and sisters. And yet at the same time we are itinerant preachers, who cannot settle for too long, but must set out to preach. We are contemplative and active. Let me explain how the Hail Mary is marked by this same tension.

Think of the great pictures of the Annunciation. They usually offer us a domestic scene. The angel has come to Mary's home. Mary is there in her room, usually reading. Often there is a spinning wheel in the background, or a brush leaning against the wall. Outside there is a garden. This is where the story begins, at home. And this is appropriate, because the Word of God makes his home with us. He pitches his tent among us.

And in a way, the Rosary is often the prayer of the home and the community. Traditionally it was said by the family and by religious communities each day. From the mid-fifteenth century we see the foundation of Rosary Confraternities who meet to pray together. So the Rosary is deeply associated with community, a prayer that we share with others. I must confess that I have ambiguous memories of family Rosary! We did not say the Rosary at home, but we often stayed with cousins who recited it together every night. But it was often a disaster. No matter how carefully the doors were locked, the dogs always burst in and made their way around the family licking our faces. And so however pious we intended to be, we usually collapsed in giggles. I came to dread the family Rosary.

But the angel's greeting does not leave Mary at home. The angel comes to disturb her domestic life. I often think of a wonderful Annuciation made by our Dominican brother Petit, who lives and works in Japan. He shows Gabriel as a great messenger, filling the canvas, and Mary is this small, shy, demure Japanese girl, whose life is turned upside down. She is propelled on a journey, which will take her to Elizabeth's home, to Bethlehem, to Egypt, to Jerusalem. It is a journey that will lead to her heart being pierced, and to the foot of the cross. It is a journey that will eventually carry her to heaven and glory.

So the Rosary is also the prayer of those who journey, of pilgrims, like yourselves. I have come to love the Rosary precisely as a prayer for my travels. It is a prayer for airports and airplanes. It is a prayer that I often say as I come into land at a new place, and I wonder what I shall find, and what I can offer. It is a prayer for taking off again, giving thanks for all that I have received from the brothers and the sisters. It is a prayer of pilgrimage around the Order.

I think that the structure of Mary's journey marks the Rosary in two ways. It is there in the words of each Hail Mary. And it is there in the structures of the mysteries of the Rosary.

HAIL MARY – THE STORY OF THE INDIVIDUAL

Each *Ave Maria* suggests the individual journey that each of us must make, from birth to death. It is marked by the biological rhythm of each human life. It mentions the only three moments of our lives which we can know with absolute certainty: that we are born, that we live now, and that we shall die. It starts with the beginning of every human life, a conception in the womb. It situates us now, as we ask now for Mary's prayers. It looks forward to death, our death. It is an amazingly physical prayer. It is marked by the inevitable corporeal drama of every human body, which is born and must die.

And this is surely truly Dominican. For Dominic's preaching began in the south of France, not far from here, against heretics who despised the body, and who thought of all creation as evil. He was confronted with one of those waves of dualistic spirituality which have periodically swept Europe. Augustine, whose Rule we have, was caught in another such movement, when he was a Manichee as a young man. And even today, much of popular thought is profoundly dualistic. Studies have shown that modern scientists usually think of salvation in terms of the escape from the body.

But the Dominican tradition has always stressed that we are physical, corporeal beings. All that we are comes from God. We receive the sacrament of Jesus' body and blood for our nourishment; we hope for the resurrection of the body.

The journey that each of us must travel is, in the first place, this physical, biological one, which takes us from the womb to the tomb. It is in this biological span of life that we will meet God and find salvation. And this simple prayer helps us on the way.

Conception

The words of the angel promise fertility, fertility for a virgin and for a barren woman. The blessing of God makes us fertile. Each of us, in our individual births, is a fruit of a womb that was blessed.

I believe that the blessing promised by the angel always takes the form of fertility, in every human life. It is the blessing of new beginnings, the grace of freshness. Perhaps we are made in the image and likeness of God because we share God's creativity. We are his partners in creating and recreating the world. The most dramatic and miraculous example of this is childbirth. But even we men, who cannot manage that miracle, we too are blessed by fertility. When we are faced with barrenness, sterility, futility, then God comes with a fertile word. Whenever God draws near to us, it is so that we may be creative, transforming, making new, whether in tilling the soil, planting and sowing, or through art, poetry, painting.

'Blessed is the fruit of your womb'. Perhaps the best way, then, that we can ever preach the miracle of this fertility is through art, through painting and song and poetry. Because these are some small share in that same blessing, that endless fertility of God.

There is a charming story, which was told by Malaroux to Picasso. He said that when Bernadette of Lourdes entered the convent, many people sent her statues of the Virgin. But she never had them in her room, because she said that they did not look like the woman whom she had seen. The bishop sent her albums of famous pictures of the Virgin, by Raphael, Murillo and so on. She looked at Baroque virgins, of which she had seen so many, and Renaissance virgins. But none of them looked right. And then she saw the Virgin of Cambrai, a fourteenth century copy of a very old Byzantine icon, which was not like any picture of Mary that Bernadette would have seen. And she said, 'That's her!'

Perhaps it is not surprising that the young girl who had seen the Virgin, recognised her again in an icon, the fruit of a holy art, a sacred creativity. Mary shows herself most clearly in the work of one who was made fertile through God's grace, a painter.

Now

But the Rosary also invokes another time, not just of birth but also now. 'Pray for us sinners now'. Now is the present moment in the pilgrimage of our lives, when we must carry on, survive, on our way to the Kingdom.

It is interesting that this present moment is seen as a time when we sinners need compassion. This is a profoundly Dominican compassion. You remember that Dominic prayed always to God: 'Lord, have mercy on your people. What will become of sinners?' Now is a moment when we need compassion, mercy. In the Sistine Chapel, in the fresco of the Last Judgement, there is a man being pulled up from Purgatory by an angel with a Rosary.

Now is the time when we must survive, wondering how long we must wait for the Kingdom. When an American Dominican went back to visit China a few years ago, he found various groups of Dominican laity who survived during years of persecution and isolation. And the only thing that they had kept during all those years was the recitation of the Rosary together. It was the daily bread of survival. And when some of our brethren went to remote areas of Mexico, and met groups of Dominican laity, who had not been in contact with the Order for years, they found the same thing. The one practice that was continued was the Rosary. It is the prayer for survivors in this present time. During Communist times when our brother Dominik Duka was in prison with Vaclav Havel, now the President of the Czech Republic, they said the Rosary together on a knotted piece of string.

Bede Jarrett, the English provincial in the 1930s, sent a member of the Province, called Bertrand Pike, to South Africa, to help in the new mission of the Order. But Bertrand felt overwhelmed and unable to cope. It was more than he could face. He lacked the courage to continue. And Bede wrote to him reminding him of a time in war when he had found his courage in his Rosary.

'Do you remember that dreadful day you had to cross between trenches at Ypres, when your courage failed you, and only after 3 or 4 attempts, did you force yourself to get by, and how you found the carved edges of your Rosary-beads had cut into your finger in your unconscious gripping of them to take a new lease of courage from holding them.'

'Yes, I remember that.'

'But, my dear Bertrand, courage and fear are not opposed. Those only have courage who do what they should do even though they have fear.'[2]

So Bertrand must tightly grip his Rosary to have courage, 'now and at the hour of his death'. It is the prayer for all of us who need courage to carry on, to triumph over fear. It gives us the courage of the pilgrim.

The hour of our death

And the final certain moment of our bodily lives is death. 'Pray for us sinners now and in the hour of our death'. In the face of death, we pray the Rosary. I have just returned from Kinshasa, in the Congo, where many of our sisters have faced death in recent years. The Provincial of the Missionary Sisters of Grenada, Sister Christina, told me about how she and her sisters had had to flee from their home in the north of the Congo during the last war. They had been hidden in the bush by friends. She is a doctor, and

2. B. Bailey, A. Bellinger and S. Tugwell (ed.s), *The Letters of Bede Jarrett* OP, p. 190.

when they were fleeing she met a man whose wife she had saved. And he said to her that now it was his turn to save her life. All around them they heard the sound of gun fire. They were told that the rebels had discovered where they were and would come soon to kill them. In the face of this death, they prayed the Rosary. It is a prayer that when we face death, knowing that we will not do so alone, Mary will then pray for us.

I think also of my father. During the Second World War, my mother and the three eldest children remained in London. I was just on the way. My mother insisted on being available in case my father could ever have leave and come home, even though night after night the bombs fell on London. And my father promised that if all of his family would survive the war, then he would pray the Rosary every night. So one of the memories of my childhood is of how every night before dinner, my father would pace up and down the drawing room, praying the Rosary. He gave thanks nightly, that we had survived that threat of death. And one of my last memories of my father was of just before he died, too weak to pray himself any more, we his family, his wife and six children, gathered around his bed and prayed the Rosary for him. It was the first time that he could not do it himself That death, surrounded by all of us was an answer to that prayer he had said so many thousands of times. 'Pray for us now and at the hour of our death.'

T. S. Eliot begins one of his poems 'Pray for us now and at the hour of our birth'.[3] And this is right. For we must face these three sure moments in our life: birth, the present, and our death. But what we long for in each moment is always the same, new birth. What we long for now, as sinners, is not the mercy that merely forgets what we have done, but which makes this too a moment of new birth, of fresh beginning. And faced with death, we again

3. 'Animula' from the Ariel Poems.

long for the words of the angel to announce a new fertility. For all of our lives are open to God's endless newness, his inexhaustible freshness. The angel comes time and time again, with new Annunciations of good news.

THE MYSTERIES OF THE ROSARY – THE STORY OF SALVATION

So the individual *Ave Maria* is the prayer of the journey that each of us must make, from birth, through the present now until death. But ultimately our lives do not have meaning in themselves, as private and individual stories. Our lives only have meaning because they are caught up in a larger story, which reaches from the very beginning to the unknown end, from Creation to the Kingdom. And this longer span is given by the mysteries of the Rosary, which tell the story of redemption.

The mysteries of the Rosary have been compared with the *Summa Theologiae* of St Thomas. They tell, in their own way, of how everything comes from God and everything returns to God. For each mystery of the Rosary is part of a single mystery, the mystery of our redemption in Christ. As Paul wrote to the Ephesians, 'For he has made known to us in all wisdom and insight the mystery of his will, according to his purpose which he set forth in Christ as a plan for the fullness of time, to unite all things in him, things in heaven and things on earth'. (Eph 1:9)

So, one might say that each *Ave Maria* represents an individual life, with its own story from birth to death. But all these *Ave Maria*s are taken up into the mysteries of the Rosary just as our individual lives are taken up into the larger story of redemption. We need both dimensions, a story with two levels. I need to give a form and meaning to my own life, the story of this unique human flesh and blood, with my moments of failure and victory. If there is no place for my unrepeatable story, then I will be merely lost in the history of humanity. For Christ says to me,

'Today, you will be with me in paradise'. I need the individual *Ave Maria,* my own little drama, in the face of my own little death. My death may not mean much for humanity, but it will be quite important for me.

But it is not enough to remain trapped on that merely personal level. I must find my life taken into the larger drama of God's purpose. Alone my story has no meaning. My individual *Ave Maria* must find its place in the mysteries of the Rosary. So the Rosary offers that perfect balance we need in the search for the meaning of our lives, both the individual and the communal.

REPETITION

I have tried to sketch a few reasons why the Rosary is indeed a deeply Dominican devotion. The *Ave Maria* bears all the marks of a perfect little sermon. And the whole of the Rosary is marked by the theme of the journey, our own and that of humanity. All this fits well the life of an Order of itinerant preachers. There are other things that I could have stressed, like the biblical basis of the mysteries. It is a prolonged meditation on the Word of God in scripture. But I have said enough!

But I must face a final objection. I have tried to suggest the theological richness of the Rosary. But the fact is that when one prays the Rosary, one rarely thinks about anything. We do not in fact think about the nature of preaching or the human story and its relationship with the story of salvation. Our minds are largely blank. We may even sometimes find ourselves wondering why we are endlessly repeating the same words in this mindless fashion. That is surely not very Dominican! Yet from the very beginning of our tradition, our brethren and nuns have delighted in this repetition. One brother Romeo, who died in 1261, is supposed to have recited a thousand *Ave Marias* a day!

First of all, many religions are marked by this tradition of the repetition of sacred words. Last Sunday, when I was wondering what to say about the Rosary, I heard a Buddhist service broadcast on the BBC, and it seemed to consist in the endless repetition of holy words, the mantra. It has often been pointed out that the Rosary is quite similar to these Eastern ways of prayer, and that the constant reiteration of these words can work a slow but deep transformation of our hearts. Since this is so widely known I will say no more.

One could also point out that repetition is not necessarily a sign of a lack of imagination. It may be sheer exuberant pleasure that makes us repeat words. If we love someone, we know that it is not enough to tell them 'I love you' just once. We will want to say it again and again, and we may hope that they wish to hear it again and again.

G. K. Chesterton argued that repetition is a characteristic of the vitality of children, who like the same stories, with the same words, time and time again, not because they are bored and unimaginative but because they delight in life. Chesterton wrote:

Because children have abounding vitality, because they are in spirit fierce and free, therefore they want things repeated and unchanged. They always say, 'Do it again'; and the grown-up person does it again until he is nearly dead, for grown-up people are not strong enough to exult in monotony. But perhaps God is strong enough to exult in monotony. It is possible that God says every morning, 'Do it again' to the sun; and every evening 'Do it again' to the moon. It may not be automatic necessity that makes all daisies alike; it may be that God makes each daisy separately, but has never got tired of making them. It may be that He has the eternal appetite of infancy; for we have sinned and grown old and our Father is younger than we. The repetition in Nature may not be a mere recurrence; it may be a theatrical encore. Heaven may encore the bird who laid an egg.[4]

Or our repetition of the Rosary!

Finally, it is true that when we say the Rosary we often may not think about God. We may go for hours without any thoughts at all. We are just there, saying our prayers. But this may be good. When we say the Rosary, we are celebrating that the Lord is indeed with us and we are in his presence. We repeat the words of the angel 'The Lord be with you'. It is a prayer of God's presence. And if we are with someone then we do not need to think about them. As Simon Tugwell wrote, 'I do not think about my friend when he is there beside me; I am far too busy enjoying his presence. It is when he is absent that I will start to think about him. Thinking about God all too easily leads us to treat him as if he were absent. But he is not absent.'[5]

So, in the Rosary we do not try to have thoughts about God. Instead we rejoice in the words of the angel addressed to each of us, 'The Lord be with you'. We endlessly repeat these same words, with the endless vital exuberance of the children of God, who take pleasure in the good news.

4. *Orthodoxy*, London, 1908, p. 92.
5. *Prayer in Practice* Dublin, 1974, p. 35.

A LIFE THAT WAS GIVEN

Our Dominican brother, Pierre Claverie, the Bishop of Oran, has clearly and consciously given his life for the Church in Algeria, and for peace and brotherhood in that land of his birth. His death is indeed a cause of suffering for his brothers and those who were close to him. Nevertheless his constancy in giving witness for peace and brotherhood is also a source of pride for those who understood the choice he had made. Just like the monks of Tibhirine, he knew the risks he ran, but it was his choice to remain in solidarity with the people of Algeria and with all those who worked for peace.

Some months ago he had spoken of the meaning of this presence:

> The Church accomplishes its calling and its mission when it is present where there is the tearing apart of humanity, that very crucifixion of the flesh. Jesus himself died suspended between heaven and earth, as it were, with arms outstretched so as to gather together the children of God, scattered as they were by sin, isolated indeed and set up one against the other, indeed against God himself. Jesus placed himself at the epicentre of this tragic break-down born of sin. For in Algeria we are on the very seismic fault-lines which mark the world: Islam-the West, North-South, rich-poor. This is the right place for us to be, for it is here that the Light of the Resurrection can shine forth.

During a visit to our brother Pierre in Oran some months ago, I was very struck both by his determination and his joy. The joy of one who knows he's set the compass of his life on the right path. In the wake of the sacrifice of so many victims in Algeria,

---

A letter sent to members of the Dominican Order on 2 August 1997, marking the murder of Pierre Claverie OP, Bishop of Oran, Algeria.

Christians and Muslims who are devoted to peace, may the sacrifice of our brother be, like that of Jesus, a source of peace for our violent world.

In the name of the Order of St Dominic, I honour Pierre's memory, for the life of our brother Pierre is a source of pride for us. May God and St Dominic welcome him into Peace.

ABBREVIATIONS

LCM – *Liber Constitutionum Monialium*: The Book of Constitutions of the Nuns of the Order or Preachers

LCO – *Liber Constitutionum et Ordinationum*: The Book of Constitutions and Ordinations of the Order of Preachers.

Constitutions may be changed only by the decision of three successive General Chapters, which meet at intervals of three years.

The first Chapter in a sequence is an elective chapter and consists of priors provincial and representatives (diffinitors) from the provinces – one diffinitor or more depending on the size of the province. Three years later, the General Chapter consists of diffinitors only, and three years after that there is a chapter of provincials. To complete the cycle and start another, there then follows, after three years, another elective chapter.